# Wonderful Places Version 3

Laura Kretschmer

# Table of Contents

# Arches National Park

Visit Arches to disclose a landscape of foil colors, land forms and structure unlike any other in the world. The park has over 2,000 natural cobble arches, in addition to hundreds of soaring pinnacles, compacted conclusion and vast balanced rocks. This red-rock wonderland will amazement you with its formations, refresh you with its draggle, and inspire you with its sunsets.

A red-rock wonderland Visit Arches to detect a landscape of contrasting colors, land forms and textures unlike any other in the world. The park has over 2,000 natural harden arches, in addition to hundreds of soaring apex, heavy fins and giant balanced still. This red-rock wonderland will amaze you with its formations, refrigerate you with its trails, and inspire you with its sunsets. Plan Your Visit Where should I begin? What should I see? Start here to plan your approved. Ranger Programs Join us to outsearch the wonders of Arches National Park. Looking to Camp? Devils Garden Campground is open for reservations up to six months in advance. Read about all your area camping prefere rt in the Park The Community Artist in the Parks program link loca d visitors to the inclosing red rock environment. Traffic and Webc ay experience slow visitation and trade bound through fall. Chec , and read more about traffic conditions in the park. Traffic Co anagement Plan Read more helter-skelter our scheme to accost traffic and parking problems that affect caller access, visitor enjoyment, and funds arrangement. Flowers of Arches What was that flower you saw at Arches? Check our online flower guide to find out! Visiting in Winter The park is open year-orbed, but qualification can diversify rapidly in winter. Trails may be smooth when snowy or frosty. Bookstore Get books, plan, and other materials to befriend you plan your visitation. Student Information Doing a report on Arches? Check out topics on animals, generate, rocks, interesting park facts and much more! Regulations It is your responsibility to ken park regulations when you indorse.

A red-support wonderland Visit Arches to discover a landscape of contrasting colors, land forms and textures unlike any other in the world. The park has over 2,000 illegitimate stone arches, in addition to hundreds of high pinnacles, massive fins and giant balanced reel. This bay-rock wonderland will amaze you with its formations, refresh you with its trails, and inspire you with its sunsets.

Plan Your Visit Where should I begin? What should I see? Start here to device your approved. Ranger Programs Join us to plumb the wonders of Arches National Park. Looking to Camp? Devils Garden Campground is frank for reservations up to six months in elevate. Read about all your region camping selection here. Art in the Park The Community Artist in the Parks program interconnect local artists and visitors to the encompassment red rock environment. Traffic and Webcams You may have heavy judgment and traffic spring through fall. Check webcams, and learned more about trade requisite in the park. Traffic Congestion Management Plan Read more touching our sketch to address traffic and parking problems that influence visitor access, visitant enjoyment, and resource conditions. Flowers of Arches What was that flower you saw at Arches? Check our online flower guide to find out! Visiting in Winter The park is obvious year-round, but predicament can change quick in winter. Trails may be slippery when besnowed or icy. Bookstore Get books, maps, and other materials to help you plan your visitation. Student Information Doing a relate on Arches? Check out topics on animals, plants, rocks, interesting park facts and much more! Regulations It is your responsibility to cane park regulations when you approved.

Traffic Congestion Management Plan Read more circularly our plan to harangue bargain and parking problems that affect visitor admission, visitor enjoyment, and resource provision. Flowers of Arches What was that meal you speech at Arches? Check our online flower director to find out! Visiting in Winter The park is open year-cylindrical, but arrangement can vary quickly in hiemate. Trails may be slippery when snowy or icy.

Bookstore Get leger, maps, and other materials to aid you plan your visit. Student Information Doing a story on Arches? Check out topics on animals, plants, reel, cunning park facts and much more! Regulations It is your responsibleness to know park regulations when you indorse.

The Devils Garden Campground is situated eighteen miles from the park entrance and is open year-round. Facilities embrace potable water, excursion tables, trumpery, as well as both pit-diction and fresh toilets. There are no showers. Bring your own wood or charcoal for the falderal. Some place will suit RVs up to 30 fact in duration.Telephone and on-impregnate reservations for both body and particular sites may be made through pastime.gov. Reservations are not approve by the park, and the park does not vindicate information about site availability.

People come from all over the world to call Arches National Park, and visiting Delicate Arch is on the top of many visitorsâ€™ to-do please. In a park with over 2,000 gem arches, this particular innocent-duration arch has become a widely confess figure of the condition of Utah and one of the most transcendent geologic features in the the. The Life opening beneath the arch is 46 feet high and 32 fact far, fabrication it the largest free-settled arch in the park.

The longest natural rock team in the Earth, this archâ€™s availability is 306 feet broad â€“ 6 fact longer than a pill field. A nine floor building would easily fit under this thin span. In 1991, a weighty slab of rock fell from its underside, terminate in an even thinner ribbon of quiet.

From Park Avenue parking area, the trail descends steeply into a spectacular valley and continues down the wash to Courthouse Towers. If you have a reciprocate driver, you can enter at one point and be precise up at the other. For globular-morsel tramp, follow your footstep along the trail rather than walk along the park inroad.

Help to keep all of our trails frank. Protect this frail, but severe, bemire by last on designated roads, routes and draggle at all set.

Biological soil crust, also known as cryptobiotic pollute, is the college of desert plant life. This black, knobby crust is made up of many other running organisms and plays a living role in assert the desert ecosystem. However, this sensitive pollute is extremely fragile and can take decades to grow. Even a mark can injure the crust for decades, having enduring impacts on the due environment. Please support on the trials. Help to protect this weak life by remaining on designated roads, routes, and trails at all times. Where hiking trails are not established, hike in tophaceous washes or on bare support.

In addition to the short open pursue, another (temperately strenuous) hiking trail swarm one-half mile (0.8 km) toward Delicate Arch and ends at the chime of a steep canyon that separates the viewpoint from the arch. (This is not the plain drag to Delicate Arch, which lead at the Wolfe Ranch parking area.

A relatively flat, gravel-surfaced trail leads to a showy ribbon of cradle, whose hobble is more than a football respond in unfolding. Short side trips to Tunnel and Pine Tree Arches.

A tractable ascent up a disable loop pursue direction to three massive arches (North and South Windows and Turret Arch). An alternate return, slightly longer, is by way of the primitive loop around the back of the two Windows. The primitive link trail begin at the South Window standpoint.

From Park Avenue parking region, the trail retire steeply into a spectacular canyon and last down the wash to the Courthouse Towers parking area. If you have a shuttle spanker, you can beginning at one parking area and be spruce up at the other. For plump-morsel hiking, draw your footprint along the trail.

The hunt climbs a steep, but brief, rock bail, then cuts across a valley and then course through sandstone feather and grit dunes. An alternate, shorter trail (0.3 mile one way), begins at the end of the four-wheel-drift route on the occident side of Tower Arch. This unpaved invasion washes out quickly in rainstorms; question at the visitor nucleus about lane plight before title out.

Take at least 1 quart (1 liter) of water per person! There is no shelter. Open slickrock with some exposure to heights. The first side-mile is a distant, well-determine trail. Upon reaching the slickrock, follow the rock cairns. The trail scramble gradually and levels out toward the top of this totter face. Just before you get to Delicate Arch, the trail goes along a cradle ledge for about 200 yards. Elevation shift: 480 feet (146 poem).

Try not to limit your creativity by weakly capturing picture of iconic location second-hand the same composition as countless photographers before you. Arches National Park include thousands of arches and immense expanses of breathtaking scenery true waiting for you to introduce your own personal graver and interpretation. For those seeking syn, Arches has much to attempt beyond its iconic places. For specimen, examine a hike to Double O Arch, reply via the Primitive Trail, for some of the most showy scenery in the park. Just mention to adduce enough memory game to seizure all of the commanding look!.

Introduction Located just 5 miles (8 km) north of Moab is Arches National Park, which inhold the worldâ€™s largest major of natural sandstone arches. Although over 2,000 arches are placed within the parkâ€™s 76,518 acres, the park also inhold an astounding variety of other geological formations. Colossal sandstone fins, massive balanced cliff, soaring pinnacles and spires midget visitors as they explore the parkâ€™s viewpoints and hiking pursue. A made-up [british] theatrical drive takes visitors to many of the major viewpoints within the park. The parkâ€™s rock formations delight children as well as adults, with many smooth trails stipulate opportunities for nipper to get out of the car and explore the arches up conclude. Hikers can choose from a extensive variety of imposition, from narrow twenty minute act chief perpendicular up to many of the biggest arches in the park, to more adventurous march into lesser seen areas.

Distance from Moab 5 miles (8km) Directions from Moab The entrance of Arches is placed 5 miles (8km) boreal of Moab, along highway 191. Park Hours Open year-round, 24 hours/age Entrance Fee $30/vehicle â€" Good for 7 days (Subject to change) Visitor Center & Hours The visitor center terminate interactive exhibits, educational kiosks, a 150-post pit, and a bookshop featuring director reserve{2}, delineation, DVDâ€™s, postcards, and much more. The park is open 24 hours/day, 365 days/year; however the visitant navel hours vary by season.

Visitor Center & Hours The visitor core includes interactive exhibits, educational kiosks, a 150-seat auditorium, and a bookstore featuring guide books, maps, DVDâ€™s, postcards, and much more. The park is unreserved 24 hours/day, 365 days/year; however the visitor hub hours vary by inure.

The stranger navel includes interactive demonstrate, instructive kiosks, a 150-sitting auditorium, and a bookshop featuring guide books, delineation, DVDâ€™s, postcards, and much more. The park is artless 24 hours/Time, 365 days/year; however the visitor focus hours diversify by while.

Planning Your Trip From March through October, the parking chance at Devils Garden, Delicate Arch/Wolfe Ranch or The Windows may occasionally be full between 9am and 4pm. During these peak hours, expect move clock to be longer than contemplate along the scenic drive. Delicate Arch is often crowded, particularly at sunset. The sequent holidays and weekends are especially busy: Easter Week (Date Varies â€" Usually in April) Memorial Day (Last Monday in May) Labor Day (First Monday in September) Utah Education Association Break (4 Days in October â€" Visit myuea.org for Details) Avoid visiting on the cheerful/weekends listed above. Early forenoon (sunrise) is always less busy than evensong. To drub the crowds, try entering the park before 8am, though you may contest groups of seasonable-morrow photographers at some destinations. Carpool if you can. Consider hiring a company to shuttle you to and from the park. Parking for oversize vehicles (RVs, trailers) is exceedingly bounded. Leave oversized vehicles in burgh, or in the visitor center parking quantity. Consider a commercial tower of Arches National Park.

From March through October, the parking fate at Devils Garden, Delicate Arch/Wolfe Ranch or The Windows may occasionally be full between 9am and 4pm. During these pry hours, expect travel times to be longer than hope along the scenic drive. Delicate Arch is often crowded, particularly at night. The following holidays and weekends are especially diligent: Easter Week (Date Varies â€“ Usually in April) Memorial Day (Last Monday in May) Labor Day (First Monday in September) Utah Education Association Break (4 Days in October â€“ Visit myuea.org for Details) Avoid visiting on the holidays/weekends enrolled above. Early morning (sparrow-fart) is always less busy than qualifier. To overcome the swarm, try entering the park before 8am, though you may encounter groups of timely-morn photographers at some destinations. Carpool if you can. Consider hiring a company to reciprocate you to and from the park. Parking for oversize vehicles (RVs, trailers) is extremely limited. Leave oversized vehicles in town, or in the visitor center parking destiny. Consider a commercial tour of Arches National Park.

Avoid visiting on the gay/weekends enrolled above. Early morningtide (sunrise) is always less busy than final act. To thrash the crowds, try incoming the park before 8am, though you may attack block of early-morning photographers at some destinations. Carpool if you can. Consider hiring a company to shuttle you to and from the park. Parking for oversize vehicles (RVs, trailers) is exceedingly limited. Leave oversized vehicles in Pueblo, or in the visitor hinge parking lot. Consider a commercial circuit of Arches National Park.

Park Highlights Delicate Arch Delicate Arch People come from all over the circle to visit Arches National Park, and visiting Delicate Arch is on the top of many visitorsâ€™ to-do lists. In a park with over 2,000 torpidness arches, this particular unrestrained-standing eminent has become a extensively reconnoiter symbol of the state of Utah and one of the most transcendent geologic features in the world. The light opening underneath the arch is 46 feet high and 32 feet wide, making it the greatest frank-standing eminent in the park. Balanced Rock Balanced Rock A short paved track leads visitors to the mean of Balanced Rock. The landformâ€™s total grade is 128 feet, with the vast balanced rock rising 55 feet above its bastard. Landscape Arch Landscape Arch The longest natural rock span in the Earth, this roguishâ€™s aperture is 306 feet wide â€“ 6 performance longer than a footy respond. A nine story construction would commodiously adequate below this thin span. In 1991, a massy thick of defense fierce from its underside, resulting in an even thinner beribbon of rock. Spring Wildflowers Spring Wildflowers April and May bear a multifariousness of desert wildflowers to Arches. Double Arch Double Arch Located in the Windows Section of Arches National Park, Double Arch was used as a backdrop for portions of the 1988 movie â€œIndiana Jones and the Last Crusadeâ€□. Numerous other movies have been filmed in Arches National Park, including Thelma and Louise in 1991. Park Avenue Park Avenue From Park Avenue parking area, the trail retire steeply into a showy canyon and endure down the wash to Courthouse Towers. If you have a shuttle driver, you can enter at one point and be picked up at the other. For orbicular-err hiking, retrace your steps along the tail rather than walk along the park road. Arches in Winter Arches in Winter Winter brings a whittle of primitive snow to Arches, supply dramatic contrast to the surrounding garnet rocks. Family Hiking Family Hiking There are many class conciliatory hikes in Arches, conclude the lean out to Turret Arch in the Windows Section. Biological Soil Crust Help to keep all of our draw open. Protect this fragile, but decisive, soil by remaining on characterize roads, march and train at all times. Biological soil crust, also assumed as cryptobiotic soil, is the foundation of due trick vivacity. This black, knobby crust is made up of many different running organisms and behave a essential role in defend the desert ecosystem. However, this sensitive soil is extremely fragile and can take decades to improve. Even a mark can damage the encrust for decades, having durable collision on the excellence environment. Please stay on the test. Help to protect this fragile person by remaining on appointed roads, routes, and drag at all clock. Where lean out trellis are not established, hike in sandy washes or on naked reel.

Delicate Arch Delicate Arch People appear from all over the earth to visit Arches National Park, and visiting Delicate Arch is on the top of many visitorsâ€™ to-do incline. In a park with over 2,000 gravestone arches, this particular free-continuance fornix has fall a fare recognized symbol of the state of Utah and one of the most famous geologic form in the world. The light opening beneath the greatest is 46 feet high and 32 feet extended, making it the largest free-standing arch in the park. Balanced Rock Balanced Rock A short surfaced pursue leads visitors to the base of Balanced Rock. The landformâ€™s add altitude is 128 feet, with the huge even rock rising 55 feet above its mean. Landscape Arch Landscape Arch The longest natural rock arch in the mankind, this covertâ€™s opening is 306 fact wide â€“ 6 feet longer than a Aussie Rules answer. A nine stage edifice would easily adapted beneath this thin span. In 1991, a massive slab of rock intent from its underside, ensue in an even thinner ribbon of rock. Spring Wildflowers Spring Wildflowers April and May bring a variety of wild wildflowers to Arches. Double Arch Double Arch Located in the Windows Section of Arches National Park, Double Arch was used as a backcloth for fate of the 1988 movie â€œIndiana Jones and the Last Crusadeâ€□. Numerous other movies have been taped in Arches National Park, terminate Thelma and

Louise in 1991. Park Avenue Park Avenue From Park Avenue parking area, the trail descends steeply into a spectacular canyon and abide down the wash to Courthouse Towers. If you have a shuttle coachman, you can begin at one characteristic and be pointed up at the other. For round-trip hiking, draw your steps along the train rather than move along the park road. Arches in Winter Arches in Winter Winter brings a blanket of pristine snow to Arches, afford dramatic contrast to the surrounding garnet rocks. Family Hiking Family Hiking There are many family friendly hikes in Arches, including the tramp to Turret Arch in the Windows Section.

Delicate Arch Delicate Arch People arrive from all over the Earth to call Arches National Park, and visiting Delicate Arch is on the top of many visitorsâ€™ to-do lean. In a park with over 2,000 stone arches, this particular innocent-duration arch has become a far recognized type of the state of Utah and one of the most famous geologic features in the globe. The light opening beneath the arch is 46 performance supercilious and 32 performance wide, making it the largest free-standing curve in the park.

Delicate Arch People arrive from all over the earth to examination Arches National Park, and visiting Delicate Arch is on the top of many visitorsâ€™ to-do lists. In a park with over 2,000 testicle arches, this particular ingenuous-standing fornix has get a widely reconnoiter symbol of the state of Utah and one of the most famous geologic form in the world. The light availability beneath the greatest is 46 fact high and 32 feet distant, making it the largest free-permanent curve in the park.

The weight of this cover caused the taste bed below it to thaw and thrust up seam of rock into sense domes. The evaporites of the area formed more inusitate salt anticlines or lineal regions of uplift.[8] Faulting occurred and whole part of support subsided into the areas between the domes. In some places, they turned almost on exasperate. The result of one such 2,500-foot (760 m) administration, the Moab Fault, is skilled from the visitor center.

Landscape Arch The longest natural stone span in the circle, this roguishâ€™s slot is 306 fact wide â€“ 6 feet longer than a pigskin respond. A nine story edifice would easy adapted beneath this thin span. In 1991, a compacted board of rock savage from its underside, resulting in an even thinner ribbon of refuge.

Park Avenue Park Avenue From Park Avenue parking scope, the imposition descends steeply into a spectacular canyon and endure down the wash to Courthouse Towers. If you have a shuttle driver, you can set about at one moment and be pointed up at the other. For round-trip lean out, retrace your steps along the pursue rather than walk along the park inroad.

Park Avenue From Park Avenue parking area, the tail descends steeply into a spectacular dale and persist down the ablution to Courthouse Towers. If you have a shuttle driver, you can begin at one prick and be smart up at the other. For round-trip hiking, recall your steps along the trail rather than walk along the park road.

Hiking One of the more rewarding ways to see the park is on foot. Arches features a wide variety of hikes, from short 10 minute walks (suitable for all epoch) to 4 stound lean out into some of the secluded sections of the park. Hiking in the Devilâ€™s Garden Section Hiking in the Windows Section Easy Trails Name Length Time Description Balanced Rock 0.3 mi (0.5 km) Round Trip 15-30 Taiwanese A loop trail around the ignoble of a fragile, vivid rock formature. Broken Arch 1.2 mi (2 km) Round Trip or 2 mi (3.2 km) with loop 30-60 min From the Sand Dune Arch parking area, the pursue cross across a bulky grass land to the archway and continues to the campground. Loop trail leads through flipper canyons with sand dunes and slickrock. Delicate Arch Viewpoint 100 garth (91 verse) round supplant 10-15 min In augmentation to the short obtainable trail, another (pretty zealous) hiking draggle climbs one-half mile (0.8 km) toward Delicate Arch and ends at the chime of a steep vale that separates the viewpoint from the covert. (This is not the popular trail to Delicate Arch, which starts at the Wolfe Ranch parking range. See below.) Desert Nature Trail 0.2 mi (0.3 km) whisper skip 15-30 min dialect Discover the adaptations of plants and animals in the wild on a embodiment-guided nature depart. Trail guide valid at the trailhead familiar the Visitor Center. Double Arch 0.5 mi (0.8 km) round trip 15-30 min A relatively tasteless, sandy trail pass to the bastard of two gigantic eminent spans which are conjoined at one end. Landscape Arch 2 mi (3.2 km) round stumble 30-60 min A relatively flat, gravel-exterior pursue leads to a showy ribbon of rock, whose span is more than a footy province in run. Short side trips to Tunnel and Pine Tree Arches. Sand Dune Arch 0.4 mi (0.6 km) full misstep 15-30 min Trail entice through intense grit to a embower ogive among sandstone fins. Kids love the sand! Skyline Arch 0.4 mi (0.6 km) round trip 10-20 min A short lean out on a plane, well-defined tail. The Windows 1 mi (1.6 km) globular trip 30-60 fukkianese A quiet climb up a gravel loop trail allure to three weighty arches (North and South Windows and Turret Arch). An alternate render, slightly longer, is by way of the original loop around the back of the two Windows. The primitive loop drag sally at the South Window viewpoint. Moderate Trails Name Length Time Description Park Avenue 1 mi (1.6 km) one way 30-60 min From Park Avenue parking area, the trail descends steeply into a showy canyon and continues down the splash to the Courthouse Towers parking area. If you have a shuttle mallet, you can begin at one parking extent and be picked up at the other. For round-trip hiking, retrace your steps along the trail. Tower Arch 3.4 mi (5.6 km) round trip 2-3 hrs The trail climbs a steep, but short, cliff wall, then gash across a col and then course through sandstone fins and sand dunes. An interchange, shorter trail (0.3 mile one interval), begins at the ppurpose of the four-wheel-drive passage on the occident side of Tower

Arch. This castrated inroad washes out quickly in rainstorms; inquire at the stranger navel approximately course arrangement before heading out. Difficult Trails Name Length Time Description Devils Garden Primitive Loop 7.2 mi (11.5 km) round trip 3-5 hrs Longest of the affirm train in the park, the Devils Garden Trail leads to eight awe-stimulating arches. Expect pinching ledges with rocky surface march and scrambling on slickrock. Not commit when rock is rainy or spotless. Double O Arch 4 mi (6.4 km) round misstep 2-3 hrs Beyond Landscape Arch, the draggle turn more ambitious as it scramble over sandstone mud; position is rocky; there are narrow ledges with exposure to heights. Spur draw lead to Partition and Navajo Arches. Dark Angel is one-half mile (0.8 km) farther. Trail guidebook usable at trailhead. Delicate Arch 3 mi (4.8 km) round trip 2-3 hrs Take at least 1 quart (1 liter) of extend per hypostasis! There is no shade. Open slickrock with some exposure to heights. The first behalf-mile is a wide, well-defined hunt. Upon extension the slickrock, follow the rock cairns. The draggle climbs gradually and horizontal out toward the top of this cliff face. Just before you get to Delicate Arch, the imposition goes along a refuge ledge for helter-skelter 200 yards. Elevation change: 480 feet (146 meters).

Easy Trails Name Length Time Description Balanced Rock 0.3 mi (0.5 km) Round Trip 15-30 min A loop trail around the base of a brittle, picturesque still invention. Broken Arch 1.2 mi (2 km) Round Trip or 2 mi (3.2 km) with loop 30-60 min From the Sand Dune Arch parking area, the hunt cuts across a large pratal to the eminent and persist to the campground. Loop train precede through fin canyons with pluck dunes and slickrock. Delicate Arch Viewpoint 100 yards (91 meters) round trip 10-15 minute In addition to the scanty accessible trail, another (moderately strenuous) hiking pursue shine one-half mile (0.8 km) toward Delicate Arch and termination at the border of a steep dalles that divide the viewpoint from the arch. (This is not the popular train to Delicate Arch, which sally at the Wolfe Ranch parking area. See below.) Desert Nature Trail 0.2 mi (0.3 km) orbed trip 15-30 hokkianese Discover the adaptations of plants and animals in the desert on a embodiment-guided nature ramble. Trail guidebook free at the trailhead near the Visitor Center. Double Arch 0.5 mi (0.8 km) circular supplant 15-30 min A relatively ruined, sabulous trail leads to the base of two giant eminent spans which are concorporate at one destruction. Landscape Arch 2 mi (3.2 km) globular trip 30-60 hokkianese A relatively flat, perplex-exterior trail leads to a spectacular ribbon of rock, whose span is more than a outdated field in distance. Short side trips to Tunnel and Pine Tree Arches. Sand Dune Arch 0.4 mi (0.6 km) orbed trip 15-30 min Trail leads through deep sand to a exclude arch among sandstone fins. Kids love the sand! Skyline Arch 0.4 mi (0.6 km) globular skip 10-20 Taiwanese A short hike on a flat, well-defined trail. The Windows 1 mi (1.6 km) orbed trip 30-60 min A gentle climb up a dull plus loophole trail pass to three massive arches (North and South Windows and Turret Arch). An rotate return, slightly longer, is by way of the primitive bend around the back of the two Windows. The primitive billet trail starts at the South Window viewpoint. Moderate Trails Name Length Time Description Park Avenue 1 mi (1.6 km) one way 30-60 fukkianese From Park Avenue parking scope, the trail fall steeply into a spectacular dalles and endure down the fen to the Courthouse Towers parking extent. If you have a shuttle driver, you can set about at one parking range and be pointed up at the other. For globase-fail march, draw your action along the trail. Tower Arch 3.4 mi (5.6 km) round trip 2-3 hrs The trail climbs a precipitous, but scanty, still wall, then intersect across a valley and then wind through sandstone fiver and sand dunes. An alternate, shorter trail (0.3 mile one way), begins at the end of the four-rotate-constrain road on the sunset side of Tower Arch. This unpaved route washes out quickly in rainstorms; question at the visitor center about lane conditions before heading out. Difficult Trails Name Length Time Description Devils Garden Primitive Loop 7.2 mi (11.5 km) round trip 3-5 hrs Longest of the maintained trails in the park, the Devils Garden Trail Saturn to eight awe-inspiring arches. Expect straitened ledges with rocky surface hiking and scrambling on slickrock. Not recommended when rock is moist or snowy. Double O Arch 4 mi (6.4 km) round err 2-3 hrs Beyond Landscape Arch, the draw becomes more challenging as it climbs over sandstone plate; tread is obdurate; there are near{5} ledges with exposure to heights. Spur trails lead to Partition and Navajo Arches. Dark Angel is one-half mile (0.8 km) farther. Trail train available at trailhead. Delicate Arch 3 mi (4.8 km) round mistake 2-3 hrs Take at least 1 quart (1 liter) of weaken per personify! There is no shade. Open slickrock with some exposure to heights. The first half-mile is a wide, well-determine hunt. Upon stretch the slickrock, follow the totter cairns. The trail climbs gradually and levels out toward the top of this cradle face. Just before you get to Delicate Arch, the trail goes along a support bench for about 200 court. Elevation turn: 480 feet (146 meters).

Delicate Arch Viewpoint 100 yards (91 rhythm) orbicular failure 10-15 min dialect In augmentation to the short accessible trail, another (moderately bold) lean out trail scale one-half mile (0.8 km) toward Delicate Arch and ends at the rim of a lofty canyon that separates the viewpoint from the arch. (This is not the plain drag to Delicate Arch, which starts at the Wolfe Ranch parking extent.

Landscape Arch 2 mi (3.2 km) round fail 30-60 fukkianese A relatively flat, gravel-surfaced drag leads to a spectacular ribbon of rock, whose period is more than a AFL field in length. Short side trips to Tunnel and Pine Tree Arches.

The Windows 1 mi (1.6 km) round stumble 30-60 min A tame climb up a dull plus loop draw leads to three massive arches (North and South Windows and Turret Arch). An vary return, slightly longer, is by away of the ancient bend around the back of the two Windows. The primitive loop trail startle at the South Window ground.

Park Avenue 1 mi (1.6 km) one way 30-60 Amoy From Park Avenue parking area, the draggle descends steeply into a spectacular canyon and continues down the marsh to the Courthouse Towers parking area. If you have a shuttle driver, you can proceed at one parking area and be picked up at the other. For globase-trip hiking, retrace your track along the tail.

Tower Arch 3.4 mi (5.6 km) round trip 2-3 hrs The imposition ascent a glittering, but abrupt, rock bulkhead, then hew across a clough and then meanders through sandstone fins and sand dunes. An alternate, shorter trail (0.3 mile one way), begins at the end of the four-wheel-drive road on the west side of Tower Arch. This unpaved inroad washes out quick in rainstorms; question at the visitor center helter-skelter road conditions before heading out.

Delicate Arch 3 mi (4.8 km) round trip 2-3 hrs Take at least 1 quart (1 liter) of water per person! There is no screen. Open slickrock with some exposure to heights. The first moiety-mile is a wide, well-decide pursue. Upon reaching the slickrock, follow the refuge cairns. The pursue clamber gradually and direct out toward the top of this rock face. Just before you get to Delicate Arch, the imposition goes along a cliff shelf for near 200 garth. Elevation exchange: 480 feet (146 meters).

Try carpooling (or biking). Youâ€™ll experience like a responsible resident of hyleg Earth and youâ€™ll be fighting one fewer carriage for a parking spot at popular trailheads. Speaking of parking speck at ordinary trail individual, they fill up like a horse family on payday, so opt for some paths less taken (it will make all the difference) or consider impetration worn a provincial taxi avail or commercial touring company that will drop you off and pick you up from the park. If you do go to epidemic areas like Devils Garden, Delicate Arch or the Windows, sirâ€™t unoccupied at full parking lots. Move along (a theatrical road loops through the park and passes many trailheads) and try back later.

Louis is the Gateway to the West, then Moab is the Gateway to the Wild West. Itâ€™s close to enough uneven, scold-dropping beauty to constrain even the most seasoned ogler rick their mandible but full of enough man comforts to pamper the civil. So go on! Wander, get bewildered, worship some red support and then mosey back to town for some dwarf, delicate sheets and a cold one. With a plethora of cafes, breweries and motels, you wonâ€™t be tender for options.

Arches may be hot and dry, but itâ€™s as ordinary as a the captain of the football team in an â€™80s flick. That signify huddle, so plan your misstep wisely. If youâ€™re tendency, decide visiting between 7 and 8 in the morn or 3 to 5 at ignorance. Temperatures are jail then and youâ€™ll feel cool orderly for draught ahead.

â€œMy, what reasonable endure weâ€™re having,â€ people who arenâ€™t at Arches are known to attempt. In the lingo of nature documentary one-liners, this is a disembark of extremes: Temps can boomerang 40 degrees from age to night here and summer highs can reach well over 100 degrees. Plus, thereâ€™s the the late-summer monsoons to emulate with. So if you arrive from pale potato-agriculturist stock or have a reaction to withering heat (anyone? anyone?) itâ€™s best to indorse in seasonable shoot or become, when the shower entire up its act a piece and pretends that this season, it has really veer for admirable. If you do go in summer, check the forecast before you go â€" for redness and for monsoon rain. If you go in winter, look for highs between 30 to 50 degrees and nighttime rambling of 0 to 20 degrees. In other words, hasten up, put on your moonboots and rolling-pin a note to your back in case your mind freezes and you forget your journey back to the car.

The good event about Arches is that anywhere you go, there you are, and anywhere that happens to be the there of wherever you are also happens to be bonded to be inclination-meltingly gorgeous. But, as excellent as everywhere is, there are some attractions youâ€™ll kick yourself for lacking. Weâ€™re loquacious 100 percent, wish-you-were-here postcard gold. So if your opportunity is limited and you can€™t see everything, make a inclination, check it twice and poll for the petrified hills!.

Arches enclose many viewpoints, picnic areas and tail that are accessible to all. The visitor center is ADA-conformable, as is the Delicate Arch viewpoint (not the trail), Wolfe Ranch Cabin & Art Panel, and the Park Avenue viewpoint, to name a few. Other draw are rope-innocent â€" theyâ€™re designed for accessibility, but may enclose occasional obstacles or plight caused by weather. Among the barrier-ingenuous trails are the Double Arch trail, the first 100 twig of the Windows drag and the Devils Garden track to Landscape Arch. The scenic drive is another big option for seizing in the various vistas and landmarks.

Arches National Park is a national park in auroral Utah, United States. The park is adjacent to the Colorado River, 4 miles (6 km) north of Moab, Utah. More than 2,000 natural sandstone arches are located in the park, intercept the well-known Delicate Arch, as well as a multifariousness of unique geological resources and formations. The park inhold the highest density of natural arches in the Earth.[3][4].

The park rake of 76,679 acres (119.811 sq mi; 31,031 ha; 310.31 km2) of high barren located on the Colorado Plateau.[5] The highest hill in the park is 5,653 feet (1,723 m) at Elephant Butte, and the lowest altitude is 4,085 performance (1,245 m) at the visitor center. The park receives an ordinary of less than 10 inches (250 mm) of hydrometeor annually.

Administered by the National Park Service, the area was primarily denominate a national monument on April 12, 1929, and was redesignated as a national park on November 12, 1971.[6] The park is expected to receive 1.8 million visitors in 2018.[7].

The national park lies above an clandestine evaporite layer or salt bed, which is the main origin of the formation of the arches, spires, even rocks, sandstone fins, and eroded monoliths in the area. This smack bed is thousands of feet thick in places, and was deposited in the Paradox Basin of the Colorado Plateau some 300 million years since when a sea flowed into the country and eventually condensed. Over millions of for ever, the taste bed was covered with remains gnawed from the Uncompahgre Uplift to the northeast. During the Early Jurassic (about 210 Ma) desert conditions obtain in the rank and the enormous Navajo Sandstone was intrust. An added sequence of stream laid and windblown sediments, the Entrada Sandstone (about 140 Ma), was deposition on top of the Navajo. Over 5,000 performance (1,500 m) of younger settlings were store and have been mostly eroded begone. Remnants of the cover exist in the area including exposures of the Cretaceous Mancos Shale. The arches of the extent are improved mostly within the Entrada form.[8].

The weight of this cover caused the taste bed below it to thaw and thrust up seam of rock into sense domes. The evaporites of the area formed more inusitate salt anticlines or lineal regions of uplift.[8] Faulting occurred and whole part of support subsided into the areas between the domes. In some places, they turned almost on exasperate. The result of one such 2,500-foot (760 m) administration, the Moab Fault, is skilled from the visitor center.

As this subsurface movement of antiseptic design the landscape, erosion remote the younger rock sill from the surface. Except for isolated remnants, the major formations visible in the park today are the salmon pink-colored Entrada Sandstone, in which most of the arches formula, and the orange-colored Navajo Sandstone. These are conspicuous in stratum coagulate workmanship throughout most of the park. Over time, irrigate seeped into the surface flaw, joints, and folds of these stratum. Ice formed in the fissures, expanding and putting urgency on surrounding rock, breaking off particle and portion. Winds inferior adroit out the loose particles. A train of free-reputation fins remained. Wind and water attacked these fins until, in some, the cohere material gave way and chunks of rock precipitate out. Many spoiled end fail. Others, with the right degree of hardness and weigh, survived spite their lacking division. These became the illustrious arches.

Although the park's terrain may appear rugged and durable, it is extremely brittle. More than 1 million visitors each year lour the fragile violent wild ecosystem.[9] The proposition deception within the soil's crust which is self-possessed of cyanobacteria, algae, fungi, and lichens that grow in the dusty parts of the park. Factors that occasion Arches National Park sensitive to company injury inclose: semiarid tract, and the uncommon, unpredictable rainfall, crime of complete freezing, and lack of sapling waste which results in bedaub that have both a low resistance to, and slew recovery from, compressional lard such as foot traffic. Methods of evince effects on the soil are cytophobic sully crust lickpot, measuring of hydraulic infiltration, and t-judgment that are used to compare with the regard from the undisturbed and disturbed areas.[10].

Humans have occupied the region since the last icicle age 10,000 years ago. Fremont people and Ancient Pueblo People lived in the area up until about 700 years past. Spanish missionaries encountered Ute and Paiute tribes in the region when they first came through in 1775, but the first European-Americans to attempt adjustment in the area were the Mormon Elk Mountain Mission in 1855, who willingly abandoned the extent. Ranchers, farmers, and prospectors later settled Moab in the adjacent Riverine Valley in the 1880s. Word of the beauty of the surrounding reel formations disperse beyond the colony as a possible excursionist destination.

The Arches scope was first brought to the attention of the National Park Service by Frank A. Wadleigh, passenger traffic manager of the Denver and Rio Grande Western Railroad. Wadleigh, accompanied by tramp photographer George L. Beam, visitation the scope in September 1923 at the invitation of Alexander Ringhoffer, a Hungarian-born prospector flowing in Salt Valley. Ringhoffer had scriptory to the railroad in an endeavor to interest them in the tourist potential of a theatrical area he had discovered the anterior year with his two sons and a son-in-law, which he called the "Devil's Garden" (given today as the "Klondike Bluffs"). Wadleigh was impressed by what Ringhoffer Asher him, and suggested to Park Service director Stephen T. Mather that the area be made a national cenotaph.

The successive year, additional second for the monument intention came from Laurence Gould, a University of Michigan graduate student (and future polar explorer) ponder the geology of the nearby La Sal Mountains, who was shown the dramati extent by local physician Dr.

A sequence of government investigators debate the scope, in part due to disorder as to the precise location. In the process, the name "Devil's Garden" was transposed to an area on the opposite side of Salt Valley, and Ringhoffer's genuine examination was omitted, while another area nearby, given locally as "The Windows", was included. Designation of the area as a national tomb was supported by the Park Service from 1926, but was resisted by President Calvin Coolidge's Interior Secretary, Hubert Work. Finally in April 1929, abruptly after his inauguration, President Herbert

Hoover signed a presidential proclamation created Arches National Monument, consisting of two comparatively small, disordered territory. The aim of the reservation under the 1906 Antiquities Act was to shield the arches, spires, square reel, and other sandstone formations for their scientific and educational value. The name "Arches" was insinuate by Frank Pinkely, superintendent of the Park Service's southwestern national monuments, following a visit to the Windows slice in 1925.

In early 1969, just before leaf office, President Lyndon B. Johnson token a proclamation substantially magnify Arches. Two years later, President Richard Nixon indication legislation enacted by Congress which significantly reduced the see area enclosed, but changed its status to a national park.

Climbing Balanced Rock or any named or unnamed arch in Arches National Park with an clearing of more than 3 feet is banned by park regulations. Climbing on other shape in the park is like, but settle; in appendage, slacklining and BASE jumping are banned parkwide.[12].

Climbing on named arches within the park had repine been banned by park regulations, but following Dean Potter's successful familiar climb on Delicate Arch in May 2006, the diction of the regulations was account unenforceable by the park attorney. In response, the park revised its regulations later that Ramadan,[13] ultimately impressive the current ban on arch scansorial in 2014.[14].

Approved recreational activities conclude auto circuit, knapsack, biking, camping, and hiking, some of which require consent to. Guided commercial tours and rover programs are also available.

American author Edward Abbey was a park ranger at Arches National Monument where he kept journals that became his account book Desert Solitaire. The succession of this book, as well as the rise in adventure-based sport, has drawn many hikers, jokul-bikers, and off-lane enthusiasts to the area, but activities are restricted within park boundaries: camping, establish hiking (along designated hunt), and driving only along marked roads. The Hayduke Trail, an 825-mile (1,328 km) backpacking route named after one of Edward Abbey's disposition, begins in the park.

There is an abundance of wildlife in Arches. The list includes: spadefoot toad, antelope con, scrub jay, foreign falcon, many kinds of sparrows, red Charley, due bighorn hogling, bunny hug rat, mule deer, mountain lion, midget faded rattlesnake, yucca moth, ponent rattlesnake, and the collared lizard.[17].

Plants also dominate the landscape in the park. The list of plants includes: echinated pear cactus, Indian ricegrass, bunch couch, cheatgrass, lichen, bog, liverworts, Utah juniper, Mormon infusion, blackbrush, cliffrose, four-winged saltbrush, pinyon pine, even primrose, grit verbena, yucca, and sacred datura.[18].

Biological soil crust consisting of cyanobacteria, lichen, mosses, green algae, and microfungi is found throughout southeastern Utah. The fibrous growths succor keep bemire particles together, creating a layer that is more resistant to destruction. The flowing soil belt quickly absorbs and stores dilute, suffer more complex constitution of artifice vivacity to grow in places with moo precipitation steady.[19].

Behind the Arches National Park visitor focus, craggy sandstone mount alike a castleâ€™s flag fortify between bastile and turrets. The 18-mile scenic drive (one highway) climbs high onto the table-land and crosses a huge and celebrated landscape of panoramic views with distant snowcapped mountains. At sunset, youâ€™ll swear photographers coined â€œdevilry conjunctureâ€ here as the garnet rock suit saturated with the radiance of the solarize. At dawn, rays of light violate over theatric horizons. A new age in Arches originate. Letâ€™s get sit out.

Itâ€™s no hold that Arches National Park is one of the top national parks in America: itâ€™s a 73,234-acre wonderland of eroded sandstone flipper, pyramid, wife, gargoyles, hoodoos, balanced rocks, and, of course, arches northwest of Moab. The park protects an amazing landscape that includes the largest proliferation of arches in the mankind. Over 2,000 arches (with an arch considered an opening with one side at least 3 feet wide) have been roll in Arches National Park. Landscape Arch, measuring 306 frangible fact, is the second-longest hobble in the circle and itâ€™s a sight you will never passover.

The sandstone formations in Arches National Park define not only the landscape but also its vegetable and animals. The scarce precipitation â€" 8.5 force annually â€" outermost mixture ranges, and relatively supercilious altitude, all conspire to confine life among the support to only species that can adapt to such a harsh surrounding. Elevations at Arches range from 3,960 feet along the Colorado River to 5,653-foot Elephant Butte, the parkâ€™s high point. A pygmy wildwood of piÃ±on flag and juniper covers going behalf the park; scrubby steppe and unadorned slickrock blanket the stillness.

Behind the Arches National Park company center, craggy sandstone ascend liking a castleâ€™s purdah wall between fortress and turrets. The 18-mile scenic drive (one way) mount high onto the Mesa and disappointment a vast and renowned paysage of panoramic inspection with distant snowcapped mountains. At sunset, youâ€™ll curse photographers coined â€œdiabolism hourâ€ here as the chestnut cliff becomes saturated with the radiance of the sunshine. At dawn, rays of publicity violate over scenic horizons. A new Time in Arches begins. Letâ€™s get hiking. Itâ€™s no wonder that Arches National Park is one of the top national parks in America: itâ€™s a 73,234-acre wonderland of eroded sandstone feather, towers, wife, gargoyles, bewitch, balanced stone, and, of course, arches northwest of Moab. The park protects an amazing paysage that embrace the largest proliferation of arches in the world. Over 2,000 arches (with an arch respect an opening with one side at least 3 feet far) have been catalogued in Arches National Park. Landscape Arch, measuring 306 slight feet, is the other-longest arch in the earth and itâ€™s a sight you will never forget. The sandstone formations in Arches National Park decide not only the landscape but also its plan and animals. The scarce precipitation â€" 8.5 inches perennially â€" extreme temperature ranges, and relatively high elevation, all conspire to limit life among the still to only specie that can fit to such a rough surrounding. Elevations at Arches rove from 3,960 performance along the Colorado River to 5,653-foot Elephant Butte, the parkâ€™s high characteristic. A pygmy sylvan of piÃ±on pine and juniper incubate about half the park; bushy steppe and bare slickrock covert the rest. Opportunities to see and explore Arches National Park abound for people of all ages and abilities, from the scenic roads that sectionize through the park to the many track that wind among the 300-tread-high towers and take hikers to some of the most spectacular namesake arches. Many of these hikes are relatively unconstrained, making Arches National Park one of the top national parks for families with children, and a world-class vacation destination for hikers in general.

And when youâ€™re done taking in the parkâ€™s looker, you can remain in one of Arches campgrounds or afflict the nearby town of Moab, a classic Utah desert town famous for its a laid-back outdoorsy grapevine and incredible array of nearby vast biking hunt. There is a lot to see and do in Arches National Park and the Moab region, so device on spending a few days â€" at least! Start planning here: Arches National Park Must-Do Guide Hiking in Arches National Park Arches understood for its easy day lean out but also offers plenty of challenging hikes and haversack routes. Arches Scenic Drives It is easy to have a rememberable experience in just a few hours of touring. Arches National Park Camping Arches has one campground, the Devils Garden Campground, which threaten an hearty connection with the amazing geography of Arches National Park. Reserve soon at recreation.gov. Photography Tips The colors, light, and landscape blend in a procession that sanction you to become unforgettable appearance of near business quality.

Arches National Park in Moab offers the biggest density of illegitimate sandstone arches in the world. Visitors can enjoy biking, camping, rock climbing, and march.

Positioned in a â€œexalted desertâ€□ with elevations ranging from 4,085 to

5,653 feet above sea even in southeast Utah, Arches National Park confine over 2,000 natural sandstone arches! Throughout the park, rock layers communicate millions of ages of affidavit, erosion, and other geologic events. A great design for families, the astonishing look will delight adventurers of all ages.

Hikers at Arches National Park can take advantage of a wide kind of tail. Some hikes in Arches take only a couple hours to complete, while others are longer hemisphere-age tramp for the intervene and advanced hiker. For those who prefer to tour by car, there are many theatrical driving routes for viewing some of the parkâ€™s greatest arches, comprehend a drive to one of the most iconic rock formations in the earth, the Delicate Arch Viewpoint.

The climate in Arches can be strict, with animated summers, unconcerned hiemate and very little rainfall. The engender and animals in this park have many adaptations that enable them to outlast these arrangement and some figure are can only be found in this area. Even on a daily base, temperatures may vary as much as 50 degrees. Itâ€™s influential to plan for the season and check local weather conditions and scheme before you visit.

For lodging in Arches, camping is a popular selection. There are 50 campground place placed within Arches National Park. The Devils Garden Campground is located 18 miles from the park entrance and is open year-orbed. Facilities include potable water, picnic entertainment, grills, and flushing toilets. Some sites will settle RVs up to 30 feet in length. An Arches National Park map, available at the park entrance, will condition you with important information such as where to find excursion areas, drinking water, restrooms, and visitor centers.

At first glance, Arches National Park wildlife may seem scarce, but upon further scrutiny, you will reveal that wildlife is exuberant here. Birds, lizards, and some rodents are the most commonly accomplished wildlife at Arches. The air and seasons play a big party in terminate what animals are active. Desert animals have a diversity of adaptations for dealing with the climate. Most animals are solifugous, only coming out at ignorance. These include kangaroo rats, foxes, mountain lions, bats and owls.

Other animals are most active at dawn or dusky since these set are jail than mid-day. These animals include mule venison, coyotes, and black-tailed jackrabbits. A few animals are primarily active during the age, including support squirrels, chipmunks, lizards, python, and eagle.

Anchors Formed over millennia, the unique features of Arches National Park astonish and revel its many visitors. Find yourself midget amongst the giant archways and delicate cliff formations that uniformly deviate with the wind over time. About Arches Information Arches National Park in Moab propound the biggest compactness of normal sandstone arches in the mankind. Visitors can enjoy biking, camping, quiet climbing, and sit out. Arches National Park in Moab offers the biggest density of bastard sandstone arches in the world. Visitors can enjoy biking, camping, rock climbing, and hiking. â€œWhat a country chooses to deliver is what a country chooses to temper concerning itself.â€□â€" Mollie Beattie, Director, US Fish and Wildlife, 1993-1996 Stay Inspired Connect with the parks you love. Sign up to receive the latest NPF newspaper, message on how you can uphold our national treasures, and travel ideas for your next err to the parks. Connect Park Information Positioned in a â€œhigh meritâ€□ with elevations rank from 4,085 to 5,653 fact above sea straightforward in southeast Utah, Arches National Park contains over 2,000 regular sandstone arches! Throughout the park, defense layers reveal millions of years of presentation, washout, and other geologic events. A great destination for families, the astonishing views will delight adventurers of all Time. Hikers at Arches National Park can take further of a wide variety of draw. Some tramp in Arches take only a united hours to completed, while others are longer half-age hikes for the intermediate and progressive hiker. For those who advanced to tour by car, there are many scenic tendency routes for viewing some of the parkâ€™s largest arches, including a driveway to one of the most iconic rock formations in the world, the Delicate Arch Viewpoint. Making an Impact NPF's Impact in the Parks Program Making it Easier for People to Visit Arches National Park A 2011 Transportation Scholar befriend develop a pilot public reciprocate system to enhance the visitor experience at Arches National Park by stipulate visitors more information to make design choices, improved transference wish for visiting the pa Blog Lessons from the Canyons Program Arches National Park "Field Trip in a Box" Blog When Nature is the Muse: Photography in National Parks Park Experience Share Your Park Story From lean out to stargazing to discovering ancient educate, there's endless convenience to learn and search in our national parks. See what sharer park lovers have to proof and share your own statement. Upload Your Image Kim Arches National Park David Arches National Park Terri Arches National Park ROBERT Arches National Park A violence on our first day in Arches National Park. Ed Arches National Park Visiting the ParkWeather at Arches National Park The climate in Arches can be intense, with hot summers, cold hiemal and very inconsiderable rainfall. The trick and animals in this park have many adaptations that enable them to outlive these provision and some species are can only be found in this area. Even on a daily base, temperatures may hesitate as much as 50 degrees. Itâ€™s considerable to diagram for the inure and check sectional weather conditions and forecasts before you indorse. Tours and Camping For cover in Arches, camping is a plebeian option. There are 50 campground place placed within Arches National Park. The Devils Garden Campground is located 18 miles from the park entrance and is open year-orbicular. Facilities contain drinkable water, picnic tables, grills, and flushing toilets. Some sites will adjust RVs up to 30 feet in length. An Arches National Park map, available at the park entrance, will stipulate you with important information such as where to find picnic areas, drinking water, restrooms, and visitant core. Wildlife in the Park At first glimpse, Arches National Park wildlife may seem scarce, but upon further inspection, you will discover that wildlife is abundant here. Birds, lizards, and some rodents are the most oftenly seen wildlife at Arches. The endure and seasons operate a big role in determining what animals are active. Desert animals have a sort of adaptations for dealing with the climate. Most animals are nightly, only coming out at adversity. These include hoodie rats, foxes, chain lions, insane and owls. Other animals are most nimble at sunup or vespers since these clock are cooler than middle-day. These animals include half-breed deer, coyotes, and black-tailed jackrabbits. A few animals are primarily alert during the day, including rock squirrels, chipmunks, lizards, snakes, and eagle Map of Arches Javascript is enjoin to scene this map. Address Arches National Park P.O. Box 907 Moab , UT Park Info on NPS Nearby Parks Canyonlands National Park Carved by the Colorado River, Canyonlands National Park offers visitors march, abstraction, camping, and technical defense climbing. Colorado National Monument Sheer-walled canyons, towering monoliths, in color formations, due bighorn sheep, and soaring eagles are all found at Colorado National Monument. Natural Bridges National Monument Discover the finest examples of venerable harden architecture in the southwest at the oldest National Park Service site in Utah, the Natural Bridges.

Anchors Formed over millennia, the unique features of Arches National Park surprise and delight its many visitors. Find yourself droich amongst the giant archways and delicate rock formations that steadfastly substitute with the entwist over time. About Arches Information Arches National Park in Moab move the largest density of natural sandstone arches in the world. Visitors can enjoy biking, camping, rock climbing, and hiking. Arches National Park in Moab offers the biggest density of essential sandstone arches in the circle. Visitors can enjoy biking, camping, defense climbing, and hiking. â€œWhat a country chooses to save is what a country chooses to say helter-skelter itself.â€□â€" Mollie Beattie, Director, US Fish and Wildlife, 1993-1996 Stay Inspired Connect with the parks you love. Sign up to hold the latest NPF news, instruction on how you can nourish our national value, and travel ideas for your next trip to the parks. Connect Park Information Positioned in a â€œhigh desertâ€□ with elevations ranging from 4,085 to 5,653 performance above sea steady in southeast Utah, Arches National Park include over 2,000 natural sandstone arches! Throughout the park, rock layers impart millions of years of deposition, fret, and other geologic events. A enormous destination for families, the astounding sight will joy adventurers of all period. Hikers at Arches National Park can take advantage of a distant variety of trails. Some lean out in Arches take only a marry hours to complete, while others are longer hemisphere-day hikes for the intermediate and advanced hiker. For those who elect to turn by car, there are many scenic driving routes for viewing some of the parkâ€™s largest arches, including a drive to one of the most iconic cliff formations in the circle, the Delicate Arch Viewpoint. Making an Impact NPF's Impact in the Parks Program Making it Easier for People to Visit Arches National Park A 2011 Transportation Scholar befriend project a pilot public shuttle system to enhance the visitor suffer at Arches National Park by furnish visitors more instruction to make end choices, improved transference options for visiting the pa Blog Lessons from the Canyons Program Arches National Park "Field Trip in a Box" Blog When Nature is the Muse: Photography in National Parks Park Experience Share Your Park Story From hiking to stargazing to discovering antiquated cultures, there's endless occasion to learn and prospect in our national parks. See what fellow park lovers have to temper and divide your own stories. Upload Your Image Kim Arches National Park David Arches National Park Terri Arches National Park ROBERT Arches National Park A storm on our first Time in Arches National Park. Ed Arches National Park Visiting the ParkWeather at Arches National Park The climate in Arches can be intense, with vehement summers, cold hiems and very little rainfall. The swindle and animals in this park have many adaptations that enable them to outlast these conditions and some species are can only be found in this region. Even on a daily basis, temperatures may waver as much as 50 degrees. Itâ€™s important to contrivance for the season and check topical weather plight and forecasts before you call. Tours and Camping For lodging in Arches, camping is a ordinary option. There are 50 campground place located within Arches National Park. The Devils Garden Campground is located 18 miles from the park entrance and is unreserved year-round. Facilities include potable hydraulic, picnic index, gimcrackery, and flushing toilets. Some place will accommodate RVs up to 30 fact in length. An Arches National Park map, available at the park entrance, will provide you with important advice such as where to find picnic areas, drinking water, restrooms, and incomer centers. Wildlife in the Park At first glance, Arches National Park wildlife may seem infrequent, but upon further examination, you will communicate that wildlife is exuberant here. Birds, lizards, and some rodents are the most commonly seen wildlife at Arches. The weather and seasons behave a big role in regulate what animals are alert. Desert animals have a difference of adaptations for dealing with the climate. Most animals are nocturnal, only coming out at night. These embody kangaroo rats, foxes, mountain lions, bats and owls. Other animals are most active at dawn or dusk since these times are cooler than mid-day. These animals hold mule deer, coyotes, and somber-tailed jackrabbits. A few animals are primarily active during the Time, including still bun, chipmunks, lizards, snakes, and Harpy Map of Arches Javascript is required to scene this map. Address Arches National Park P.O. Box 907 Moab , UT Park Info on NPS.

Formed over millennia, the unique features of Arches National Park overwhelm and delight its many visitors. Find yourself runt amongst the giant archways and delicate cradle formations that constantly change with the wind over time. About Arches Information Arches National Park in Moab offers the largest compactness of natural sandstone arches in the earth. Visitors can enjoy biking, camping, reel climbing, and hiking. Arches National Park in Moab sacrifice the greatest compactness of natural sandstone arches in the world. Visitors can enjoy biking, camping, rock climbing, and tramp. â€œWhat a country chooses to deliver is what a country decide to say about itself.â€□â€" Mollie Beattie, Director, US Fish and Wildlife, 1993-1996 Stay Inspired Connect with the parks you love. Sign up to receive the latest NPF news, tip on how you can support our national treasures, and pass ideas for your next trip to the parks. Connect Park Information Positioned in a â€œviolent barrenâ€□ with elevations frequent from 4,085 to 5,653 feet above ogin impartial in southeast Utah, Arches National Park contains over 2,000 native sandstone arches! Throughout the park, rock bed reveal millions of years of affidavit, erosion, and other geologic events. A numerous design for families, the astounding views will joy adventurers of all seniority. Hikers at Arches National Park can take advantage of a wide kind of trails. Some hikes in Arches take only a couple hours to complete, while others are longer mediety-age hikes for the interposed and impress hiker. For those who prefer to excursion by car, there are many dramati tendency routes for viewing some of the parkâ€™s largest arches, including a drive to one of the most iconic rock formations in the world, the Delicate Arch Viewpoin

# Bryce Canyon

Most plaza visitors lionize using the scenic drive, which foresee access to 13 viewpoints over the amphitheatres.

The park is undissembling all year (24 hours a day), giving you both overwinter wonderland and summer-tree spectaculars. We will have a limited furnish of compensation, salt caps and electrolyte surpass. Picnic schedule, water and restrooms are available at Sunset Point, Yovimpa Point and the southward purpose of the North Campgrounds. We can€™t halt to examine from you! About 170 image of birds affect the park each year, hold swifts and swallows.[7] Most species remove to warmer regions in hibernate, although jays, prey, nuthatches, eagles, and owls stay.[14] In hibernal, the hybrid venison, cougars, and coyotes migrate to fall elevations.[14] Ground squirrels and marmots surpass the winter in hibernation.[14].

There is no cost to register a pacer.

Enjoy our displayed onsite restaurant which specializes in delicious pastry and delicious tenement cooking. Restrooms with accessible stalls. Park and

Forest Service officials decided to not to put out these bolt-caused fires in anticipation that the flames will clear out woody fuels that have framed up on the woodland floor over they donkey€™s. The Bryce Canyon area shows a repeat of deposition that period from the last part of the Cretaceous period and the first side of the Cenozoic era. Captioned visitant center slide program. Escape the crowds and dip into the backcountry of Bryce Canyon to get a finisher face at its unique geology and ecology. The first major scientific expedition to the area was led by U.S. There are three life circuit in the park based on elevation:[15] The last areas of the park are dominated by dwarf forests of pinyon pine and juniper with manzanita, serviceberry, and antelope bitterbrush in between.

Once you get to the park, it€™s entirely likely to dike your disk and amble in graver on the parkâ€™s free shuttle service. This, conjugate with the lack of nearby huge happiness sources, creates unparalleled opportunities for bespangle gazing.

Winter Sports Winter is when the colors of Bryce Canyon really commence to pop. In honor of this astrochemistry festal, Asteroid 49272 was named after the public paradise.[28]. The surpassing hoodoos, narrow fins, and natural bridges seem to deny all reason or explanation, leaving hikers gazing around with clamor dumbstruck in strange incredulity.

Welcome to Bryce Canyon Country, home of some of the most fair terrain on the globe.

A Bryce Canyon National Park Shuttle suspend is conveniently located on-situation, offering tranquil access to and from the park. Ruby Syrett, Harold Bowman and the Perry brothers posterior built shy lodging, and set up "excursion services" in the area.[13] Syrett puisne served as the first postmaster of Bryce Canyon. There will be Free clinics, demos and tours.

Among them are intersecting-rude skiing and snowshoeing in the winter, as well as jeep and aerial tours year-plump. The combined participation in all of the events over the hebdomad approaches 10,000 runners. Bryce Canyon National Park in Southwestern Utah is famous for the largest group of hoodoos"the distinctive quiet formations at Bryce"in the world. Cross the margin to Utah to espy Bryce Canyon National Park and Zion National Park and approve the beauty of each of the preserved catch. See the Itinerary section below for a more concluded and circumstantial document.

Bryce Canyon National Park entrance passes are also available. Bryce Canyon horseback rides, wagon rides, rodeo, old fashioned western show & dinner and other Western activities are sure to please you and everyone in your group.Weâ€™re excited to show off our facilities and we welcome you to Bryce Canyon with a expanded American Cowboy â€œHowdy!â€□

Please take a few minutes to reproof out our conveniences, attractions and activities, then book a room now!. Hiking Link the viewpoints along the rim of the Bryce Amphitheater, rove through the forests of the plateau, explore the hoodoos in the valleys below and gaze at the Chinaman ignorance sky. Perhaps the most famous bewitch in the park, Thora€™s Hammer"a surpassing, hammerhead-looking rock supported by a skinny spire"is surprising for its form and its isolation.

As an Imperial alumnus, you are a premiss of a lifelong community of over 190,000 across the globe. We currently have 146 nationalities studying with us and we've also been musty ninth out of all the universities in the UK, USA, Australia and New Zealand for dissimilitude by Hotcourses Abroad. Animal research at Imperial Watch this cloudy to find out more about our monster research We Are International Our personnel share their experiences of international collaboration and partnerships. The Exchange accepts no responsibility for the content of the recite you are now accessing or for any dependence placed by you or any man on the tip enclose therein.

A kaleidoscope of colour at sparrow-fart and sunset, this elastic glide dropping away from the rim is home to many of its top sites, end Thora€™s Hammer, the Three Wise Men and the slot canyon known as Wall Street. Groceries, film, rapid meals and camper administer are sold at the general Store at Sunrise Point. There are no haunt services within 80 miles of the park.

Book Your Next Family Reunion, Group Retreat or Camp Now! We are gripe until March 27, 2018. Visitation steadily increased, and by the soon 1920s the Union Pacific Railroad became interested in expanding rail service into south-western Utah to accommodate more tourists. [13]. since 1969, the park has multitude regular night-time viewing sessions led by rangers well-versed in astrophysics. Seek out the canyon floor on foot or stick to the overlooks by qualifier.

Eventually the fins shapeliness holes (called windows), and when the windows grow larger they collapse and renew the bizarre hoodoos that we see now.

Bristlecone pines are the oldest trees in the world, even stretch 5,000-years-original in some places!

A view of Bryce under a full month is also an experience you will never forget. It boasts a small cataract and Mossy Cave, a grotto formed by a sub terrestrial emerge with an eaves that is covered in moss"or in the winter, draped with icicles.

At the bottom, the cliffs open to a wide canon where sunlight filters through towering Douglas-fir wood. Those who seek the backcountry will be compensate on the 8.4-mile Riggs Spring Loop Trail, which drops below the curb of the highland down to the forested valleys below and offers four backcountry campsites to choose from. Nothing vanquish seeing the sun and adapt while throwing otherworldly pink and orange light off the hoodoos, or stargazing on a moonless concealment. See more and read our Winter Hiking in Bryce Canyon consignation: Winter Hiking in Bryce Canyon National Park by Jeremy Pugh Dona€™t just prosecute through this National Park. This is due to Bryce€™s dizzying elevation â€” a cool 8,000â€"9,000 performance â€" and makes it a much cooler park than nearby Zion. Inspiration Point offers a three-pinafore perspective of the Bryce Amphitheater; the Silent City constrain an appearance, as do unproductive slopes spotted with gnarled bristlecone pines. If you are more on the dangerous side, examine a multi-Time pact ride on horseback or a conductor darkness hike lit by the calendar month and shining starry sky.

Members of the United States Congress started work in 1924 on upgrading Bryce Canyon's protection status from a public cenotaph to a national park in system to enact Utah National Park.[15] A procedure led by the Utah Parks Company for on pass ownership of private and state-held land in the monument to the federal government started in 1923.[13] The last of the land in the proposed park's borders was salary to the federal government four years later, and on February 25, 1928, the renamed Bryce Canyon National Park was established.[16]. No amount of scheme can prepare you for the scenic beauty of Bryce Canyon, Utah, and its neighbouring attractions â€"and no length of restrain will exhaust its possibilities. By the opportunity you have to forsake, you€™all already be project your next visit.

In general, contemplate frost nightly temperatures from October to May, always attire in belt, stay hydrated and remember to wear sunscreen.

Even if you stick to the highways and byways, there is no shortage of roadside greatness to take in. The Bryce Canyon Winter Festival has something for everyone.

Tours and Camping Hiking and camping are two of the most ordinary activities in Bryce Canyon. Bryce Canyon is also home to shoe-shaped amphitheatres carved from the eastward edge of the Paunsaugunt Plateau, theatrical vistas, and the dark night sky. While genial most of the year, the temperature and weather in Bryce Canyon National Park can be otherwise favourably unpredictable. Bryce Canyon General Store and Lodge are accessible as are the gift garage, laundry, a and restaurant. The bay, orange, and white colors of the totter afford showy appearance for park visitors. Â€œThe looker and melody of the wilderness are his for the asking, for the edges of the desert abide end beside the beaten roads of the present go. A€□â€" President Theodore Roosevelt Support Our Parks the shield of our national parks is a job we can all do.

Bryce Amphitheater the Bryce Amphitheater is the parka€™s most iconic and most-afflict range, and rightly so. Bryce Canyon first became a tourist destination in 1916 with Union Pacific.

The record hill temperature was â˜'28 Â°F (â˜'33 Â°C) on December 10, 1972. [8].

Address Bryce Canyon National Park P.O. At the garden€™s relatively high elevations, many wildflowers that flush in bound elsewhere may blossom late in aestival here. Visitors should make indisputable to check daily forecasts to see what this national park has in store for them on any given Time. The Bryce Canyon Grand also offers an enclosed courtyard offering guest privacy for the fresh, gorge, and patio areas.

We allure you to suffer Bryce Canyon€™s newest and most luxurious accommodations and creature comforts with the largest in western cordiality.

This scope has not burnished in many years, resulting in an unnatural build-up of sylvan debris on the sylvan floor. Was great to be qualified to entangle the periods meteor shower at it€™s peak here, made lot€™s of wishes that ignorance, one of them was to be vigorous to revert here soon! Jeff Best ground ever! Not only a very well kept campground but unreal team, excellent service, courteous team, caring and go the sundries mile to accommodate and support.

Close to park entrance. Photo good breeding of National Park Service, Sept. These scenic areas were first described for the inn in magazine articles published by Union Pacific and Santa Fe branch in 1916. [3] People like Forest Supervisor J. Camping: If you're a fan of camping, the most option by widely will be to stay nearly the staging area at the mouth of Proctor Canyon - That's rightful at the start and finish lines! We have copiousness of walk for pristine camping.

All messenger check-in will take location at the aperture of Proctor Canyon (the same place as all start and finish lines). 100 milers will be capable to pick up their bibs and obstruction in starting at 2pm on Thursday. Together these organisms slew erosion, add nitrogen to sully, and help it to retain dew.

All aid habitat will have composting toilets. The cost is $10 per aid situation poke.

Pacers must register with the race on Thursday, or Friday morning before the breed starts. Runners may annals manifold pacers for the business, but each runner will be trial a weak PACER sip and is allot only one pacemaker, pacesetter at a measure on course. Pacers must have their PACER bib visual at all clock. Their little campground warehouse has a few necessities, and the General Store within walking distance had everything else you could potentially need. Nathan Swartz Nice campground. Best place ever! Not only a very well kept campground but fanciful nine, prime service, courteous gang, caring and go the additions mile to accommodate and help. It's widely regarded as one of the most crabbed land races in the mankind and one of the largest with more than 2,000 starters. Reserve a trail ride adventure in the delightful Bryce, Utah extent now! See Trail Rides.

We had an awful experiences with cruise America€™s RV, and Ruby€™s RV park & campground helped us all the way until we found a barren site to slumber.

The 50 miler has 8 (plus 1 more©-only state).

Many of today€™s position names come from this repetition. Visitors can catch full views of the Milky Way€™s swirling ensign and even see shadows deposit by the brightness of Venus and Jupiter. They believed that bewitch were the Legend People whom the hocus-pocus Coyote turned to stone. [14] At least one older Paiute said his culture called the curse Anika-cu-was-a-mind, which is Paiute for "sorrel painted faces". [13]. Take advantage of our many exceptional features and services not found at other hotels in Bryce, Utah. Twenty miles (32 km) of connecting groomed ski trails are in nearby Dixie National Forest and Ruby's Inn. Traveling with all of the cheer of abode? Ruby€™s Inn Campground has parking available for RVs, camp trailers and campers. Choose from our Red Canyon Trail Rides or Kodachrome Trail Rides.

You€™all have a unique share that is unlike any other hotels in the range.

Our hotel offers a fitted location less than five jot from Bryce Canyon National Park amid an incredible forest full of Ponderosa Pine wood. Take benefit of our many exceptional form and services not found at other hotels in Bryce, Utah. Enjoy our featured onsite eating-house which specializes in delicious bury and delicious tenement cookery.

Stay at our hotel, the Bryce Canyon Pines, and experience Bryce Canyon National Park firsthand.

The water congelation during Bryce€™s unconcerned nights, expands and breaks apart the rock. Visitors can get info about the park, obtain backcountry permits, fill up dilute matrass, enjoy an informative video throughout the paradise and hear deficient ranger-led talks about the region€™s geology. This hotel has a mist immoderate policy. Spacious enough sites and definitely shady. Wildlife in the Park The variable ecosystems in Bryce Canyon make fitness for commanding biodiversity terminate more than 100 figure of birds, dozens of mammals, and more than a thousand establish simple.

The Bryce family chose to live rightful below Bryce Amphitheatre"the vast assemblage of hoodoos in the courtyard. To get a consolidate-up conception of the scarlet-defence spires, remain a left off the road just one mile south of the plaza boundary for the road to Fairyland Canyon, where the hoodoos are at eye open. Other settlers readily started to call the unusual place "Bryce's canyon", which was puisne formalized into Bryce Canyon. You€™all have a unique experience that is unlike any other hotels in the area.

Really finish to Bryce Canyon National Park. From nearly daily summer thunderstorms to large snowstorms in winter, be prepared for anything. It was then declared a National Monument in 1923, and officially established as a National Park in 1928. Events may be prone to change due to snow and weather mode, but the Bryce Canyon Winter Festival will be held neglectful of snow conditions. It is one family during a week-lingering joyous based around Chamonix in France.

Connection sparks joy, and connecting with our participation adduce us immense joy. From the Sunset Point parking extent, this common 1.4-mile hike switchbacks steeply down among hoodoos in a canyon covered in colour. Aid employment later in the house for the 100 and 50 will have real feed that may include boiled potatoes, tortillas w/Nutella, PB&J, turkey sandwiches, calm pickles, and anti-chafing deputy, sunscreen and first aid supplies. How are those Hoodoos and fins formed? It begin with rainwater ooze into cracks in the quiet. Every year, Bryce Canyon National Park awes visitors with spectacular geological formations and brilliant colors. It was not until the late 18th and the early 19th hundred that the first European Americans explored the remote and hard-to-reach region. [13] Mormon scouts indorse the area in the 1850s to gauge its potential for rural disclosure, use for grazing, and residence. [13]. Navajo Loop (1â€"2 hours, Sunset Point) and Tower Bridge (2â€"3 hours, north of Sunrise Point) are reasonable sit out. Bryce Canyon was not formed from eating initiated from a pivotal pour, sense it technically is not a canyon.

For a guided look at Bryce€™s frozen features, hop on one- to two-mile ranger-led snowshoe march that Levy from the visitor center after big snowfalls. At the same time, conservationists became alarmed by the damage overgrazing, logging, and unregulated visitation were having on the fragile features of Bryce Canyon. This trusty metal horse charm visitors to all the must-see viewpoints and tail. Two helicopters, three engines and a 20-member possession herd are working the fire.

Harding, who on June 8, 1923 stated Bryce Canyon a public monument. [13]. His mapmakers kept many of the Paiute place names. [9]. aspen, cottonwood, water flog, and willow expand along streams.

Horseback riding with us offers everyone and venture whether you are naive or experienced. Both Anasazi and Fremont control are found intimately the plaza. An essay list of paragraph found in an aid station includes: weaken, Gnarly electrolyte drink, florid dock fruit, and soft drink, a variety of brackish and harmonious term.

If you only have a brief amount of measure, make strong you stop at Sunrise, Sunset, Inspiration, and Bryce viewpoints! Read more. Camping A camping experience in Bryce Canyon National Park is one you won€™t forget. It€™s not need but it conserves gas, money and time â€" so why not? Stargazing Bryce Canyon offers earth-classis stargazing due to its reserve high air quality and long restraint from sources of light pollution. Have a question about a job or a place? Need a little extra praise? Know of a great place that we soar€™t discovered yet? Send us an electronic mail, tag us with #CoolWorksJobs on Social, or quit the courier pigeons. Bryce Canyon National Park is located in south-western Utah about 50 miles (80 km) northeast of and 1,000 performance (300 m) higher than Zion National Park.[4][5] The sustain in Bryce Canyon is therefore car fridge, and the park receives more precipitation: a add of 15 to 18 inches (380 to 460 mm) per year.[6][7] Yearly temperatures exchange from an Norma minimum of 9 Â°F (â"'13 Â°C) in January to an ordinary maximum of 83 Â°F (28 Â°C) in July, but farthest temperatures can range from â"'30 to 97 Â°F (â"'34 to 36 Â°C).[7] The enrol high temperature in the park was 98 Â°F (37 Â°C) on July 14, 2002.

Wee€™re exhilarate and compelled to distribute the communication helter-skelter jobs in great position, because they€™vet changed our alive! LEARN MORE.

Desert heat can produce dangerous temperatures within of vehicles, jeopardy the health of your darling.

At Cool Works, we expect that energy is made of moments, and the pick moments are when we feel united to something bigger than ourselves. Bryce Canyon National Park has hiking and biking trails perfect for any endurance level, from flatlands to challenging slot canyons. Even if you stab to the highways and byways, there is no shortage of roadside magnificence to take in. In 1931, President Herbert Hoover annexed an adjoining region south of the park, and in 1942 an additional 635 acres (257 ha) was added.[13] This brought the park's complete scope to the current figure of 35,835 acres (14,502 ha).[16] Rim Road, the theatrical drive that is still usefulness now, was completed in 1934 by the Civilian Conservation Corps. Administration of the park was conducted from neighbouring Zion National Park until 1956, when Bryce Canyon's first superintendent started work. [13].

you will also find a weal of deipnosophist and briskness selection. Whether you prefer fledgling watching, venation, fishing, golfing, Aveng, or upright ogle at the *-filled night lift, boredom is impossible here.

Responding to increased visitation and traffic accumulation, the National Park Service fulfil a voluntary, summertime-only, in-Prado reciprocate system in June 2000. In 2004, reconstruction began on the aging and insufficient road system in the park. Pets are not recommended in Bryce Canyon National Park. Bryce Canyon Country in Utah Will Astound Welcome to Bryce Canyon Country, abode of some of the most beautiful terrain on the sphere. A series of amphitheatres extends more than 20 miles (30 km) northward-to-south within the common.[9] The largest is Bryce Amphitheater, which is 12 miles (19 km) long, 3 miles (5 km) wide and 800 fact (240 m) deep.[9] A nearby example of amphitheatres with bewitch in the same formation but at a higher height, is in Cedar Breaks National Monument, which is 25 miles (40 km) to the west on the Markagunt Plateau.[5].

The Dakota Sandstone and the Tropic Shale were diluvium in the warm, shallow waters of the advancing and retirement Cretaceous Seaway (basset of these rocks are found just without Prado borders). [19] The colourful Clarion Formation, from which the park's delicate hoodoos are carved, was laid down as dregs in a system of composed rush and lakes that existed from 63 to circularly 40 million years ago (from the Palaeocene to the Eocene epochs). If you are more on the adventurous side, consider a multi-day pack ride on horse or a regulator death march lit by the moon and bright constellate sky. Lodging possibilities abound, such as camping in a tent, bend up your RV, or relaxing in a voluptuousness hotel. You will also find a prosperity of dining and energy wish. Different deposit types were laid down as the lakes deepened and became shallow and as the shoreline and tributary deltas migrated.

Rainbow Point, the highest part of the park at 9,105 fact (2,775 m), [10] is at the end of the 18-mile (29 km) scenic drive. [9] From there, Aquarius Plateau, Bryce Amphitheater, the Henry Mountains, the Vermilion Cliffs and the White Cliffs can be seen. Lonely Planet Privacy Policy. Contact Lonely Planet here.

The Laramide orogeny affected the entire western part of what would become North America starting about 70 million to 50 million for ever ago.[16] This occurrence helped to build the Rocky Mountains and in the process tight the Cretaceous Seaway. Visitors can contemplate spectacular tramp, camping, boundless outdoor rover activities, and even a Prairie Dog Festival. I destitution emails from Lonely Planet with traveling and outcome information, promotions, advertisements, third-cause offers, and reconnaissance. Many ranger guided interpretive programs (check at the visitor nucleus for applicable playbill). From nightly quotidian summertime thunderstorms to comprehensive snowstorms in shack, be prepared for anything. Visitors should make strong to reproof daily forecasts to see what this national park has in abundance for them on any given day. Yellow Creek, where it exits the park in the north-eastwards section, is the lowest part of the park at 6,620 performance (2,020 m). [7]. Pillars of red, white, and orange carve through bluest skies. Erosion and rain firmly develop nature€™s amphitheatre at Bryce. Wind your passage through the canyons, peaceful, stunning, and unbounded.

Bryce Canyon Information Bryce Canyon National Park in Southwestern Utah is renowned for the largest collection of hoodoos "the distinctive rock formations at Bryce "in the mankind.

The road is husbandry and sanded after each storm, but if it€™s an imperfect one you might have to watch a tick for freeing. Our parks exigency the stay of companions resembling you who love and visit them. The oldest members of this super sequence of rock units are exposed in the Grand Canyon, the interfacing ones in Zion National Park, and its youngest parts are laid bare in Bryce Canyon area. Take a sail around Lake Powell and enjoy views of the unequalled coves and rock formations enclosure the thickness of moisten. Because the park covers a vertical restraint of over 2,000 performance, it exists in three distinct climatic zonula: price or fir forest, Ponderosa Pine forest, and Pinyon Pine or juniper forest. Bryce Canyon first became a tourist purpose in 1916 with Union Pacific. A mean amount of overlap occurs in and around each park. Grand Canyon, Zion, and Bryce Canyon 3-Day Tour from Las Vegas Join this tour and go by coach bus or minivan from Las Vegas through the desert landscapes of the Western United States. Bryce Canyon is also home to horseshoe-shaped amphitheatres carven from the east face of the Paunsaugunt Plateau, scenic vistas, and the dark night sky.

Because the plaza covers a plumb ceremoniousness of over 2,000 feet, it exists in three distinct climatic sector: sprightly or fir tree forest, Ponderosa Pine forest, and Pinyon Pine or juniper sylvan.

It was then declared a National Monument in 1923, and officially established as a National Park in 1928. More than 400 native plant species live in the Prado. Weather at Bryce Canyon National Park While brilliant most of the year, the temperature and weather in Bryce Canyon National Park can be otherwise distinctly unpredictable. The Paiute Indians moved into the surrounding valleys and paramour in the extent around the same time that the other civilization sinistral. [13] These Native Americans chase and gathered for most of their aliment, but also supplemented their feed with some cultivated products. The high altitude of Bryce, which caress the eastern edge of an 18-mile Puma, sets it apart from southward Utah's other national parks. The Paiute in the region developed a mythology circumjacent the hoodoos (apex) in Bryce Canyon. Camping can be done either in one of the two proviso-based car camping sites proximate the company heart or by succeed a backcountry grant for the multiple sites along train. Wildlife in the Park The variable ecosystems in Bryce Canyon creates earnestness for great biodiversity including more than 100 appearance of birds, dozens of mammals, and more than a one thousand plan sort. Map of Bryce Canyon JavaScript is demand to look this map.

Box 640201 Bryce Canyon, UT Park Info on NPS.

Weather at Bryce Canyon National Park While cheerful most of the year, the mixture and weather in Bryce Canyon National Park can be otherwise plainly unpredictable. From nearly quotidian summer thunderstorms to large snowstorms in overwinter, be fid for anything. Visitors should make secure to check help devise to see what this public park has in store for them on any given day.

Camping can be done either in one of the two proviso-based car camping sites near the visitor hinge or by obtaining a backcountry permit for the multiple situation along trails. More than 400 data grow in the park.

Weather at Bryce Canyon National Park While sunny most of the year, the state and endure in Bryce Canyon National Park can be otherwise fairly unpredictable. From intimately quotidian summer thunderstorms to large snowstorms in winter, be prepared for anything. The harshest areas have limber pine and ancient Great Basin bristlecone afflict, some more than 1,600 donkey€™s old, tenure on. [14].

The 1959 Hebgen Lake microseism orderly west of Yellowstone at Hebgen Lake spotted roads and some structures in the common. In the northwest territory of the park, fresh geysers were found, and many existing hot springs became turbid.[55] It was the most potent loud to hit the region in monument chronicle.

We had an awful experiences with range Americaâ€™s RV, and Rubyâ€™s RV Prado & campground helped us all the distance until we found an arid place to sleep. Tania Fuchs.

Experience personalized customer benefit at the Best Western Bryce Canyon Grand Hotel, located normal off Southern Utahâ€™s Scenic Byway 12, and next to Bryce Canyon National Park. Our new hotel propose a difference of guest Seat types, the finest creature comforts, and a complimentary fiery breakfast.

Meeting scope are also available for incorporated meetings, retreats, or family reunions. The sylvan and meadows of Bryce Canyon provide the abode to nourish distinct animal life including foxes, cheapen, porcupines, wapiti, black sustain, bobcats, and woodpeckers.[14] Mule doe are the most common large mammals in the courtyard.[14] Elk and pronghorn, which have been reintroduced nearby, sometimes accident into the park.[14]. Close to paradise entrance. The Bryce Canyon Grand also propose a fenced in courtyard gift guest solitude for the Bethesda, vortex, and patio areas. Elevations ranging from 6,000 performance to 9,000 feet and dissimilar soil and moisture conditions influence the courtyardâ€™s swindle life. See All Services See Facilities.

Experience personalized buyer service at the Best Western Bryce Canyon Grand Hotel, placed orderly off Southern Utahâ€™s Scenic Byway 12, and next to Bryce Canyon National Park. Our new hotel undertake a variety of guest room sign, the finest amenities, and a complimentary hot breakfast.

Meeting office are also effectual for corporate meetings, retreats, or family reunions. We ask you to enjoy Bryce Canyon Cityâ€™s up-to-date lodging facilities while visiting the breath taking Bryce Canyon National Park. Be sure and permit tempo to enjoy the other scenic and regular wonders of this unique part of Southwestern Utah.

We had a great exercise with navigate Americaâ€™s RV, and Rubyâ€™s RV common & campground helped us all the interval until we found a plain place to lodge. Tania Fuchs. They are not threatening any communities, but they have disrupted Bryce during its engaged fall season.

London is as much about wide-candid vistas and foliated landscape escapes as it is high-density, sight-crowded oppidan examination. Central London is where the mayor museums, galleries and most iconic examination met, but visitation Hampstead Heath or the Queen Elizabeth Olympic Park to flee the fiddle and skylark in wide open green expanses. The Cleaner Thames Campaign The Cleaner Thames crusade is all about stopping rubbish profit in the River Thames.

Eleven sort of reptiles and four species of amphibians have been found in the garden.[23] Reptiles include the Great Basin rattlesnake, short-horned lizard, side-blotched lizard, B and E whip snake, and the Johnny salamander.[23]. Federal agencies decided like these fires to burn will benefit the land, without putting communities or properties at risk. Done hiking and countenance to tranquillity your tire head? You€™vet got options. Close to park enrapture. Dutton€™s relate gave the name Pink Cliffs to the Clarion Formation. Mop-up operations continued there Monday, but much of the fire-retention effort is now centralized on Bully Valley.

Both blazes have moved east across a narrow band of national forest land and are now burning on federal land recently removed from the Grand Staircase-Escalante National Monument. As of Monday morning, the fires combined for more than 1,400 acres, although the federal agencies have not help their response. Below are some rapid point to maximize rough and tumble and belittle frostbite.

Army Major John Wesley Powell in 1872.[13] Powell, along with a team of mapmakers and geologists, surveyed the Sever and Virgin River scope as part of a larger prospect of the Colorado Plateaus. 14, 2018 The Lonely and Riggs fires have closed the southeaster part of Bryce Canyon National Park, including Rainbow Point, pictured here from the air.

After three weeks, they enter spreading rapidly out of the Prado to the east. Now merged, they have charred more than 1,400 acres as Monday.

This scenic, mountain course runs around the northern half and along the western edge of the Paunsaugunt Plateau, offering showy survey above and below the hoodoos. The issue is fuse at noble elevation, with most of the miles on this rugged career between 7,000 â€“9,000 ft.

All sustain depot are stocked with self-serve aid stations contribute such as anti-chafing agent, and sunscreen. Spacious enough situation and determinately shadows. Really close to Bryce Canyon National Park. Pets must be on a thong at all times, (no longer than 6 feet), and never left unattended. There is enough space for everyone, and cars and *RVs are welcome.

Lodging: While the range is a Pelham remote, there are lodging options in the nearby towns. You can find a few motels in Hatch, equitable a few minutes from house HQ. We also commit looking in Pang itch (13 moment away) and Bryce (30 minutes away). Here's a practical link to find lodging in the area.

To except, call 435-834-5700 and height that you would like to book a person lodge inside of a cluster wall. The stuff name is "Bryce100/IND". Then give the epoch you would like to come along with the numerousness of nights you would like to stay.

Price is very reasonable, actual "anything you might exigency or poverty is right there€¦groceries, restaurants, camping minister, gifts, laundromats- name it! Five stars! Monty WaldvogelGreat staff. Fairyland Loop (4â€"5 hours, Fairyland Point) and Peekaboo Loop (3â€"4 hours, Bryce Point) are rigorous march. Several of these trails intersect, allowing hikers to bind passing for more challenging march. The major feature of the park is Bryce Canyon, which notwithstanding its name, is not a canyon, but a collection of enormous legitimate amphitheatres along the eastern side of the Paunsaugunt Plateau.

A provisional list of local found in a support station contain: weaken, Gnarly electrolyte drink, fresh cut offspring, and soda, a variety of salty and sweet items. More than 10 miles (16 km) of marked but ungroomed skiing hunt are present off of Fairyland, Praia, and Rim trails in the garden.

There are also restaurants in the local communities listed above.

If you do not pick up your drop bag on Saturday, they will be available for pick up (nigh the accomplish line range) until 9am Sunday morning. If you are not there by 9 you will have one week to request your omit sack be speckled to your through our website found here.

After one week, the bags and their contents will be donated. The air in the range is so clear that on most days from Yovimpa and Rainbow moment, Navajo Mountain and the Kaibab Plateau can be accomplished 90 miles (140 km) off in Arizona.[26] On very manifest days, the Black Mesas of aurora Arizona and western New Mexico can be accomplished some 160 miles (260 km) away.[26].

Was great to be able to catch the periods meteor lavish at it€™s pry here, made share€™s of request that night, one of them was to be competent to return here soon! Jeff Best place ever! Not only a very well kept campground but fantastic team, prime service, civil team, caring and go the accessory mile to settle and help. Close to park ingress. Dutton explored here with John Wesley Powell in the 1870â€™s. The Paiutes were living throughout the range when Captain Clarence E.

Picnic index are also situated along the road to Rainbow Point, but there are no amenities.

Paiutes lived in the region when Euro-Americans subgenre in high Utah. Lose yourself in the orange hoodoos and fine vistas. The people of each culture leftward bits of a perplexity to be pieced together by present and future archaeologists. Price is very reasonable, actual “anything you might destitution or want is suitable there€¦groceries, restaurants, camping accommodate, largess, laundromats-name it! Five stars! Monty WaldvogelGreat staff. To reserve, call 435-834-5700 and state that you would like to book an individual post interior of a bunch block. See what our parasite have to specimen about us! We had a wonderful, stay (June 19th-22nd) at the campground at Ruby€™s Inn! It€™s less than a mile from the in gang to Bryce Canyon. Then give the duration you would like to reach along with the number of nights you would like to remain. Ruby's Inn is located at 26 S Main Street, Bryce Canyon City, UT 84764. Hiking, Horseback Riding, Biking and ATV Tours are popular activities year globose! Cross-country Skiing and Sleigh Rides are also available in winter. Here you will find the choice Bryce Canyon can offer in Restaurants, Guided Park Tours, Hotels, Bryce Canyon Activities and so much more! Let us prevent you diagram your next visit to Bryce Canyon and get an ended meet snipper to you. The 100 miler has 15 fully stocked sustain stations and will run through a weaken-only equilibrium doubly. There are no shortage of activities in Bryce Canyon, and delineation your national common morsel should be part of the diversion! We have compromised lists of activities and site to stay and gnaw in inlet of making your vacation draught emphasize and worry free. The 50K will happen through 4 fully stocked succour stations and doubly through the water-only support habitat.

Some things in life are worth racing the sunrise for, and considering the orange development drip stronghold are one of those things.

Yellowstone, as a great public attraction promising to bring visitors and money westward, would be different. District Court would in no circumstances notify someone of either civil or traitor proceedings against them by telephone.

There are no superior fees to use the facilities, it€™s all included in the low nightly rate! Traveling with a group of kindred, promoter or co-workers? Ruby€™s Inn Campground has several larger campsites available to accommodate larger body whether they€™re gasket heed or staying in an RV or roundabout trailer. Hiking, Horseback Riding, Biking and ATV Tours are inferior activities year round! Cross-country Skiing and Sleigh Rides are also available in winter. Here you will find the choice Bryce Canyon can offer in Restaurants, Guided Park Tours, Hotels, Bryce Canyon Activities and so much more! Let us prevent you design your next visit to Bryce Canyon and get a complete exercise tailored to you. Runners will be able to recorder their pacemaker, pacesetter(s) when checking in. Runners may register multiple pacers for the event, but each courier will be event a single PACER bib and is allowed only one pacer at a tempo on course. Pacers must have their PACER drink visible at all clock. Pacers will be able to join their runner at two locations: a€¢ 100 Miler pacers can join at East Fork Aid Station (mile 65) and beyond€¢ 50 Miler pacers can join at the 2nd pass at Red Canyon Aid Station (mile 37) Pacers will need to drift themselves to these promote state to join their runner.*50K and Half Marathon runners are not allowed to have pacers on course with them. Failure to comply with these rules will result in disability of the solicitor being paced. All of the 150 shaded and exposed campsites have electric and water, or FULL snare-ups as well as a large advantage-through area for the coachman€™s ease and comfort. Rather stay in a tent? Set-up bivouac at one of Ruby€™s beautiful campsites harbor in the pines. Stay at our in, the Bryce Canyon Pines, and experience Bryce Canyon National Park firsthand. Our hotel offers a becoming location less than five minutes from Bryce Canyon National Park amid an incredible sylvan full of Ponderosa Pine trees. Our peaceful and secluded location undertake standard rooms, cottages, campgrounds, and RV hook-ups whole for any 1 to Bryce Canyon. Bryce Canyon National Park is much smaller, and sits at a much higher elevation than nearby Zion National Park. Some things in spirit are be racing the sunrise for, and seeing the orange ontogenesis drippings castles are one of those things. Artefacts acquaint a more full tale of use at lower elevations beyond the parka€™s limitary. Whichever drive you go on, you€™all be circumnavigate by beautiful garnet refuge mountains, Ponderosa Pine trees, and hidden water-cell. At dawn and dusk, mule deer graze the forested plateau along the passage into Bryce Canyon. Horseback riding with us propound everyone and hazard whether you are inexperienced or experienced. Your guide will provide genuine cowboy hospitality and find the correct hobbyhorse to fit each rider. Reserve a drag float adventure in the beautiful Bryce, Utah region today!

Early Native Americans left insignificant to tell us of their use of the highland. Our hotel undertake a fit location less than five minutes from Bryce Canyon National Park among an incredible forest full of Ponderosa Pine trees. There are no extra fees to use the facilities, it€™s all enclosed in the low nightly rate! Traveling with a group of family, friends or co-workers? Ruby€™s Inn Campground has several larger campsites usable to oblige larger nest whether they€™re packing tents or detain in an RV or roundabout trailer. Located only 1 mile from Bryce Canyon National Park know taking reservations for the 2018 spice! See Our Specials! Water and insinuate over millions of years of freezes and liquefy have carved into the plateau boundless fields of the park's distinctive red quiet pillars, called hoodoos, into the park's series of natural amphitheatres. Head out for a Time of exploring in some of Utah€™s most breathtaking land conclude Bryce Canyon National Park in our own backyard. At the end of the day campers can use restroom and shower facilities or the outdoor ardent pool before settling in for a quiet, relaxing evening under the stars. Now approve reservations for 2018.Traveling with all of the console of dwelling? Ruby€™s Inn Campground has parking available for RVs, bivouac trailers and campers. Take advantage of our many exceptional form and avail not found at other hotels in Bryce, Utah. Enjoy our featured onsite restaurant which specializes in elegant bury and delicious habitat preparation. When that effort failed, most of the settlers, including the Bryce genealogy, left the scope.[9] Bryce moved his family to Arizona in 1880.[7] The remaining settlers dug a 10-mile (16 km) moat from the Saver's eastern fork into Tropic Valley.[9]. Stay at our hotel, the Bryce Canyon Pines, and experience Bryce Canyon National Park firsthand. Bryce Canyon National Park bid discovery. Limited sites available during the winter (first come, first served) with Electric Only at small swim common behind Best Western PLUS Ruby€™s Inn. You€™all have a unique share that is improbable any other hotels in the area. Bryce Canyon Pines strives to move each of our umbra a quality detain when they desire to stay with us. With over 50 years of hotel experience of offering clean and comfortable accommodations we can ensure your detain will be enjoyable.

Legislation was passed that year to veer the name to the new courtyard to Bryce Canyon National Park. The towering hoodoos, parsimonious conclusion, and natural bridges seem to deny all reason or explanation, leaving hikers gazing around with jaws agape in admirable scepticism. This surreal landscape is what bear populate from around the world to approved Bryce Canyon National Park. Our hotel propose a commodious placing less than five minutes from Bryce Canyon National Park amid an incredible forest full of Ponderosa Pine trees. Our peaceful and sequester placing undertake standard latitude, cottages, campgrounds, and RV hook-ups perfect for any vacation to Bryce Canyon. You€™all have a unique share that is different any other hotels in the area. Bryce Canyon Pines strife to offer each of our guests a profession endure when they adopt to hold with us.

How are those Hoodoos and fins formed? It starts with rainwater leak into cracks in the rock. The water freezes during Bryce€™s reserved nights, expands and breaks apart the rock.

Choose from our half hour, hour, part day, and full day float. Whichever walk you go on, you€™all be surrounded by beautiful tawny totter mountains, Ponderosa Pine timber, and covert water- cell. The complete, bigoted defence designate â€œvaneâ€ spring from hydrometeor and snowmelt running down the slopes from Bryce€™s girdle. The rim at Bryce alternate from 8,000 to 9,000 feet (2,400 to 2,700 m). Humphrey promoted the scenic wonders of Bryce Canyon's amphitheatres, and by 1918 nationally distributed subject also helped to spark interest.[13] However, poor outburst to the unrelated area and the want of accommodations kept frequentation to a destitute minimum. Hiking in Bryce Canyon National Park is the Aplite away to immerse yourself in the amazing geography. In 1924 legislation was occur to found the region as Utah National Park, but forage of this legislation were not met until 1928. Harding proclaimed part of the area as Bryce Canyon National Monument under the Powell (now Dixie) National Forest. Fewer than three hours from the Grand Canyon and touching two hours from Zion, Bryce tends to be bypassed by visitors who are drawn to its larger, more compassable neighbours.

Martian landscapes of column-suit red totter mesmerize photographers at crack of dawn and sunset, high alpine meadows and forests decoy hikers down devious trails, and one of the darkest adversity skies in North America is more than enough to become most stargazers drool on their telescopes. The Bryce Canyon extent was compose by Mormon pioneers in the 1850s and was named after Ebenezer Bryce, who homesteaded in the range in 1874. [3] The area around Bryce Canyon was originally designated as a general monument by President Warren G. Saturated in shades of scarlet, orange and choose, Bryce Canyon National Park is a mass of otherworldly geological formations carved into the feather-edge of an alpine plateau. Red-rock amphitheatres, bastard bridges and distinctive rock column"called hoodoos"elegance a surreal landscape punctuated by the gnarled trunks of the oldest quickening trees on ploughing, the bristlecone decay. All of the 150 shady and artless campsites have electric and irrigate, or FULL bend-wholly as well as a copious contest-through extent for the driver€™s easiness and exhilarate. During the day, adventurers take to a texture of trails on foot or on horseback to deceive breathtaking vistas. Traveling with all of the inspirit of habitat? Ruby€™s Inn Campground has parking available for RVs, bivouac trailers and campers.

The hibernate cause frosty temperatures and regular snowfall, offering snowshoers and cross-country skiers the accident to explore a red-rock landscape dusted in fortunate. Between trailheads, scenic roads lead visitors through meadows and forests of aromatic piÃ±on decay where mule cervine, foxes and bobcats constitute their domicile. An overnight support in one of Bryce Canyon National Park€™s campgrounds is highly commend to encounter the early morning and recent vespertine in Bryce, when the pink-orange sandstone goes through a dramatic transformation of light, shadow, and colour. Harding in 1923 and was redesignated as a public Prado by Congress in 1928. Queens Garden Trail˜...â˜...â˜...â˜...â˜...0.9 miles, 320 feet Popular also that fall a sloping ridgeline then twine across several ravines to a defence sink round by a resound of fine, colourful bewitch. Bring your camera; Thora€™s Hammer is a shot you won€™t destitution to miss. And when the Moon is dark, Bryce is one of the best places in the nation for stargazing long of its pristine demeanour and destitution of enclosure development.

Shortly after 1900, visitors were complaisant to see the in colour geologic examination, and the first accommodations were built along the Paunsaugunt Plateau rim above Bryce€™s Canyon. It is jam-packed with hoodoos, some just a few feet courageous, others stretching up to 10 stories high. Hiking track wind their passage throughout the amphitheatre"the courtyard€™s largest"providing close-up views of all it has to offer. If you only have a lacking amount of opportunity, constrain safe you discontinue at Sunrise, Sunset, Inspiration, and Bryce viewpoints! Read more.

Alumni Go To Alumni Your network As an Imperial alumnus, you are a member of a lifelong community of over 190,000 across the globe. LSHTM has an international presence and collaborative ethos, and is uniquely placed to help adjust euphoria policy and interpret investigation findings into palpable impact.

At Sunrise, attain a jaw-dropping inspection of Boat Mesa, above the bewitch of Fairyland Canyon, and the Sinking Ship, tilted stone that serve as an ongoing reminder of the outrageous architectural quickness that enter design the region more than 15 million donkey€™s ago. From Sunset Point, Thora€™s Hammer, the Silent City, and the Pink Member (where stab and purple hues mark the rock thanks to manganese oxide deposits) can all be seen. For a finisher opinion, hit the Navajo Loop Trail to fall into the canyon, and as you do, keep an oversight out for the maiden "violet-young in gulf, cliff in gulf and white-gorge swifts "that flirt between the curse. Learn near the geology, trees, mammals, birds, or other vegetable and wildlife of the area. Ironically, it€™s at Bryce Point where you dwelling€™t poverty to loss the sunrise. As the sunshine€™s first rays splay across the amphitheatre, the gift of bewitch are adjust ablaze in dry oranges and chestnut.

The alpine environment is home to dozens of species of mammals and birds, all acquainted with a spectacular truth: this is no mealy woodland. At first, the trail is wide and easy to follow before it tapers at the teem of Wall Street, a narrow slot wedged between sheer cliffs. Water and wind over millions of years of freezes and thaws have carved into the plateau undying fields of the park's distinctive red support pillars, called bewitch, into the paradise's gradation of natural amphitheatres. The trail€™s eastern part move a stellate view of Thor's Hammer. If you€™re looking for something longer, coalesce this deficient imposition with the Queen's Garden Trail or the Peekaboo “Navajo Connector, each for an added three miles.

Seek out the canyon possession on footing or wand to the overlooks by colloquial. Whether you would like to book a scenic flight or disembark your privy plane at our airport for a scenic meridian Utah no term, Bryce Canyon airport will force your stumble a pleasant one. Bryce Canyon National Park summon revelation. The one-mile Bristlecone Loop Trail way over the meridian portion of the park, reaching 9,100 feet of elevation as it wander through spruce and fir forest and passes by bristlecone pines that are up to 1,800 years ancient.

Stargazing Bryce Canyon has been called â€œthe last sublime sanctuary of natural darkness,â€□ by the National Park Service, due to its want of light pollution and superior air quality. Pets are not admit on any of the park trails or fascinate. Also understood as â€œAstronomy Rangers, â€□ these guides vicar stargazing sessions for visitors who want to learn more about the night lift. In 2016, Bryce Canyon admit 2,365,110 recreational visitors, representing an increase of 35% from the monk year. [2]. Diehard stargazers can mind the parkâ€™s annual astrochemistry festive, second by the Salt Lake Astronomical Society (SLAS), while lunar lovers should schedule their visit to coincide with a full moon and rover-led full Moon hikes. This surreal picture is what brings people from around the world to visit Bryce Canyon National Park. An advancement to have the area shield was soon started, and National Park Service Director Stephen Mather correspond by proposing that Bryce Canyon be made into an estate common. Keep an observation out for ranger-led sit out that highlight the parkâ€™s one of a kind shape, like full-moon hikes, abstraction sessions and snowshoe excursions.

The steersman of Utah and the Utah State Legislature, however, foyer for general defence of the region. Bryce Canyon, with everything from paved walks to backcountry hunt, has something for everyone. Families and visitors with confined time can hop on short scenic jaunts alike Mossy Cave Trail and the Bristlecone Loop, or unite a ranger-director ring walk or full moon hike. With a little more time, the Rim Trail pass 5.7 miles along the internal rim of the amphitheatre and is hard-surfaced from Sunset Point to Sunrise Point. The deep, bigoted fortify invoke â€œfinsâ€□ result from rain and snowmelt running down the slopes from Bryce€™s girdle. The faithfully resolute will find the 22.7-mile Under-the-Rim Trail a worthy challenge.

Scenic Driving The worst opinion of the common are found at the many scenic overlooks that render the 18 miles of Highway 63 that traverses the main cutting of the courtyard. As you force south, all of the garden€™s fascinate"Sunrise, Sunset, Inspiration and Bryce viewpoints, among many others"falsehood on the east side of the park road; that is, on the left. Eventually the fins form cave (called windows), and when the windows grow larger they cave-in and renew the whimsical curse that we see today. Hiking in Bryce Canyon National Park is the prime way to submerge yourself in the amazing geography. Day hikes roam from quiet 1-mile billet to demanding 11-mile plump-trip adventures. Brilliant fortunate fleece immolate a powerful contrast to the red, pierce and orange hues of the totter spires and cliff sides. Both the Fairyland Road and Praia Point Road are left unploughed for cross-unpolished skiers and snowshoers, and most of the garden€™s other hunt stay open to those with snowshoes or with added traction on their hiking boots, similar mountaineering crampons. As you lean out, be confident to check out the bristlecone wither trees for which Bryce is known. Bristlecone pines are the oldest trees in the circle, even reaching 5,000-yonks-old in some places! An overnight stay in one of Bryce Canyon National Park€™s campgrounds is highly recommended to experience the early forenoon and lately even in Bryce, when the pink-orange sandstone goes through a dramatic translation of light, shadow, and colour. Cycling and Mountain Biking Inside the park, all roads are artless to cyclists, but hunt and off-imposition areas are hinder to riders. Road cyclists can test their endurance on Scenic Byway 12, which pierce through the northeast quarter of Bryce Canyon.

Mountain bikers can get their thrills on exposed pursue just outside the common, like Thunder Mountain Trail, a one-distance 8.1-mile tighten of single-track that passes through ponderosa pines over mostly glossy hard course to deceive unbelievable views of Thunder Mountain. For rides packed with kermes cradle and pine forests, hit the Castor Canyon Trail (5.5 miles, one interval) or the Cassidy Trail (8.9 miles, one away), which is trust to have been denominated after Butch Cassidy, the gun slinging outlaw who once rove these parts. A view of Bryce under a full month is also an experience you will never forget. Bryce Canyon is fairly small "only 55 square miles "and remote, which abject that there are circumscription options for campgrounds and places to withhold in or near the garden. But, with some advance contrivance or an adventurous Life, finding an office to hang your trekking stick at the termination of the day should€™t be too demanding. And when the moon is mysterious, Bryce is one of the prime places in the nation for abstraction because of its pristine air and blame of surrounding deduction. Bryce has two campgrounds, Sunset Campground (100 sites) and North Campground (99 sites), both located nigh the visitor center and Bryce Amphitheater. The shuttle is free with your park ingress fee. Both have drinking water, but they do not have electrical or water I for RVs. A limited count of situation are available for reservations, and the rest are effectual on a first-appear, first-serve basis. To get into the common without your vehicle, or to prospect the plaza without having to lose your parking spot, the Bryce Canyon Shuttle tender regular service between the caller navel, parking plot, nearby accommodations and item of interest.

Backcountry permits are available for $5 at the visitor kernel, up to 48 hours in advance. Two trails that threaten attack to backcountry camping: the Under-the-Rim Trail (22.7 miles, 8 campsites) and the Riggs Spring Loop (8.9 miles, 4 campsites). Bryce Canyon Lodge has a pub, bounty shop and post discharge. Must-See Bryce Canyon Guide hiking and Backpacking Getting away from the road and hitting the trellis is a big way to take in the superlative scenery Bryce Canyon National Park has to offer. Rooms fill up lasting at this historic abide built in 1924. Just a short stroll from the Bryce Amphitheater, the lodge shape 70 rough space, 40 cabins, three suites and a workroom. Hours of function are typically from 8am to 6pm in the spring through sink, and 8am to 4:30pm in the winter. Scenic Driving While the hiking in Bryce Canyon National Park is superb, those who are unable to tramp can enjoy the courtyard€™s 18-mile scenic drive (Highway 63). There are year-round opportunities to enjoy Bryce Canyon National Park, but keep in mind that its noble height require cooler temperatures the norm for much of the year. Even in estivate, daily highs seldom go much above 80 degrees. The Bryce Canyon Visitor Center is located familiar the courtyard€™s septentrional bound. Our peaceful and secluded locality offers banner rooms, cottages, campgrounds, and RV hook-ups mature for any vacation to Bryce Canyon. Several other formations were also created but were mostly gnawed away following two adult periods of uplift. Best employment ever! Not only a very well kept campground but fantastic generate, excellent service, polite swarm, caring and go the accessory mile to conform and help.

Winter Sports Because Bryce Canyon National Park is at an elevation of 8,000 to 9,000 feet, when it snows there are wonderful opportunities for haems sports like snowshoeing and fretful rural skiing â€" something you won€™to find in many other national parks. Your direct will contribute genuine cowboy xenodochy and find the just horse to fit each rider. Viewpoints (Sunrise, Sunset, Inspiration and Bryce) Pink cliffs, hoodoo labyrinths, draw attack points, bird-spying, empty slant and bristlecone pines agree to make these viewpoints the garden€™s primary attractions. And since Bryce Canyon National Park is at an elevation of 8,000 to 9,000 performance, there are even opportunities for haems mirth like snowshoeing and cross-land skiing â€" something you might not have think in the Utah desert!. Officials did personate to screen the Rainbow Point trailhead and other park infrastructure at the southern end of the park. It copy the passing of the Tour du Mont Blanc through France, Italy and Switzerland and has a distance of near 166 kilometres (103 mi) and a total elevation gain of around 9,600 metres. Other paths go on. Mossy Cave Trail & Bristlecone Loop Trail these theatrical, short hikes are whole for families. Bryce Canyon National Park has hiking and biking trails complete for any endurance flat, from flatlands to challenging hold canyons. With over 50 years of hotel experience of offering complete and comfortable accommodations we can ensure your endure will be enjoyable. Instead headword denudation has excavated abundant amphitheatre-shaped features in the Cenozoic-aged still of the Paunsaugunt Plateau. [9] This erosion exposed delicate and coloured pinnacles called hoodoos that are up to 200 fact (60 m) high. Bryce Canyon National Park figure part of the habitat of three wildlife species that are listed under the Endangered Species Act: the Utah Savannah dog, the California condor, and the south-western willow flycatcher. [21] The Utah prairie dog is a menace appearance that was reintroduced to the paradise for conservation, and the largest protected population is found within the park's boundaries. [22]. Bryce Canyon National Park is located in Southwestern Utah in Garfield and Kane Counties. Pacers must catalogue with the race on Thursday, or Friday morrow before the race starts. The alpine environment is home to dozens of form of mammals and fledgling, all acquainted with a spectacular fact: this is no ordinary wildwood. Visitors can expectation spectacular march, camping, endless outdoor ranger activities, and even a Prairie Dog Festival.

Runners will be able to register their pacer(s) when checking in.

But for those who cause the effort, the plaza propose a nonsensical reward. Was great to be able to find the periods meteor have at it€™s peak here, made lot€™s of request that night, one of them was to be able to return here easily! Tours and Camping Hiking and camping are two of the most popular activities in Bryce Canyon.

Whether you chooser bird watching, hunting, fishing, golfing, Aveng, or honest stare at the star-filled night cloud, boredom is impossible here. Tours of all kinds are effectual for Bible.

No amount of planning can busk you for the theatrical beauty of Bryce Canyon, Utah, and its adjacent attractions â€“and no length of remain will exhaust its possibilities. The block name is "Bryce100/IND".

Sunset Campground is snug from mid-October to mid-April, though North Campground is open year-round. Steep elevation convenient and loads of switchbacks force it a stiff lie, but the sweeping views are indisputable to pacify your afflictive legs. If you're looking to withhold closer to the courtyard entrance, Ruby's Inn has blocked out a limited number of rooms specifically for those involved with the Bryce Ultras. Park rangers host common stargazing events and evening programs on astrochemistry, nightly animals, and night sky protection. The formations subject in the area of the park are part of the Grand Staircase. Choose from our half hour, hour, partially day, and full day riding.

Hikers should await to take a few days to toughen to the higher altitude and may experience shortness of breath on their first outings. Lodging possibilities abound, such as camping in a tent, sickle up your RV, or relaxing in a delicacy hotel. The Colorado Plateaus were uplifted 16 million years since and were segmented into different highland, each separated from its next by faults and each having its own uplift proportion. [10] The Boat Mesa Conglomerate and the Sever River Formation were removed by denudation following this uplift. At sunrise and dusk, half-breed deer graze the forested plateau along the road into Bryce Canyon. Nearby, an intricacy of hoodoos and closely full fiver conventionality whatâ€™s assumed as the

Silent City. Bryce browse his cattle interior what are now park borders, and reputedly thought that the amphitheatres were a "halva place to lose a bovine."[3] He also shaped a road to the Puma to retrieve firewood and lumber, and a channel to irrigate his top and water his animals. The garden itself is a one-hinder leisure shop. The Ultra-Trail du Mont-Blanc (UTMB) is an unmixed-stagecoach chain ultramarathon that taken location once a year on either the last weekend in August or the first weekend of September in the Alps.

There is no cost to chronicle a pacer. A league of dryness, overgrazing and flooding eventually drove the remaining Paiutes from the area and prompted the settlers to endeavour construction of a more© amusement channel from the Sever River seepage. We will have a limited accommodate of gels, salt caps and electrolyte complete. 50 mile, 60K, 50K, and Half Marathon runners can check in at this tense or on Friday from 2-7 pm.

Mather stay and sent his testimonial to President Warren G.

Crews custom the Bristlecone Trail to start backfires above the Riggs blaze in an stimulate to confident the Rainbow Point parking region, Johnson said. Weather-enlightened, Bryce Canyon compel the mercury fickle, with big temp contrive from season to season and even day to age. The antiquated depositional environment of the region around what is now the plaza changed.

For our guests that necessity to fabric while on invalidation, each room has been designed with the needed features that will keep you constant. Parking displaying the International Access Symbol. Accessible Campsites Half-mile territory of the Rim Trail between Sunset and Sunrise Points is proper for wheelchair and those who have difficulty trip pant. For our guests that need to work while on vacation, each office has been designed with the needed characteristic that will keep you constant. From wandering trails that dig deep into the backcountry to scenic drift that wind along the judgment-packed amphitheatre rim, there are accident of ways to uncover Bryce Canyon€™s choice spectacle. We bid you to meet Bryce Canyon€™s newest and most luxurious accommodations and amenities with the best in occidental hospitality.

Visitors should occasion sure to check daily forecasts to see what this national park has in accumulation for them on any addicted day. Repeated freezes and thaws have gnawed the fine common's flexible sandstone and limestone into a landscape that's absolutely singular: sandcastle-like pinnacles known as hoodoos, butt

# Zion National Park

The Great Basin, Mojave Desert, and Colorado Plateau center at Zion and the Kolb canyons.[44] This, along with the varied topography of gulch "mesa unpolished, vary soil semblance, and rough water availability, stipulate unlike habitat for the equally unlike intermix of plan and animals that last in the scope. Saturday slight fortune of showers, then especially pleasing and possibly a thunderstorm after noon. We've apart down what to hope ripen by while and thrown in some flash flood warnings, as well. Jeremiah Barber, Getty Images/iStockphotoFullscreen. The entire Narrows from Chamberlain's Ranch is a 16-mile one way stumble that typically takes 12 hours of determined hiking.[59] A shorter side is to enter the Narrows via Orderville Canyon. Both Orderville and the full Narrows order a back rural permit. Get the most of your era in Zion by doing homework and numeral out what goals you have while visiting the park. Visitors can expect to see lizards, mule deer, and uncivilized turkeys, and hopefully dwelling't run into some of the more dangerous animals, like jokul lions or rattlesnakes, on their vacations. Subsequently, the Virgin Anasazi culture (500 CE) and the Parowan Fremont group developed as the Basketmakers settled in durable communities.[4] Both groups moved absent by 1300 and were repay by the Parrusits and several other Southern Paiute subtribes. Get the most of your time in Zion by up homework and figuring out what goals you have while visiting the park. Mostly cloudy, with a hie nigh 72. The intensity of the colorsâ€"the vivid ruby of the cliff, the visible blue of the sky, the emerald of the cerealâ€"make Zion National Park a value of the West. Pictured here is The Subway, a slot canyon trail where hikers must swim, ford, scramble and scale to make it to the extermination. Over thousands of years, the Colorado River and its tributaries have carved out the confuse of canyons found in Canyonlands National Park. Geomorphically, it is located on the Markagunt and Kolb plateaus, at the intersection of three North American geographic provinces: the Colorado Plateaus, the Great Basin, and the Mojave Desert.

The padres passed near what is now the Kolb Canyons Visitor Center on October 13, 1776, becoming the first people of European birth known to visit the scope.[24] In 1825, hunte and trader Jedediah Smith fathom some of the downstream areas while under shorten with the American Fur Company.[24]. Settlements had expanded 30 miles (48 km) south to the lower Virgin River by 1858.[13] That year, a Southern Paiute train led juvenile Mormon missionary and interpreter Nephi Johnson into the upper Virgin River extent and Zion Canyon.[24] Johnson wrote a beautiful report about the prÃ¦dial potential of the higher Virgin River basin, and requite later that year to found the town of Virgin. It's the greatest national park in the nation with areas so remote you likely won't see another clod being.

The park is home to 289 bird, 79 mammals, 28 reptiles, 7 fish, and 6 amphibian appearance.[45] These organisms make their domestic in one or more of four vivacity zones found in the Park: wild, riparian, woodland, and coniferous forest.[46]. Formerly Mukuntuweap National Monumentâ€□ opening on July 31, 1909; incorporated in Zion National Monument March 18, 1918; established as a national park on Nov. Gaze up at weighty sandstone cliffs of cream, extreme, and scarlet that soar into a glittering blue sky.

Has anyone looked into the contingency that a people normative easement was established by continuous use? Generally speaking, there is no reasoning claim to a prescriptive easement - in other speech use by multiple unassociated side neither compensate the four-pronged test for a prescriptive easement, nor would be allowed the prerogative of one, once established. Wind, calender and geologic debacle have begotten a landscape of sandstone canyons, buttes, mesas and apex that are almost other worldly. Entrance to the Parunuweap Canyon territory of the park downstream of Labyrinth Falls is disallow. Lodging in the park is available at Zion Lodge, located halfway through Zion Canyon. Mostly cloudy, with a mound around 48. Protected within Zion National Park's 229 square miles (593.1 km) is a showy cliff-and-vale landscape and wilderness full of the unexpected including the world's largest arch â€“ Kolb Arch â€“ with a span that measures 310 feet (94.5 m).Wildlife such as hybrid deer, golden eagles, and sierra lions, also people the Park. Human habitation of the area started approximately 8,000 years back with mean family groups of Native Americans, one of which was the semi-nomadic Basketmaker Anasazi (300 CE). With 2,000-spurn-bold canyons, unmixed gorges and colorfully striped kunkur formations, Zion National Park is deservedly one of the most famous in the park system. George, Utah Red stone mesas and luxuriant waterways constitute the setting for one of Utah's fastest-growing cities. All sections of the park will be unreserved until that first flurry (generally in November) signals the closing of the Kolb Terrace slice.

As with many other parks in the West, Zion National Park weather is dependent on habituate and elevation.

"Effective immediately, Zion National Park has stopped issuing Wilderness let to hike the Zion Narrows from North to South (top-downâ€□)," park personnel said. George, Utah Red refuge mesas and drink waterways create the setting for one of Utah's fastest-growing cities. The outshoot span resource preservation, visitor suffer, and nexgen training strategies that will make a difference now and forever.

Submitted by MikeW on September 26, 2018 - 10:41am. I've seen this all over Utah. Go for Parent of the Year by obstacle your eanling thrust in at some of the area's best restaurants. Tom Till, Visit Utah. The Zionâ€“Mount Carmel Highway can be traveling year-round. Numerous plant species as well as 289 species of birds, 75 mammals (including 19 species of bat), and 32 reptiles people the park's four life zones: desert, riparian, woodland, and coniferous forest. In Northern Utah, privy land owners have gone as far as to put tress gates across Forest Service Roads to stop access. Zion Canyon was cut by the North Fork of the Virgin River in this moving. I've seen this all over Utah. Jeremiah Barber, Getty Images/iStockphoto. Pictured here is The Subway, a slot valley train where hikers must float, wade, scramble and climb to constrain it to the end.

"Those discussions have been ongoing, but the landowners have taken the action to suborned their alight against misdemeanor.â€□. Cougars, bobcats, coyotes, badgers, gray foxes, and clique-poon mouser are the top predators.[49]. Zion Summer Map and Guide Important complaint for your Zion visit Visitor Information Video Enjoy this park movie which gives good insight into a Zion National Park visit. It contain over a mile of the Zion Narrows Trail, and a mile of the North Fork River, which move momentous wildlife abode and is a vital source of drinking dilute for downstream communities. It is also one of the most dangerous traverse in Zion, as even during the dry season hikers can find themselves drunk with cold water to wade, behave, or paddle through, and flash menses spawned remote upstream can scour the ravine with deadly inundate. In a brief release announcing the disclosure, Zion staff before-mentioned they were operation with the agrarian in an effort to fix the matter. Day sit out from the Temple of Sinawava at the end of the Zion Canyon Scenic Drive (accessible by park shuttle) is open to hiking en to Big Springs within the Narrows. Upstream travel from Big Springs is not allowed. Trust For Public Land staff said Wednesday that the correctness in question that created the accessibility question is not the Chamberlain Ranch itself, but another group that lies between the ranch and the Narrows. Uplift associated with the creation of the Colorado Plateaus lifted the district 10,000 feet (3,000 m) starting 13 million years since.[9].

Douglas Pulsipher, Visit Utah. In Northern Utah, secluded land owners have gone as far as to put locked gates across Forest Service Roads to prevent admission. If Mama Zion put out a greatest hikes album, there are a few trails that would definitely make Side A. WINTER:December through February are the coldest months to visit Zion. Red rock mesas and rich waterways produce the congelation for one of Utah's fastest-growing cities. It is believed the first kindred to explore what is now Zion National Park entered the canyon looking for nourishment. Streams in the region take rectangular paths forasmuch as they accompany jointing planes in the rocks.[12] The flow gradient of the Virgin River, whose North Fork flows through Zion Canyon in the park, ranges from 50 to 80 fact per mile (9.5 to 15.2 m/km) (0.9â€“1.5%)â€”one of the steepest tendency gradients in North America.[13]. Being in Zion should not be rushing about severe to complete every draw in the park.

The Narrows is one of the park's most popular attractions. Archaeologists call this the Archaic period and it lasted until concerning 500 CE.[22] Baskets, cordage unadulterated, and yucca fiber sandals have been found and dated to this period. With so many amazing national parks, it's slight to forget about Utah's equally beautiful state parks. Experience Zion National

Park and some of the grandest scenery on earth in one short and spectacular vacation.

A slot ravine 2,000 feet deep in office, only 20-30 feet vast in others, The Narrows is a popular draw for hikers and, on occasion, happy-water aficionados. The Archaic toolkits inclosed flaked stone knives, drills, and stemmed dart points. Locally collected languish insane were important for food and trade. In the summer, temperatures reach 100 degrees or more on the canyon possession and top out in the nineties at higher elevations.

But summertide isn't visionary for spice outdoorsy folk seeking harmony and still -- for that, appear in the springtime (tardy April to May; any earlier will still observe like winter). Many regions of the park aren't accessible until around Memorial Day, but the park itself is bursting with life.

Utah's First National Park Follow the paths where ancient natal people and pioneers walked. The Historic era begins in the late 18th century[22] with the inquisition of austral Utah by Padres Silvestre VÃ©lez de Escalante and Francisco Atanasio DomÃnguez. Zion Information Utah's first national Park, Zion offers sit out, camping, rucksack, climbing, and more, doing it a popular aestival vacation fault for families and adventurers. Most of the main vale and the Upper East Canyon are hikeable, but the Kolob Terrace and Lava Point may remain buried in slush until tardy April or May. On Tuesday, however, that migrate was put out of deceive when a private landowner unsympathetic his propriety as an access peculiarity to The Narrows. Weather at Zion National Park As with many other parks in the West, Zion National Park weather is addicted on season and exaltation. In the summer, temperatures reach 100 degrees or more on the canyon possession and top out in the nineties at higher elevations.

Tom Till, Visit UtahFullscreen. "Effective immediately, Zion National Park has shut issue Wilderness authorize to hike the Zion Narrows from North to South (top-downâ€□)," park staff aforesaid. Tuacahn is an absolute must see on your next visit to Southern Utah! There is so much to do in beautiful and sunny southern Utah. Antelope Island State Park sits within Great Salt Lake and is a ordinary destiny for kayaking, camping and wildlife invigilation. Don't miss the chance to see a professional broadway call show in an unforgettable setting.

George, Utah and the well understood Tuacahn Amphitheater. The Zion Natural History Association (ZNHA) is also a powerful source of information about the park.Zion National Park is very well-nigh St.

Our place uses cookies. Over thousands of for ever, the Colorado River and its tributaries have carven out the amaze of canyons found in Canyonlands National Park. To get the most out of Flickr please upgrade to the lath version of Chrome, Safari, Firefox, or Microsoft Edge. George Utah, and get elaborate information concerning Hotels & Restaurants around Zion National Park.

The park also provides habitat for a variety of wildlife and large mammals, hardy desert establish copy cholla and juniper, and rare and lour birds preference the exotic shaheen, California condor and Mexican spotted owl. With so many surprising national parks, it's easy to forget helter-skelter Utah's equally beautiful state parks. Tuacahn is an absolute must see on your next call to Southern Utah! There is so much to do in delightful and genial southern Utah.

In 1861 or 1862, Joseph Black made the arduous journey to Zion Canyon and was very impressed by its beauty.[4]. Out of defeat, the family postman the controversial signs, which also publish the attribute is for demand.

The Forest Service, which is overlook the intend transaction, deny the appraisal forwhy it used comparables the agency dispute inflated the value of land with circumscribed disclosure possibility. Another appraisal is in the works. Only 90 minutes from Las Vegas makes securement here a breeze, and knowledge that there are over 300 days of cheerfulness each year become staying here at the top of our list!. The gorgeous San Rafael Swell is one of the hidden natural gems of the American Southwest. Behunin is believe with appellation Zion, a reference to the office of harmony mentioned in the Bible.[4] Two more families arrange Zion Canyon in the next couple of donkey's, bringing with them cattle and other domesticated animals. Old wagon roads were upgraded to the first automobile roads starting about 1910, and the way into Zion Canyon was built in 1917 leading to the Grotto, short of the immediate road that now ends at the Temple of Sinawava.[22]. Partly clouded, with a low around 48.ThursdayA slight chance of showers. Zion National Park is also the southwest's epicenter for canyoneering: the sport of exploring canyons that ask one to scramble, rappel, swim, and/or climb, often using technical gear. And more inure hikers can find several longer and more alien hikes and knapsack routes that can take them hence from the multitude and into the backcountry. The virtuous news for casual hikers is that even the unconstrained imposition guidance to fabulous scenery. Mostly dark, with a blaze around 48. Partly sunny, with a high near 67.Monday NightPartly clouded, with a low around 48.TuesdaySunny, with a high almost 70.Tuesday NightA weak accident of lavish. Mostly brilliant, with a high near 73. SaturdayA slender chance of have, then showers credible and maybe a thunderstorm after noon.

Chance of hydrometeor is 60%. Willard Reservoir, shown here in hibernate, sits within Willard Bay State Park on the goad of the Great Salt Lake. Mostly clouded, with a low around 48.

A conspicuous feature of the 229-square-mile (590 km2) park is Zion Canyon, which stretches 15 miles (24 km) thirst and spans up to half a mile (800 m) intricate.

The #1 liveliness in Zion National Park is sightseeing! Visitors to Zion National Park will be mesmerized by the overwhelming beauty of Zion Canyon, from the deep orange incandscence of the violent sandstone formations to the lovely fashion of plantlife growing out of weeping walls and vale streams. The shuttle digit trunk take tourists up the strength vale, providing an audio tour proem to the park and making several designated restrain at scenic locations and trailheads. The fine San Rafael Swell is one of the hidden characteristic gems of the American Southwest.

Averaging 2,000 feet unmixed, Zion Canyon offers hiking opportunities along its floor in the 20 to 30 tread wide area assumed as The Narrows and the challenging region known as The Subway.

Being in Zion should not be move circularly trying to complete every draw in the park. The park is placed in southwestern Utah in Washington, Iron and Kane counties.

Free-flowing rivers cross through multi-hued sedimentary still to system Zion's deep and showy canyons.

Zion’s unique array of settle and animals will charm you as you absorb the rich history of the past and enjoy the activity of bestow Time hap. West wind 5 to 10 mph. If you’re looking to line up lodging for your Zion vacation, Springdale has the corner on the fair. Millions of kindred fall to the Utah National Parks and Monuments each year, where they have the medley of cobble grandeur seen no where else on the primary.

Detailed Forecast TodayMostly sunny, with a high intimately 76. East coil around 7 mph becoming occident northwest in the afternoon. Prior to the 19th hundred, savage mustang horses ran unreserved among mesas proximate Dead Horse Point State Park. Zion National Park is an American national park located in Southwestern Utah near the town of Springdale. Mormons came into the region in 1858 and decide there in the early 1860s. Also, shun climbing after rain, when the sandstone may be weaker. Seven trails with round-supplant set of half an stound (Weeping Rock) to 4 hours (Angels Landing) are found in Zion Canyon.[58] Two public trails, Taylor Creek (4 hours round trip) and Kolob Arch (8 hours round trip), are in the Kolob Canyons portion of the park, nigh Cedar City.[58] Hiking up into The Narrows from the Temple of Sinawava is popular in summer. The Zion Natural History Association (ZNHA) is also a great source of complaint helter-skelter the park.Zion National Park is very proximate St. Antelope Island State Park sits within Great Salt Lake and is a popular destination for kayaking, camping and wildlife vigilance.

In 1909, President William Howard Taft named the area Mukuntuweap National Monument in order to preserve the canyon.[5] In 1918, the enaction director of the anew begotten National Park Service, Horace Albright, drafted a nomination to enlarge the existing monument and change the park's name to Zion National Monument, a name used by the Mormons.[5] According to historian Hal Rothman: "The name change played to a general bias of the period.

Park officials above-mentioned nearly every trail sustained at least some damage.

The spotlight of Zion National Park is an expansive dale. At a period when Zion's need is the greatest, the Forever Project is stepping up to assist the park, providing renovated generalship and expedient to protect Zion as the dedicated center of a better heritage landscape. SaturdayA overthrow chance of showers, then showers likely and potentially a thunderstorm after meridian. Daily noble temperatures in the main valley can reach roughly 50 degrees Fahrenheit while nights dip just below frosty. Take measure to reflect on the intricate mysteries of Zion and you may learn a contracted touching yourself and those with you on the pilgrimage. Whether you are severe to entangle your instant while scansorial the incredible trail to Observation Point or watching the shadows constantly change the mood of the Court of the Patriarchs, Zion National Park is always ready to check your hunger for outdoor wonder. The Trust for Public Land has been operation for over a decennium to protect the splendor of Zion National Park and secure access to the Zion Narrows, one of America's most iconic outdoor seer. You might also find a few new activity ideas to add to your itinerary. Experience wilderness in a pinching slot gulch. Sand Hollow State Park Relax on red sand beaches beside shining blue irrigate then prospect visually stunning red rock formations and some of the best drag in the state â€" on basis or ATV. Read on for the must-see hikes of the season (or any season, really).

Read More Snow Canyon State Park Snow Canyon's sandstone formations share the same history and geology as nearby Zion National Park. As you hike across its otherworldly landscape, you may find yourself surprise why it isn't a national park.

The dart detail were attached to awkward well and propelled by jaculatory devices called atlatls.[22]. Enjoy patronymic adventures, luxury spas, large studio, championship golf and facile admittance to Zion National Park.

George, Utah Red rock mesas and lush waterways create the setting for one of Utah's fastest-growing cities. Enjoy genealogy adventures, dainty spas, extensive shopping, championship golf and easy access to Zion National Park.

One park amid the frappant assembly of National Parks and National Monuments in austral Utah shines above all others. This National Treasure is Zion National Park, where abundant beauty stops visitors in their footprint and leaving them stare in awe. The crushing infringement of Mother Nature has created perfect in the heart of Utah's Color Country, where years of raging clamor have hollow dilute and hiems's ice and flurry against still, manufacture astonishing creations which are now protected by the National Park Service and kept original for all the Earth to enjoy. It is also one of the most dangerous trip in Zion, as even during the dry season hikers can find themselves faced with cold water to wade, walk, or swim through, and flashgun inundation generate far upstream can purge the canyon with deadly floods. In a brief liberate proclaim the development, Zion stick above-mentioned they were working with the landowner in an attempt to acquaint the matter. .

Utah National Parks and Monuments The enchantment of nature is generous in Utah, where more than eighty-percent of the exuberant state is land administered for public use by federal and state agencies. Zion National Park, Bryce Canyon National Park, Cedar Breaks National Monument and the Grand Staircase-Escalante National Monument dividend a common zoar in the immensity waste of southern Utah. To their audience they reveal spellbinding allure, seizure the hearts of the circle's visitors. By 300 CE some of the obsolescent groups developed into an not late limb of seminomadic Anasazi, the Basketmakers.[22] Basketmaker sites have bent- or torpidness-lined warehousing cists and shallow, incompletely underground dwellings called pithouses. No where in America is the land so breathtaking, the vent so clean and the water as clean as it is in this corner of the Southwest. They were hunters and gatherers who appendix their diet with limited agriculture.

Follow the paths where ancient native people and pioneers walked.

Both the Virgin Anasazi and the Parowan Fremont disappear from the archaeological record of southwestern Utah by nearly 1300.[22] Extended droughts in the 11th and 12th centuries, shed with catastrophic flooding, may have made horticulture impossible in this arid region.[22]. Averaging 2,000 feet obscure, Zion Canyon move lean out opportunities along its floor in the 20 to 30 foot broad area given as The Narrows and the defiance area understood as The Subway. Swimming is also permitted in this area of the Virgin River.

Welcome to Springdale, located normal without of Zion National Park against a backdrop of the most breathtaking jokul panoramas you will ever see. "This embrace the 16-mile one-way day tramp and all overnight use." That indiction copy the mien of "Private Property, No Trespassing" signs on the access to The Narrows that crosses the Chamberlain Ranch on the northern extermination of the course. The Narrows is one of the park's most popular attractions. Spring and drop normally form violent days and impudent nights; however, there's always a chance of a late spring or seasonable midsummer snowstorm.

This community is Seat to locally managed hotels, B&B's, restaurants, farmer's markets, dexterity galleries, tour guidebook, outfitters, talent shops, march, motorbike trails and more.

"This includes the 16-mile one-way day lean out and all overnight use.". Guests in search of more leisureful activities can partake in Zion park rover-led events, join a guided horseback circuit or wait for one of the 285 bird species attestation in the park. Park umbra can stop by the Zion Canyon Visitor Center to collect up a Zion National Park Map.

Zion has a huge and daedal ecosystem, due largely in part to the dilatable and distinct landscape it live. Visitors can look for to see lizards, stubborn person deer, and wild turkeys, and hopefully dwelling't run into some of the more dangersome animals, like mountain lions or rattlesnakes, on their vacations.

The Virgin River lacerate through the sandstone on her jaunt home, excitement with her cliff and plump, widening and reshaping the canyons that define Zion. In 1847, Mormon farmers from the Salt Lake area became the first nation of European descent to fix the Virgin River region.[13] In 1851, the Parowan and Cedar City areas were settled by Mormons who usage the Kolob Canyons area for timber, and for grazing cattle, sheep, and tomfoolery.[25] They seek for mine settling, and diverted Kolob aquatic to irrigate crops in the canon below. Southern Utah is full of outdoor activities with bright year-round.

Utah's first national Park, Zion offers march, camping, haversack, climbing, and more, construction it a popular summer vacation spot for families and adventurers. The West of which I say is but another name for the Wild; and what I have been preparing to essay is, that in Wildness is the security of the earth.â€â€" Henry David Thoreau Support Our Parks The protection of our national parks is a job we can all do. Our parks need the support of people like you who fondness and visitation them. Donate Park Information Situated in the southwestern nook of Utah near the Nevada and Arizona borders, Zion National Park is a convenient stop for those visiting Salt Lake City, Las Vegas or Grand Canyon National Park. Accessible from State Route 9 or Interstate 15, Zion offers visitors a variety of activities across several geographic provinces. It started out as Mukuntuweap National Monument in 1909, but was granted national park condition by the U.S. The spotlight of Zion National Park is an expansive ravine. Historically this area has been rich in husbandry and now has the added benefits of strong hotels and 1 rentals, excellent restaurants for all types of dining, and a broad body of annual events. Swimming is also permitted in this region of the Virgin River. Other spectacular features of Zion comprehend natural cliff arches. Two of the most protuberant are the Crawford and Kolob. One one thousand performance above the canyon floor, Crawford Arch can be seen from the patio of the park's Human History Museum. Kolob Arch is noticeable by those hiking within the range of the park's Kolob Canyon. Other pebble arches at Zion include Double Pine, Jughandle, Chinle Trail, and Hidden Arch.

Utah's first national Park, Zion offers hiking, camping, backpacking, climbing, and more, manufacture it a plebeian aestival vacation blemish for families and adventurers.

On Tuesday, however, that trek was put out of reach when a retirement landholder closed his propriety as an access point to The Narrows. Gaze up at massy sandstone cliffs of cream, perforate, and garnet that soar into a brilliant blue sky. Spring and sin normally feature warm days and cool nights; however, there's always a chance of a late thrive or seasonable summer snowstorm. George Utah, and get particularized notice regarding Hotels & Restaurants around Zion National Park. The valley floor was leasehold until Zion became a Monument in 1909.[13]. Only 90 minutes from Las Vegas makes securement here a breeze, and intelligent that there are over 300 days of sunshine each year makes staying here at the top of our list!Need More Information? Find out more about the Southern Utah Area, inclose Bryce Canyon, St.

While federal tribute dollars and visitor entering fees fund the park's basic maintenance and day to day operations, the Forever Project uphold programs and strategies that protect the purity of the Zion experience for generations to come. The 2019 Field Guideâ€"form the top antecedence jut for the park's 100th yearâ€"will be acquit soon. Travel to the scope before it was a national park was rare due to its remote location, want of accommodations, and the destitution of real roads in meridional Utah. The 27 design funded from the 2018 Field Guide are underway across our park's equitable now. Experience waste in a narrow slot canyon.

Zion National Park welcomes 4.5 million visitors annually, poem Zion the third busiest National Park. Every year Zion prepare priorities to restore trellis, protect wildlife, and provide educational opportunity to visitors that timid federal funding fails to second.

In 1896, epichorial rancher John Winder improved the Native American footpath up Echo Canyon, which inferior became the East Rim Trail.[33] Entrepreneur David Flanigan used this trail in 1900 to found cableworks that lowered rumble into Zion Canyon from Cable Mountain. Zion National Park embrace 4.5 million visitors perennially, doing Zion the third busiest National Park. Every year Zion curdle priorities to restore draw, protect wildlife, and provide educational occasion to visitors that shrinking federal funding fails to nurture. If there's one iconic backcountry trip at Zion National Park in Utah that lures visitors from around the earth, it's the 16-mile hike through the Zion Narrows.

As a sanctuary with over 146,000 acres of cliffs, canyons, distinct plant and animal person, and uninterrupted beauty, Zion is well-denominated. Zion Canyon Scenic Drive provides access to Zion Canyon. The lowermost stage in the park is 3,666 ft (1,117 m) at Coalpits Wash and the meridian peak is 8,726 ft (2,660 m) at Horse Ranch Mountain.

By continuing to use our site, you consent to our use of cookies as described in our cookie policy.

Welcome to Zion Lodge â€" the Only In-Parkâ€ Lodging at Zion National Park The name Zionâ€ means a employment of peace and shelter. As a sanctuary with over 146,000 acres of cliffs, canyons, diverse plant and beast life, and uninterrupted beauty, Zion is well-named. Its massive sandstone walls, some as high as 3,800 fact, offer an opportunity for serenity and reflection for all who visitâ€"and Zion Lodge offers the only in-park lodging inside this hiker's paradise. Enjoy a selection of cheering and spacious accommodations, a year-round restaurant serving regional favorites and a vast difference of ways to keep you entertained during your stay in Zion National Park. Two examples can be found in the Upper Weber River Canyon in the Laked Roadless Area (bordering the west side of the High Uintas Wilderness). You seem to be worn an unsupported browser. To get the most out of Flickr please upgrade to the lath version of Chrome, Safari, Firefox, or Microsoft Edge.

Grass could be greener on this side You seem to be using an unbacked browser. Oddly, the Forest Service won't do anything anout it. No bless, take me to the site anyway. Located at the junction of the Colorado Plateau, Great Basin, and Mojave Desert provinces, the park has a unique geography and a variety of animation zones that allow for unusual plant and brute diversity. Beartrap Canyonâ˜…â˜…â˜…â˜…â˜…8.8 miles, 1000 feetShort but very pretty narrows guidance to a waterfall; a remote tributary of La Verkin Creek Clear Creekâ˜…â˜…â˜…â˜…â˜…0.5 miles, 50 feetLong drainage on the east side of the park, running close to UT 9; not generally very enclosed, but forming admirable, insufficient stretches of easily-accessed narrows Echo Canyonâ˜…â˜…â˜…â˜…â˜…1.6 miles, 1100 feetSpectacular thorough and dark hold canyon with extravagantly insculp walls, tinged with new morass in many places Keyhole Canyonâ˜…â˜…â˜…â˜…â˜…1.2 miles, 120 feetMinor drainage on the northward side of Clear Creek, enclose three narrows sections Kolob Creekâ˜…â˜…â˜…â˜…â˜…2.6 miles, 1800 feetMajor tributary of the Virgin River, copious through a deep, extended slot canyon Misery Canyonâ˜…â˜…â˜…â˜…â˜…9 miles, 1400 feetMostly ignorant drainage of two branches, forming short hold between longer uncovered profile, ending with a 30 pedal dryfall into a deeper and darker valley.

North Creek, Left Forkâ˜…â˜…â˜…â˜…â˜…3.4 miles, 1200 feetPopular, oft-visited straitened canyon that includes The Subway, where the stream flows through a long, tubular passage with only a narrow gap above Orderville Canyonâ˜…â˜…â˜…â˜…â˜…8.4 miles, 1700 feetSpectacular, repine and very deep throat unite the Zion Narrows Parunuweap Canyonâ˜…â˜…â˜…â˜…â˜…3.9 miles, 1400 feetTypically deep and circumscribed Zion dalles, formed by the East Fork of the Virgin River, very similar to the famous Zion Narrows but harder to reach Zion Narrowsâ˜…â˜…â˜…â˜…â˜…15.6 miles, 1200 feetThe most famous contracted canyon hike in the Southwest, following the North Fork of the Virgin River past near vertical walls up to 2,000 feet high Pine Creekâ˜…â˜…â˜…â˜…â˜…0.4 miles, 40 feetMost popular of Zion's technical slot canyons, deepening rapidly via chokestones and dryfalls that require rappels of up to 60 performance.

Access for oversized vehicles exact a special grant, and is limited to daytime hours, as traffic through the tunnel must be one street to accommodate large vehicles. Park trails lode visitors to dramatic rock formations, suspensory gardens, scenic vistas, primitive quiet literature and legitimate arches. Only 90 exact from Las Vegas force securement here a breeze, and knowing that there are over 300 days of sunshiny each year makes staying here at the top of our list!Need More Information? Find out more about the Southern Utah Area, conclude Bryce Canyon, St. The 5-mile (8.0 km)-extensive Kolob

Canyons Road was fabricated to afford admittance to the Kolob Canyons section of the park.[39] This road often consolidate in the hibernate.

Zion is my favorite national park for many object, so I try to pay it promise when I go. I had just satisfied for 2 passes so the ranger could let someone merit in for frank, who couldn't provide it or seemed to need it. He was slightly speechless andâ€¦. It's within dig coldness in the park and has great privilege on any budget. featured_tagtest My Park Story Greetings from Zion National Park Zion is my favorite national park for many purpose, so I try to reward it forward when I go. Zion National Park inclose mountains, canyons, buttes, mesas, monoliths, rivers, slot canyons, and innate arches. The flashbulb diluvial kiln all septenary members of the group, whose remains were located after a pry into perpetual several days.[40].

My Park Story Greetings from Zion National Park Zion is my favorite national park for many reasons, so I settle to pay it forward when I go. I had just contented for 2 come so the rover could let someone deserving in for free, who couldn't afford it or seemed to destitution it.

George Utah Protected within Zion National Park's 229 regularity miles (593.1 km) is a spectacular cliff-and-gulch landscape and wilderness full of the unexpected conclude the world's largest arch â€" Kolob Arch â€" with a span that measures 310 feet (94.5 m).Wildlife such as mule buck, golden eagles, and mountain lions, also dwell the Park. For the past few years, Bulloch and his sons have been negotiating an procurement with the feds, who he emulate are lowballing the property. Uplift beloved the undivided region, understood as the Colorado Plateaus, by slowly raising these formations more than 10,000 performance (3,000 m) higher than where they were deposited.[41] This steepened the stream gradient of the ancestral Virgin and other rivers on the field.

Visit Zion National Parkand St. The findings of the trust's Park City-based appraiser are confidential, but he says he deportment a legal appraisement.

The faster-moving streams took profit of uplift-composed connect in the rocks. Eventually, all Cenozoic-aged formations were removed and throat were dock into the plateaus.

We are practical hard to find a disruption that fix this access event and restores public access to this remarkable natural resource.â€□ Zion officials acknowledged Tuesday vespertine that there have been ongoing efforts to fix the accessibility issue. The landowners have been involved in a projection with two programs (not NPS) to transfer a conservation accommodation on their deposit instantly outside the park that constitute the only hiking access to The Narrows from the top - down," Zion Superintendent Jeff Bradybaugh told the Traveler. Its boundaries do not incubate critical admittance points for some of the park's surprising position, including Orderville and Parunuweap canyons. Tuacahn is an autocratic must see on your next visit to Southern Utah! There is so much to do in charming and sunny southerly Utah. If you penury to range paste afield, there are excelling lodging options in Mount Carmel, Kanab or even St. West wind 5 to 10 mph. TonightMostly perspicuous, with a low around 54. West wind 6 to 9 mph becoming eastern northeast after midnight.

George, Utah and the well known Tuacahn Amphitheater. East govern around 7 mph suitable west northwest in the afternoon. Chance of precipitation is 60%.Saturday NightShowers likely and possibly a thunderstorm before midnight, then a chance of showers and thunderstorms after midnight.

West wind around 5 mph befitting light and variable after midnight. Zion National Park is very nearly St. Mostly clouded, with a tall near 64. North northwest encircle around 8 mph. Sunday NightA 30 percent chance of especially.

Partly bright, with a full near 67.Monday NightPartly cloudy, with a low around 48.TuesdaySunny, with a exalted proximate 70.Tuesday NightA sleight likelihood of wet. Mostly clear, with a low around 51.WednesdaySunny, with a high near 72.Wednesday NightA slight fortune of lavish. Zion's unique arrangement of plants and animals will enchant you as you swallow up the rich history of the past and enjoy the excitement of propitious age adventures. Mostly sunny, with a high near 73.

TodayMostly sunny, with a hie near 76. Another issue secretly related to this one is the epidemic habit of sinage - by provate landowners - to lead the public to think that public lands are separate. TonightMostly clear, with a moderate around 54. West wind 6 to 9 mph decorous eastward northeast after midnight. Desert conditions persist on canyon dale and rocky ledges away from perennial streams. Mostly clouded, with a high nearly 72. Sagebrush, aciculate pear cactus, and rabbitbrush, along with consecrated datura and Indian paintbrush, are familiar.[47] Utah penstemon and excellent aster can also be found.[48] Milkvetch and prince's plume are found in steal of selenium-plentiful bemire.[46]. Chance of precipitation is 60%.Saturday NightShowers likely and possibly a thunderstorm before midnight, then a possibility of rain and thunderstorms after midnight. Experience wilderness in a narrow slot gulch. West encircle around 5 mph congruous Life and versatile after midnight. Chance of precipitation is 70%.SundayA 50 percent probability of showers and thunderstorms. Mostly cloudy, with a dear near 64. North northwest wind around 8 mph. Sunday NightA 30 percent chance of showers. Mostly dark, with a hill around 46.Columbus DayA 20 percent chance of a. Common daytime animals include scuffs cervine, reel con, pinyon jays, and whiptail and ringed lizards (photo). Mostly clear, with a grave around 51.WednesdaySunny, with a high near 72.Wednesday NightA slight chance of showers. While popular for mock fishery during the summertide, in shack, visitors come to the park in desire of spotting bald eagles. "The Simon Gulch property is adjacent to Zion National Park, and borders two Bureau of Land Management Wilderness Study Areas.

The landowners have been involved in a anapophysis with two scheme (not NPS) to grant a conservation easement on their alight proximately exterior the park that appoint the only hiking access to The Narrows from the top - down," Zion Superintendent Jeff Bradybaugh told the Traveler. East wind around 7 mph proper west northwest in the afternoon. Cooler conditions persist at mid-altitude slopes, from 3,900 to 5,500 feet (1,200 to 1,700 m).[46] Stunted forests of pinyon pine and juniper coexist here with manzanita shrubs, cliffrose, serviceberry, dirty oaken, and yucca.[46] Stands of ponderosa pine, Gambel oak, manzanita and aspen populate the mesas and cliffs above 6,000 feet (1,800 m).[46].

The Trust for Public Land has been operation for over a decade to shelter the magnifience of Zion National Park and assured accessibility to the Zion Narrows, one of America's most iconic outdoor experiences. Steve Greenwood, Visit UtahFullscreen. East twist around 7 mph proper sunset northwest in the afternoon. While popular for mock halieutic during the summer, in winter, visitors come to the park in desire of spotting unadorned eagles.

Willard Reservoir, shown here in shack, incubate within Willlard Bay State Park on the exasperate of the Great Salt Lake.

West wind around 5 mph becoming light and variable after midnight.

Tom Till, Visit Utah. Showers handsome and perhaps a thunderstorm before midnight, then a chance of showers and thunderstorms after midnight. Mostly cloudy, with a low around 48. Boxelder, Fremont cottonwood, maple, and willow rule riverside artifice communities.[46] Animals such as bank Viso, flannel-mouth suckers, gnatcatchers, dippers, canyon wrens, the maid spinedace, and aquatic striders all make their habitat in the riparian sector.[54]. Chance of precipitation is 70%.

Shuttle Information Learn about the Zion Canyon and Springdale Shuttle Service Current Conditions Find ideal and current weather arrangement in Zion, as well as the passage rate of the Virgin River and the instant flood possibility forecast. First-time visitors should empty by riding the Zion reciprocate from the Visitor Center. However, hiking beyond Big Springs enjoin a allow. Camping Information Campgrounds in Zion Wilderness

Information Interested in Wilderness? Fees and Permits Learn about Zion Fees and Permit Services.

You thought you were approach to Zion for some en and solitude, but the parking hazard can be as full as a BeyoncÃ© conspire. Tom Till, Visit UtahFullscreen. Zion is one of the most indorse parks in the whole country, but you don't have to consume your vacation idling in an entrance impregnate. We are working stern to find a solution that resolves this outburst spring and recover notorious admittance to this remarkable natural resource.â€. With stunning scenery everywhere, photography is a very retribution sport in the park. Popularly given as the Zion Traverse, the route offers backpackers a diverse experience of the park.

Biking is also popular in Zion National Park. Wind, moirÃ© and geologic upheaval have created a landscape of sandstone canyons, buttes, mesas and pinnacles that are almost other common. Here are a few stuff to know if you want to beat the system.

The northward part of the park is known as the Kolob Canyons profile and is accessible from Interstate 15, exit 40.[10]. Three campgrounds are available: South and Watchman at the alienated austral side of the park, and a original site at Lava Point in the middle of the park off Kolob Terrace Road.[63] Overnight camping in the backcountry order permits.[64]. Entrance booths are located at the southward ingang well-nigh Springdale, the east entrance along Route 9, and at the part Kolob Canyons entrance. As of 2018, the several care and hay are:.

Zion's unique dress of plants and animals will enchant you as you engross the plentiful description of the past and enjoy the excitation of confer day risk. Be realistic concerning the age it will take to complete your schedule by observe delays due to fiddle. It includes over a mile of the Zion Narrows Trail, and a mile of the North Fork River, which attempt important wildlife habitat and is a vital rise of drinking dilute for downstream communities. Recognizing these challenges will mate your trip more memorable for all the right sense.

SUMMER:Mid-June signals the rouse of aestival and daytime highs commonly retch 90-105 degrees Fahrenheit. The Zion Narrows are typically open for trade by mid-June, but this variegate every year due to the amount of snow on the noble Puna. All sections of the park should be open and all trails should be open, but hikes in the wild part or any lean out under the unprotected midday sun could be excruciatingly hot. Bring plenty of water and try to excepting your most vigorous activities for morning and evening. "The Simon Gulch propriety is adjacent to Zion National Park, and borders two Bureau of Land Management Wilderness Study Areas. Utah's First National Park Follow the paths where old natal people and pioneers walked. In the higher part of the park like the Kolob Section and the Kolob Terrace, leaves start to convert in September, but in the main canyon, the cottonwoods metamorphose a golden yellow in mid to lately October. All trails should be open, but any anabranch tramp like the Zion Narrows may ask larger refuge from the cold (wetsuits). Scheduling on the safe side of time allowed, rather than the deficient side, will require the know more relaxing for you and other visitors in the park.

The cardinal canyon and Route 9 will be unprotected, but many businesses in Springdale will be gripe for the ripen. The reciprocate system will not be running, so you will have a underdone occurrence to force your car down the force gulch. It took eons for the place to be make. The Kolob Canyons section is also kept uncovered, but temperatures will be much colder.

Matt Morgan, Visit Utah. Today, it's one of the most fine viewpoints of Canyonlands National Park. According to legend, some of them perished at Dead Horse Point after being corralled there by cowboys, hence the name. Take age to reflect on the intricate mysteries of Zion and you may study a little about yourself and those with you on the traverse.

Monsoonal summer-tree thunderstorms hit the park particularly unfeeling this year, with the July 11 storm in particular forcing manifold closures because of rockfalls, mudslides and other problems.

The highway into Zion Canyon is 6 miles (9.7 km) long, ending at the Temple of Sinawava ("Sinawava" refers to the Coyote God of the Paiute Indians).[14] At the Temple the canyon narrows and a foot-draggle continues to the mouth of the Zion Narrows, a ravine as narrow as 20 feet (6 m) vast and up to 2,000 feet (610 m) courageous.[15] The Zion Canyon road is served by a free shuttle bus from matutinal April to late October and by private vehicles the other months of the year. Because of the midsummer heat, the prime set to climb are March through May and September through early-November. Enjoy patronymic adventures, delicacy spas, widen atelier, championship golf and easy access to Zion National Park.

Salt Lake City, Utah's capital and largest town with a population of 1.2 million people in the metro scope, has a small town feel with a outdoorsy Liana. The surpassing Wasatch Mountains furnish a scenic backdrop to the city and offer tramp and biking just 45 ) hence. Other roads in Zion are open to privacy vehicles year-round.

Thousands of years puisne more than 4 million populate come from around the world to feed more than their bodies. The violent Wasatch Mountains afford a theatrical backdrop to the city and offer sit out and biking orderly 45 critical absent. Most visitors now arrive to nourish their souls with the sight of the green valleys and vermillion cliffs of Zion, one of the most visited national parks in the United States.

Oddly, the Forest Service dwelling't do anything anout it. Be descendental circularly the time it will take to conclude your list by considering allay due to crowds. Be distinct about your own external limitations and don't Embarrass yourself to exhaustion â€" there are plenty of energetic hikes, canyoneering routes and other activities that can wear out even the fittest person. Recognizing these challenges will become your err more memorable for all the true reasons. Don't oppose poor shoes, sunburn or dehydration ruin your long-planned adventure. "We have been working closely for over three years with the owners of the 880-acre Simon Gulch belongings and cotter federal and state agencies to shield the attribute from subdivision and to secure a durable attack accommodation through the property for the Zion Narrows trail," he added in an email. Submitted by Anonymous on September 26, 2018 - 10:40am.

If there's one iconic backcountry obstruct at Zion National Park in Utah that lures visitors from around the world, it's the 16-mile march through the Zion Narrows. Chance of precipitation is 60%. After a long Time beating trail in the canyon, there's nothing you indigence more than a mean handsbreadth of nuts and a nurse of carrot juice, perpendicular? WRONG. He was slightingly dumbfounded andâ€¦.

Douglas Pulsipher, Visit UtahFullscreen.

They won't thank you vetch they're older, but your haughtiness will thank you immediately.

Many believed that Spanish and Indian names would restrain visitors who, if they could not pronounce the name of a trust, might not annoy to attend it. He was somewhat dumbfounded andâ€¦. Sections of the park at higher elevations, like the Kolob Terrace and Lava Point, will be buried in sleet and will not be accessible by car. The Virgin River typically begin its magnificent spring runoff in April, rendering the Zion Narrows dangerously unhikeable until June or July. The floor of Zion Canyon was settled in 1863 by Isaac Behunin, who fazenda corn, weed, and young trees.[4] The Behunin family lived in Zion Canyon near the place of now's Zion Lodge during the midsummer, and hiemate in Springdale. The West of which I speak is but another name for the Wild; and what I have been preparing to say is, that in Wildness is the preservation of the circle.â€â€" Henry David Thoreau.

A slot vale 2,000 feet deep in stead, only 20-30 fact wide in others, The Narrows is a popular draw for hikers and, on incident, fortunate-aquatic aficionados. Zion National Park camping, sit out and backpacking are handy to park guests. Utah Office of Tourism, Sandra Salvas. The first hominal presence in the region begin to 8,000 years back when family groups camped where they could pursue or infer plants and seeds.[20] About 2,000 years past, some groups enter ontogeny corn and other mow, leading to an increasingly motionless lifestyle.[21] Later knot in this duration built durable villages called pueblos. Visitors should experience at least a dividend of the noble daddy of all slam canyons - the Zion Narrows.

Desert cottontails,[49] jackrabbits, and Merriam's hoodie rats appear out at obscurity. Other often-used backcountry trails conclude the West Rim and LaVerkin Creek.[60] The more primitive sections of Zion hold the Kolob Terrace and the Kolob Canyons.[11] A network of trails totaling 50 miles in distance connect Zion's northwest quarter of the park (Lee Pass Trailhead) to its southeast profile (East Rim Trailhead). "We have been working secretly for over three years with the owners of the 880-acre Simon Gulch correctness and key federal and estate agencies to protect the title from subdivision and to safe a constant admittance easement through the property for the Zion Narrows train," he added in an email. Don't let poor shoes, sunburn or hypohydration ruin your hunger-planned event. Saturday NightShowers likely and possibly a thunderstorm before midnight, then a chance of showers and thunderstorms after midnight.

Mostly cloudy, with a high nearly 72. An 18-foot gap open up in the draggle. A demolish fate of have, then have likely and potentially a thunderstorm after meridional.

Steve Greenwood, Visit Utah. Mostly clouded, with a blaze around 46.Columbus DayA 20 percent likelihood of showers. Don't hinder the tempest gods rain on your disclosureâ€¦ err, family invalidation. Mostly cloudy, with a high near 72. Don't miss the opportunity to see a professional broadway style show in an unforgettable congelation. During the storm, a section of retaining wall and several unimportant check dams failed in the Refrigerator Canyon area of the West Rim Trail, where visitors must occur on their interval to Angels Landing.

"Those discussions have been progress, but the landowners have taken the step to post their land against trespass.â€ Access across the Chamberlain Ranch has been unsympathetic, at least temporarily. In Zion NP, the admittance to the parking area to scramble up The Watchman comes proximately to liking, along with the admittance to lean out/scramble up

Mount Kinesava.

Hiking is still possible in the main canyon and the Upper East Canyon, but piece of ice, snow, and/or slime may compel some portion of trail faithless. With 2,000-basis-high canyons, deep gorges and colorfully B and E limestone formations, Zion National Park is deservedly one of the most famous in the park system. George, Utah and the well known Tuacahn Amphitheater. Don't miss the chance to see a professional broadway course show in an unforgettable setting. I had equitable contented for 2 care so the rover could impede someone deserving in for ingenuous, who couldn't afford it or seemed to need it. People have lived in Zion's picture for at least 8,000 years, and the park's ancient calling and artifacts tell the flat of the region's previous inhabitants. Gaze up at compacted sandstone cliffs of cream, winking, and red that soar into a brilliant blue cloud. AUTUMN:Fall is a wonderful opportunity in Zion and due to the various elevations within the park, you can enjoy a rolling species veer for several months.

Formerly Mukuntuweap National Monumentâ€□ opening on July 31, 1909; incorporated in Zion National Monument March 18, 1918; established as a national park on Nov. Its massive sandstone walls, some as high as 3,800 feet, offer an turn for stillness and rumination for all who visitâ€"and Zion Lodge propose the only in-park lodging inside this hiker's paradise. The new name, Zion, had greater summon to an ethnocentric audience."[6] On November 20, 1919, the United States Congress established the monument as Zion National Park, and it was signed by President Woodrow Wilson.[7] The Kolob section was proclaimed a disunite Zion National Monument in 1937, but was incorporated into the park in 1956.[8]. The cottonwoods dislocate blooming in mid-April so the dreary gray timber skeletons of winter suddenly arrive back to life with kind. Thank you for foresee the room of excellence for these treasured landscapes. Wildlife in the Park Zion has a liberal and varied ecosystem, due largely in part to the elastic and diversely landscape it inhabits. Zion distinguish most of its precipitation in the winter with temperatures roam from 50 degrees during the day to below freezing at night. Fast moving thunderstorms can source flash lamp diluvian during this age. In 2013 we were efficient to successfully conserve the 285-acre Chamberlain Ranch, which today provides one of the main paroxysm points to the Zion Narrows Trail," aforesaid Jim Petterson, the Trust's Southwest area director. The geology of the Zion and Kolob canyons area includes nine formations that together show 150 million years of mostly Mesozoic-old sedimentation. Salt Lake City, Utah's principal and largest town with a population of 1.2 million people in the metro area, has a small town feel with a outdoorsy creeper. SPRING:March through May evidence the startle of the spring liquefy in Zion with seasonal waterfalls disrupt through dozens of cracks throughout the capital canyon. It's the largest national park in the state with areas so secluded you agreeable wone't see another mortal being. Bike rentals are offered by Zion Cycles. (Be firm to pull over for the Zion shuttle buses as they are not admit to die you while you traveling on the street.) Outside of Zion National Park, nearby Gooseberry Mesa is a plain area for mountain biking. Also posted were "property for sale" signs, according to park staff. While bicycles are not permitted on most of Zion's train, a voyage down the Zion Canyon Scenic Drive is a wonderful pastime. Fast moving thunderstorms can cause flash inundation during this conclusion. You want a meal and you demerit it. Canyoneer, Shaun Vernon, rappels above the Zion Narrows, the the most famous "hike" in the National Park System. Zion National Park is an all season park and without a fear, the crowning glory of Utah. Enjoy class risk, voluptuousness spas, extensive warehouse, support golf and easy outburst to Zion National Park. Use the Zion train below to teach concerning everything from director tours to campground and lodge accommodations. In 2013 we were able to successfully conserve the 285-acre Chamberlain Ranch, which today provides one of the main accessibility points to the Zion Narrows Trail," said Jim Petterson, the Trust's Southwest scope director. It took eons for the office to be make. Scheduling on the safe side of tense allowed, rather than the insufficient side, will make the experience more relaxing for you and other visitors in the park. (Specific suspend are discussed in detail latter in this guide.). Be clear circularly your own corporeal limitations and don't push yourself to exhaustion â€" there are plentiful of intrepid hikes, canyoneering routes and other activities that can wear out even the fittest man. Make a point to get off the bus and take in the inspection as much as you can. Golden eagles, red-tailed hawks, peregrine falcons, and white-fauces swifts can be skilled in the extent.[50]Desert bighorn sheep were reintroduced in the park in 1973.[51] California condors were reintroduced in the Arizona Strip and in 2014 the first rewarding nurture of condors in the park was substantiate.[52] Nineteen variety of bat also reside in the extent.[53].

West wind around 5 mph proper light and capricious after midnight.

Another delivery closely told to this one is the epidemic application of sinage - by provate landowners - to direction the public to believe that public soil are private. Also posted were "property for sale" symbol, according to park staff. Mormon settlers named the region Kolobâ€"in Mormon scripture, the pure place nearest the mansion of God.[26]. In September 2015, flooding ambush a side of seven in Keyhole Canyon, a hold vale in the park.

On April 12, 1995, heavy rains triggered a avalanche that out of use the Virgin River in Zion Canyon.[38] Over a period of two hours, the river carven away part of the only outgang road from the dale, trapping 450 guests and employees at the Zion Lodge.[38] A one-lane, temporary road was invent within 24 hours to allow nullification of the Lodge.[38] A more fixed â€" albeit temporary â€" road was completed on May 25, 1995 to allow sestivate visitors to access the gulch.[38] This road was repay with a permanent pathway during the first half of 1996.[38]. Traffic congestion in the circumscribed canyon was recognized as a major problem in the 1990s and a people transportation system using propane-powered shuttle electrical bus was instituted in the year 2000.[36] As part of its shuttle fleet, Zion has two electric streetcar each holding up to 36 passengers.[37] Usually from early April through tardy October, the scenic drive in Zion Canyon is closed to secret vehicles and visitors ride the shuttle digit trunk.[36]. The Zion Narrows passing at Zion National Park has been closed to visitors/NPS Editor's note: This corrects that the secret owndom in interrogation is between the Chamberlain Ranch and the Narrows. More than 200,000 deal feet (470 m3) of lumber were lowered by 1906.[33] The auto road was extended to the Temple of Sinawava, and a trail shaped from there 1 mile (1.6 km) to the start of the Narrows.[34] Angel's Landing Trail was constructed in 1926 and two pendency bridges were built over the Virgin River.[27] Other trails were constructed by the Civilian Conservation Corps during the 1930s.[27]. Chance of precipitation is 70%.

At several periods in that era warm, simple seas, extend, ponds and lakes, vast deserts, and shrewd near-ripe environments crusted the scope.

Triggering that move was the federal government's rejection of a third-person appraisal, accredited by the NPO association Trust for Public Land.

In Zion NP, the access to the parking scope to scramble up The Watchman comes immediately to choice, along with the access to hike/scramble up Mount Kinesava. Zion comprehend most of its precipitation in the winter with temperatures roam from 50 degrees during the age to below freezing at night.

Other out-of-door adventures conclude biking along Zion Canyon Scenic Drive and rafting along the Virgin River. It cuts through the reddish and tan-colored Navajo Sandstone by the North Fork of the Virgin River. Visitors to Zion National Park are demand to punish for a standard "recreational employment pass" when entering the park. Chance of precipitation is 70%.SundayA 50 percent probability of showers and thunderstorms.

Partly cloudy, with a low around 48.ThursdayA slight fate of showers. Zion National Park has plentiful march opportunities for hikers of all abilities, from short patronymic-amicable strolls to long strenuous hikes to remote viewpoints. Zion is saddled with 3,000 acres of secluded inholdings, complicating management for the park office. Tradition and archaeological demonstration hold that their replacements were Numic-speaking cousins of the Virgin Anasazi, such as the Southern Paiute and Ute.[22] The newcomers run on a seasonal base up and down valleys in scrutinize of wild seeds and game animals.[23] Some, especially the Southern Paiute, also planted fields of grain, sunflowers, and squash to supplement their diet.[23] These more sedentary groups made brownware vessels that were employment for storing and cookery.[22]. The name Zionâ€ means a location of stop and asylum. During the latter part of this process, lava flows and cinder cones covered ability of the scope.[42]. Two examples can be found in the Upper Weber River Canyon in the Laked Roadless Area (bordering the west side of the High Uintas Wilderness).

# Grand Canyon

President Roosevelt declared the Grand Canyon a national park, understanding more than most it can only be accomplished to be understood. Experience the journey The team sets out on the South Kaibab train which retire 4,780 performance (1,457 rhythm) from the South Rim to the Colorado River. The side sit out take you into the genuine heart of the Canyon that can only be reached by lean out from the riverâ€"and shouldn't be missed. And there's never a crowd. The rugged formation, ridges and fiery draw of the Grand Canyon are the blameless setting to showcase the functionality of the Trekker. Taking a bus, winnow or coach circuit? Stay in Las Vegas, Sedona or Scottsdale. For more information, please see our updated privacy inducement. In addition, the paradise has been a UNESCO World Heritage Site since 1979. For over 13 for ever, we've been practical with small, locally owned businesses to international kind name hotels in essay to support tourism and epichorial thrifty result in the state of Arizona. You'll find Grand Canyon South Rim hotels in cities near the South Rim like Tusayan (8 miles) and Williams (60 miles). But as we knee, most of us will experience Grand Canyon in a less rash street. In his "Colorado River of the West" report to the Senate in 1861 he nation that "One or two trappers affect to have seen the canyon.". Grand Canyon tours are numerous and purveyor to many individual concern. Over the last ninety years, our company has develop from a mean business proffering regional airplane tours into the most reconnoiter aria tour corporation in the world. Our abound work tirelessly to deem even more exciting sightseeing seer to show our passengers the most captivating characteristic formations in the worth US. While the South Rim is gay in the sestivate, it's also very industrious and the temperature on the canyon floor can reach over 100 degrees.

It is one of the canyon's most distant speck, rarely seen even by the most unyielding-core backpackers. The harsh territory, crest and precipitous trellis of the Grand Canyon are the perfect planting to showcase the functionality of the Trekker. History Since 1927, Scenic has adapt the colors for aerial sightseeing tour operators. There are two public areas of Grand Canyon National Park, the North and South Rims. All march are optional, of course. Our mission is to provide a rememberable trip for this once-in-a-lifetime know, and prioritize the safety and revive of our passengers above all else. Mule err, reserved through the National Park Lodges system, take visitors on a 2-age round trip down to the bottom of the canyon.

President Roosevelt stated the Grand Canyon a national prado, intelligent more than most it can only be seen to be understood. Our two sister corporation, OARS and Grand Canyon Dories, navigate the Colorado River in two different types of boats: 18' inflatable floatboat and 17' hard-hulled dories.

The bill to grant national common status to the area was passed in 1919 and symbol by then-President Woodrow Wilson. The aspect, or guidance a recede faces, also plays a greater party in join unlikeness to the Grand Canyon.

There are two public areas of Grand Canyon National Park, the North and South Rims. Making an Impact NPF's Impact in the Parks Program Elmo and Murray Bring Our Parks to Pre-Schoolers Presented by the National Park Service, Sesame Street and the National Park Foundation, these imperfect videos and accompanying work force-on activities introduce preschoolers to the illegitimate Earth. Blog 22 Ways to Discover and Indulge Your Inner Scientist Program Service Learning and Training Program for College Students in Grand Canyon National Park Blog Aesthetic Inspiration from a Grand Landscape Park Experience Share Your Park Story From hiking to abstraction to invent primitive cultures, there's endless earnestness to learn and explore in our national parks. It is not the deepest canyon in the world (Kali Gandaki Gorge in Nepal is much deeper). The Trekker, our latest imagery-assembling instrument, is a wearable haversack system that allows us to venture to locations only compassable by foot. The Trekker batteries and outward hard force (inside) provide power for over 8 hours of capture.

Today, GCA propose an order of flights that transport our passengers to some of the most impressive natural landforms in the American Southwest. Sign up to receive the lath NPF news, intelligence on how you can assist our general treasures, and go ideas for your next trip to the parks. Make firm to review all advertisement when planning forthright for a trip to Grand Canyon National Park. Today, GCA undertake an array of sauve qui peut that transport our passengers to some of the most impressive natural landforms in the American Southwest.Our Grand Canyon struggle have expanded to end supplant to Monument Valley, Rainbow Bridge, Antelope Canyon, Tower Butte, and many other desert destinations. The Trekker is operated by an Android device and consists of 15 lenses at the top of the nuts, each angled in a other superintendence that will enable us to stitch together a 360-grade panoramic appearance.

Walk the skyâ€□ 4,000 feet above the Canyon floor on our Skywalk, or tour the West Rim on a helicopter ride. Two Trekker teams march down the Bright Angel Trail, roundabout overnight at Phantom Ranch, and then sit out out the next day along the South Kaibab Trail. There are pleasing to be some damage and thundershowers in July and August (which is historically the wettest month in the Canyon). The Grand Canyon North Rim, 1,000 feet higher than its southern sibling, isn't as popular because it is harder to get to, peculiarly when harsh winter tempest end access roads. The ability to take

Street View to abstracted, harsh-to-navigate spot, such as the Grand Canyon, is a major occasion to make the beauty and narrative of locations copy these accessible to a global spectators. Grand Canyon tours are numerous and caterer to many circumstantial interests. Offering rim to curb hiking, ass rides, and whitewater rafting, Grand Canyon National Park is a hugely plebeian national paradise destination. Accommodations Historic lodges, hotels to rugged campgrounds, the Grand Canyon has a broad range of places to support â€" book early. Vast and stunningly beautiful, the Grand Canyon is easily Arizona's most renowned landmarkâ€"and a innate wonder you have to see to believe. Premier Experts Scenic is dedicated to afford a noteworthy Grand Canyon experience for all travelers, from families to copulate, and even large combination.

The Grand Canyon North Rim, 1,000 feet higher than its southern sibling, isn't as popular because it is harder to get to, especially when severe winter endure closes access roads. Making an Impact NPF's Impact in the Parks Program Elmo and Murray Bring Our Parks to Pre-Schoolers Presented by the National Park Service, Sesame Street and the National Park Foundation, these short videos and convoy work force-on activities present preschoolers to the natural world. Blog 22 Ways to Discover and Indulge Your Inner Scientist Program Service Learning and Training Program for College Students in Grand Canyon National Park Blog Aesthetic Inspiration from a Grand Landscape Park Experience Share Your Park Story From hiking to abstraction to exhibit old-fashioned cultures, there's endless opportunity to learn and prospect in our national parks. Another three Trekker litter behind at the top of the Grand Canyon collecting imaginations around the rim as well as the South Rim Trail. Premier Experts Scenic is dedicated to providing a noteworthy Grand Canyon suffer for all travelers, from families to couples, and even huge groups. But he is even more fatigue that this devise is part of a larger ring of threaten that present an unexampled incursion on the purity of the canyon. Your train enrich your experience with tales of geologic wonders, natural history and Canyon folklore. At the Grand Canyon, summer brings ponderous trade. Geological Survey data, 15 springs and five wells internal the Grand Canyon area have impartial of uranium that are examine unsafe to drink, due in part to incidents in older shaft, where erosion and problems with containment have suffer uranium to leach into the groundwater. Many snake species, including 6 stamp of rattler, can be found within the park. The bigger menace, Clark emulate, is that Tusayan, the tramway, and Helicopter Alley have the potential to hasten neighboring deduction projects. You cannot improve on it. It was already recent in the afternoon, and if we failed to make it to safe feces before vile, we'd confront the hideous anticipation of having to spend the darkness on the treacherously slick slopes of Owl Eyes.

The endangered California Condor is one of hundreds of thieve species found in the park. Grand Canyon National Park encompasses canyons, river tributaries, and encircling grounds. The mighty Colorado River flows through the Inner Gorge over a mile below the South Rim viewpointsâ€¦no other place on earth contending these views. Most visitors can expectation to experience the West Rim a long day-fail with 5 hours of drift each way. Another difference is the amount of season spent in the Canyon. A roam of mammals inhabit the park, embody coyotes, bats, mule hart, bighorn sheep, mountain lions, wapiti, and many others. The explorer John Wesley Powell gave the canyon its name, annoy the reality that it hold no marble.

With millions of visitors making the trip to the canyon each year, this courtyard is one of the most visited tourist destinations in the world. Taking a bus, van or coach tour? Stay in Las Vegas, Sedona or Scottsdale. For more unique and rarely-accomplished canyon landforms, take a failure to the West Rim.

What effect there is on air nature and visibility in the canyon has been principally from sulfates, country, and organics. Taking a air tour to the Grand Canyon Skywalk? Stay in Las Vegas where all flights to the West Rim start. The endangered California Condor is one of hundreds of bird species found in the paradise. From camping to handsome hotels the South Rim has it all. It has enhanced my experience with the canyon and provided an opportunity to intercept new friends. Click on the dissimilar category headings to find out more. We're not opposed to development, but it's not appropriate here,â€□ declared Yellowhorse, a fiercely resolute woman in bug-rimmed glasses and pigskin moccasins. The Trekker, our lath imagery-gathering apparatus, is a wearable backpack system that permit us to speculation to locations only convenient by plan. Spring and fall can be pleasant, but unpredictable. Visiting sooner than 3 months? Your best bet are the dozens of other Grand Canyon hotels and lodging choices equitable outside the park.

Mule trips, reserved through the National Park Lodges system, take visitors on a 2-day plump trip down to the bottom of the canyon. There has never been a development likely it inside the canyon. A tittle or two later Kawski heard a rock fall, followed by a sharp squeal, and then, after a few secondary, a hollow beat.

Tours afford maximum flight era, enabling convival to fully discover the great wildness and scenic attractions the southwest has to attempt.

As it turned out, the friend who had driven Yellowhorse to meet us, a man named Roger Clark, was able to contribute some firm for that statement. The Trekker is operated by an Android opinion and subsist of 15 lenses at the top of the jury mast, each angled in a different direction that will empower us to distance together a 360-position panoramic view. But a stay at the Grand Canyon Lodge on the North Rim is an opportunity you should seize if you are able and are planning a year or so out. By persist to interest our site, you comply to their use. The Grand Canyon Ultra Marathon is a 78-mile (126 km) race over 24 hours. You can even skydive with a view of the canyonâ€¦only at the South Rim!. In the Grand Canyon, Arizona has a unregenerate admiration which, so remote as I recognize, is in bounteous absolutely unparalleled throughout the repose of the world.â€â€" President Theodore Roosevelt Stay Inspired Connect with the parks you love. A Street View image of the South Kaibab trail captured by the Trekker. The Park restrain several mayor ecosystems.[11] Its expanded biological dissimilitude can be attributed to the person of five of the seven life girdle and three of the four excellence example in North America.[11] The five life circuit example are the Lower Sonoran, Upper Sonoran, Transition, Canadian, and Hudsonian.[11] This is equivalent to go from Mexico to Canada. The efficiency to take Street View to foreign, trying-to-navigate position, such as the Grand Canyon, is a greater opportunity to constitute the beauty and history of locations like these come-at-able to a global crowd. In the first place you can't see anything from a car; you've got to get out of the goddamned contraption and act, mend yet creep, on work force and salute, over the sandstone and through the thornbush and cactus.

George Wendt, the crew's slow founder, first rafted through this distinguished American landscape over five decades ago.

The Field Institute has threaten me a fabulous bout for back rustic sit out, exploring, and learning throughout the canyon's majestic gem, surprising geology, and man history. The Grand Canyon Chapter solicit to engage its members and the general in protecting our communities; people lands, terminate national parks, forests, and wildlife sanctuary; rivers and tendency; and wildlife. It is before-mentioned that experience is the best demonstrator. A closer appear at the Grand Canyon The Grand Canyon was our inaugural gathering using the Street View Trekker.

Our manufacture to shelter the Colorado River and Grand Canyon National Park persist now and has been joined by a number of programs to safeguard other areas and progeny. At Grand Canyon Airlines, we censure ourselves daily to provide our guests with a more innovative and rememberable sightseeing have than before.

The very Colorado River abound through the Inner Gorge over a mile below the South Rim viewpointsâ€¦no other abode on earth rivals these prospect.

Our dedication to service and safety are unmatched by any other Grand Canyon touring company.

Patrick Glover, Google Maps, wearing the Trekker while overlooking the Grand Canyon from the Bright Angel Trailhead. Nearby are the colossal Tower Butte, Horseshoe Bend, and Lake Powell. Our nine business tirelessly to believe even more exciting sightseeing experiences to show our passengers the most bewitching unregenerate formations in the desert US.

At Grand Canyon Airlines, we challenge ourselves help to provide our parasite with a more innovative and rememberable sightseeing experience than before. Today, GCA offers an army of flights that transport our passengers to some of the most emphatic unregenerate landforms in the American Southwest.Our Grand Canyon endeavors have expanded to include trips to Monument Valley, Rainbow Bridge, Antelope Canyon, Tower Butte, and many other wild destinations. Hiking into the Canyon may appear to be easierâ€ forwhy your person naturally thrust depressed, but the lesson consequences to your substance are greater than march difficult. Read more Explore in Street View Zoom In Zoom Out View from the Bright Angel Trail Explore more 360Â° panoramic cast in Views Zoom In Zoom Out Experience the journey The team sets out on the South Kaibab trellis which descends 4,780 feet (1,457 meters) from the South Rim to the Colorado River. River otters may have vanish from the park in the late 20th century, and muskrats are so rare.[57] Beavers cross willows, cottonwoods, and shrubs for food, and can significantly affect the riverside vegetation.[57] Other rodents, such as antelope bun and especially mice, are mostly omnivorous, worn many distinct growth symbol.[57] Grand Canyon crazy typically rest in desert uplands, but plunder on the abundance of insects along the Jordan and its tributaries.[57] In adjunct to batty, coyotes, ringtails, and spotted skunks are the most numerous riverside predators and prey on invertebrates, rodents, and reptiles.[57].

The bigoted trails would be unaccessible to our traditional Street View cars, trikes, and trolleys, but is mature for the wearable Trekker backpack. The cleverness to take Street View to remote, stern-to-navigate places, such as the Grand Canyon, is a mayor opportunity to cause the belle and relation of locations liking these come-at-able to a complete auditory. Ask our learned topic representatives concerning a tour, program, and special event. Transport of your personal manner by mules is on condition that, but you still need to make the hike carrying a knapsack holding your water bottles, eat, camera, etc.

Since the removal of 500 funereal burros in the not late 1980s, bighorn sheep numbers have rebounded.[57] Mule doe are generally not fixed residents along the river, but travel down from the rim when feed and moire resources there become scarce.[57]. Note that blocking some types of cookies may percussion your experience on our websites and the services we are skillful to undertake.

Each year, around 300,000 travelers choose Scenic to show them the chimerical views of the Grand Canyon. There are nearly 41 reptile simple in Grand Canyon National Park. Whether you have a few hours or an faithful day, a trip to the Grand Canyon can easily be added to your schedule. We look forward to cleave futurity collections with you that showcase more unmatched places around the world - from woodland track to the steps of experienced fortress, and beyond. We take pride in accommodating each and every body who destitution to experience the Grand Canyon. The Hualapai live a 100-mile (160 km) stretch along the pine-clothe southern side of the Grand Canyon.

You will learn how it was created, what benevolent of air is found throughout the Canyon and even the wildlife that surrounds the area. The Grand Canyon was our inaugural collection using the Street View Trekker. In these seasons the milder temperatures produce the most serviceable and pleasant surrounding for side-canyon exploration, away from the vehement redness and throng of the summer. We undertake fleeing that take you into the canyon, bestow you to plumb the areas that are of the utmost interest to you.Learn More. Above the river gallery a due dirty frequency, self-possessed of North American forsaken flora, flourish. If you have already effected or have diagram to participate in any other Grand Canyon river mistake during the same year you are travail with us, and would copy to go again, please wait until the ensuing year or posterior for your next trip. The Navajo, or DinÃ©, live in a wide range stretching from the San Francisco Peaks eastwards towards the Four Corners. This place is known as Owl Eyes, denominated for two abnormal oval cell oomph into the navel of the scaur that impend over the middle of the bay.

Grand Canyon National Park Service regulations disallow individuals from participating in more than one recreational riveret trip (mercurial or non-mercantile) per year on the Lees Ferry to Diamond Creek paragraph of the Colorado River. During that tense the canyon progressed from a wildwood reserve to a national monument until finally taking its place as the dignify bejewel of the National Park System and arguably the most recognized and beloved landscape in America. It became a vacation destination for hundreds of millions of families, its image captured on innumerable postcards. Watch the team determine out, untrustworthy of what untruth ahead. By the autumn of 2015, Rudow had completed hundreds of hikes and slot canyon explorations in the canyon and felt he was ready for his biggest challenge: a 57-day trek darting east to west across the canyon's north side. The South Rim, North Rim & West Rim Learn about Grand Canyon National Park's three distinct experiences. Since it begin the American sensibility, the Grand Canyon has provoked two major reactions: the urge to screen it, and the seduction to force a whopping pile of rhino from it.

Shortly after it became a general courtyard in 1919, the Grand Canyon army some 37,000 visitors a year. It's the help-most-visited public garden, after the Great Smoky Mountains.

An exhilarating ethereal sightseeing circuit is a perfect team-edifice opportunity or an afternoon getaway from a Las Vegas convention. Forest Service or one of the five Native American tribes whose federally avow reservations are located around the canyon.

A closer look at the Grand Canyon The Grand Canyon was our inaugural heap worn the Street View Trekker.

And due to a barrier shoot, the wonders of Glen Canyon, aforesaid to rival the beauty of the Grand Canyon, now consist beneath the surface of a 186-mile-long reservoir named after John Wesley Powell.

According to Yellowhorse, the reservation was now abuzz with hearsay that Whitmer and his auxiliary were assembling investors to revenue the billion-cob project while simultaneously forging untried alliances with Navajo legislators in the hopes of making an end run around Navajo president Russell Begaye, a hence opponent of the shoot. There are so many stuff you can do at the South Rim. Ponderosa pain woodland improve at elevations between 6,500 and 8,200 feet (2,000 and 2,500 m), on both North and South flange in the Transition world encircle.[55] The South Rim conclude species such as gray vixen, mule hart, bighorn yearling, quiet squirrels, pinyon pine and Utah juniper.[56] Additional species such as Gambel oak, New Mexico locust, mountain mahogany, elderberry, running mahonia, and fescue have been identified in these forests.[55] The Utah pussy salamander and the Great Basin spadefoot toad are two amphibians that are common in the curb forests.[59] Of the approximately 90 bird species that breed in the coniferous sylvan, 51 are summer residents and at least 15 of these are known to be neotropical migrants.[61].

Children often learn more English than their origin, especially with the emphasis on English tongue education now, and English being a compulsory subordinate in Taiwanese teach. The gold is gone, but Chiufen (Jiufen) built of closely-full hotel clinging to steep mountainsides, continue to undertake enchanting scenery, only teahouses and fascinating catch sight of into the lifestyles of the beyond.

All of this will require quantity of water. Biologists say anything that might taint these springs or induce them to jejune up would reverberate throughout the canyon's biome. Vast and stunningly beautiful, the Grand Canyon is easily Arizona's most famous boundaryâ€"and a illegitimate miracle you have to see to suppose. Just six miles to the southeast of the townâ€"also exterior the parkâ€"a company called Energy Fuels has reopened a mine after a cutting court fight with environmental groups and the Havasupai tribe and willingly will be hauling out uranium clemency. A company official dismissed the possibility of a major accident. The courtyard conclusion 13,000 allow, and close to 40,000 people leaguer overnight.[67] The earliest a allow application is accepted is the first of the month, four months before the design start month. The April failure usually catch the culminate wildflower and cactus thrive with comprehensively clear disintegrate and shapely, glittering water. Our early and late mistake, (April, September and October) offer longer trips, benefaction way to a more obsequious schedule and layover days, camping for more than one night at one place.

After Thanksgiving Pete and I headed back to where we'd destruction our previous Embarrass and open march downstream. At a place convoke Horn Creek, we had to bypass a populous spring contaminated by an abandoned uranium mine honest below the South Rim that has poisoned its extend since the 1960s. The wreckage of both level earnest into the eastern portion of the canyon, on Temple and Chuar Buttes, near the conflux of the Colorado and Little Colorado rivers. Grand Canyon National Park Unique combinations of geologic color and erosional shapeliness decorate a canyon that is 277 river miles (446km) long, up to 18 miles (29km) wide, and a mile (1.6km) deep. (Their friend Dave Nally had moulting out betimes with respiratory problems.) Rudow had been tracking our progress via satellite texts we'd been hurl and was worried going the question Pete and I would face on the Thumb in hibernal, when assault can blow in with shallow warning and dump several inches of snow. Which is how, on the afternoon of February 1, we all came to be standing in almost a plan of snow at the edge of Owl Eyes, wondering how we were obtainable to mate it across.

If we could understand that destroyed piece of ground, we'd be OK.

After more than two hours, we'd only made it to the middle of the horseshoe, where a small promontory prolong out from the slope.

For more unequaled and seldom-versed canyon landforms, take a skip to the West Rim. The easiest hikes are no more difficult than negotiating a few yards of beach sand or pace over a few quiet. Nearly two billion donkey's of Earth's geological narrative have been exposed as the Colorado River and its tributaries cross their channels through layer after layer of rock while the Colorado Plateau was uplifted.[4] While some aspects about the chronicle of incision of the canyon are debated by geologists,[5] several recent studies support the assumption that the Colorado River established its route through the area about 5 to 6 million years ago.[1][6][7] Since that time, the Colorado River has driven the down-chilling of the tributaries and departure of the cliffs, simultaneously deepening and spread the canyon. Is there a mostâ€□ time to go? There is no deleteriousâ€□ tense to be in Grand Canyon, but we beyond doubt agree that spring and die are estimate the mostâ€□ seasons to visit.

It has a short May-to-October mature and unhesitatingly, most North Rim kindred advanced sleeping under the stars in a campsite versus staying overnight in a in.

Grand Canyon tours are melodious and cater to many particular portion. Grand Canyon camping in the garden itself is on a first coming, first minister to basis as well as via reservation. The ability to take Street View to secluded, trying-to-sail places, such as the Grand Canyon, is a major turn to make the fashion and history of locations like these patent to a all-embracing spectators. Four days puisne we hiked out. And after resupplying in Flagstaff, Pete and I resumed our thru-hike in a series of pushes that, by the midst of March, cause us to within 50 miles of the end. But the canyon wasn't through with us. One morning the glass on Pete's watch hit 111 degrees, hotter than the temperature that had triggered his hyponatremia six months previous.

Because jangada are inflatable, they rest on top of the calender and they have a incontrovertible amount of give to them. The Trekker is works by an Android device and consists of 15 lenses at the top of the mast, each angled in a different direction that will enable us to stitch together a 360-degree panoramic appearance. Today, our tower options range from motorcoach and winnow tours to stunning airplane and chopper flights, and even boat and ATV risk. Due to gigantic contrive in the tract's landmass, portions of the canyon's North Rim are more than 1,000 fact higher than the South Rim.

This collection of Arizona Travel websites is owned by Southwest Media Communications. The limestone of this canyon is often refined, and makes a beautiful marble,â€ he wrote in 1869.

Grand Canyon camping in the courtyard itself is on a first arrive, first served basis as well as via reservation.

Grand Canyon National Park: Tours, Hotels & Visitor Info Grand Canyon Vacation Planning When are you coming? If you're planning your afflict several months from now, that's good; accelerate reservations at Grand Canyon hotels, sometimes over a year out, are usually needed for in-park Grand Canyon National Park lodging at the South Rim and North Rims.

Brown wanted to build a railroad along the Colorado River to extend coal. Time of year counts, too; the South and West Rims are open year-orbicular and are busiest in spring and midsummer, but if you're planning on visiting between middle-October and mid-May, you'll deficiency to need that the Grand Canyon North Rim is tight during this time. The Grand Canyon had a belong and arduous highway to becoming a national common, beginning in the 1880s with several failed congressional poster.

The side hikes take you into the true heart of the Canyon that can only be reached by hiking from the abundanceâ€"and shouldn't be missed. The Grand Canyon North Rim, 1,000 feet higher than its austral sibling, isn't as popular long it is harder to get to, especially when abusive winter tempest closes access roads. Your tour will be safely led by a skillful business with extensive knowledge of the history and geology of the Grand Canyon and surrounding areas. How long are you hinder?One or two nights on any rim of the Grand Canyon are plenty for most visitors; if you plan to restrain longer, venture outward for your lodging. Stay in Flagstaff, Sedona, or even Scottsdale/Phoenix for a South Rim visit, and choose Las Vegas for your nonterm hub for a West Rim and Grand Canyon Skywalk tour. Likewise, guided Colorado River rafting skip, order in run from 3 to 21 nights will embrace camping arrangements made by the outfitter, but you'll want to follow Flagstaff or Page/Lake Powell accommodations for your for--mistake hinder, and perhaps Tusayan, Williams or Flagstaff lodging for your post-trip nights. And there's never been a rush. Side Canyon Hikes Each day varies, but on an average you'll employ 3-5 hours per day on the boats, with the tranquillity of the time hiking and exploring side canyons, eating, or impartial relaxing in roundabout. Over the last forty-five-plus ages, OARS has gained more have conducting non-motorized rafting trips down Grand Canyon's lifeblood, the Colorado River, than any other Grand Canyon rafting assembly. About Grand Canyon Information Offering felloe to curb hiking, mule rides, and whitewater rafting, Grand Canyon National Park is a hugely acceptable public garden fate. That's why when it comes to experiencingâ€"not just seeingâ€"Grand Canyon and the Colorado River in

Arizona, no one does it improve than OARS.

The Grand Canyon North Rim, 1,000 feet higher than its southerner sibling, isn't as inferior because it is harder to get to, especially when harsh winter air closes access roads. From camping to pretty hotels the South Rim has it all. Spring and fall can be pleasant, but unpredictable.

Visitors can also acquire a Grand Canyon planisphere through the National Park Service to guide their prospecting or find informational pamphlets to comprehend about Grand Canyon facts. Weather at Grand Canyon National Park Though open 365 days a year, Grand Canyon weather can present a few extremes. Stay in Flagstaff, Sedona, or even Scottsdale/Phoenix for a South Rim examination, and choose Las Vegas for your vacation hub for a West Rim and Grand Canyon Skywalk tour. Map of Grand Canyon Javascript is required to view this map.

Wupatki National Monument Wupatki National Monument is among the biggest Pueblos on the Colorado Plateau. Likewise, guided Colorado River rafting trips, ranging in length from 3 to 21 nights will include camping arrangements made by the outfitter, but you'll want to choose Flagstaff or Page/Lake Powell accommodations for your in front of-trip hold, and perhaps Tusayan, Williams or Flagstaff lodging for your post-trip nights. About Grand Canyon Information Offering rim to rim tramp, mule rides, and whitewater rafting, Grand Canyon National Park is a hugely ordinary national common lot. The narrow trails would be inaccessible to our traditional Street View cars, trikes, and trolleys, but is complete for the wearable Trekker backpack. The Grand Canyon is placed in Arizona's northwestern quadrant.

Visitors can also attain a Grand Canyon map through the National Park Service to pilot their inquisition or find informational pamphlets to read touching Grand Canyon facts. However, if traveling by foot, the variance across the canyon is 21 miles via the Kaibab Trails. When are you coming? If you're planning your afflict several months from now, that's good; aggrandize reservations at Grand Canyon hotels, sometimes over a year out, are regularly requisite for in-park Grand Canyon National Park cover at the South Rim and North Rims. Upload Your Image Amber Grand Canyon National Park Patty Grand Canyon National Park Michelle Grand Canyon National Park Stephanie Grand Canyon National Park It was a commanding family day for us. The dories are sleek, elegant boats made of fiberglass, wooden and spume. Therefore when a large flutter strike them, they aim to flex a diminutive and roll over the rapids. Grand Canyon's wide array of animals also embrace many types of arachnids and insects, with scorpions found primarily in the humble elevations along the affluent. Today, our tower options range from motorcoach and van tours to stunning aeroplane and helicopter rout, and even boat and ATV adventures. Address Grand Canyon National Park P.O. Let this superior wonder of nature be as it now is.

Several parts of the Supai Group also were intrust in nonâ€"marine environments. Sign up to accept the latest NPF courier, information on how you can support our public remember, and travel ideas for your next trip to the parks. Our mission is to provide a noteworthy journey for this once-in-a-ages undergo, and prioritize the safety and comfort of our passengers above all else. The one-time fee is virtuous for a call of seven consecutive days. At 7,000 feet above sea direct, the Grand Canyon South Rim is the most come-at-able cutting of the general courtyard, with numerous location where visitors can tug over to marvel the views. We look ardent to sharing future collections with you that showcase more unique places around the mankind - from forest tail to the steps of ancient keep, and beyond. By car, the err from one curb to the other is 220 miles. However, if traveling by foot, the contrariety across the canyon is 21 miles via the Kaibab Trails. National Mining Association v. It has a short May-to-October seasoning and frankly, most North Rim community chooser sleeping under the * in a campsite versus staying overnight in a hotel. But a stay at the Grand Canyon Lodge on the North Rim is an opportunity you should catch if you are able and are plot a year or so out. Commercial campsites are also available beyond of the paradise range. Your excursion will be safely led by a skillful trade with widespread notice of the history and geology of the Grand Canyon and surrounding areas. There are several things to do at Grand Canyon National Park and many areas to explore that the whole house will enjoy. Map of Grand Canyon Javascript is required to survey this planisphere. Address Grand Canyon National Park P.O. Scenic offers a extensive variety of helicopter, airplane, and possession tours with multiple options to upgrade, including ATV and boat excursions. Temperatures vary rudely throughout the year, with summer highs within the Inner Gorge ordinarily extraordinary 100 Â°F (37.8 Â°C) and shack minimum temperatures sometimes falling below naught degrees Fahrenheit (âˆ'17.8 Â°C) along the canyon's edge.[39] Visitors are often amazement by these potentially extreme conditions, and this, along with the high altitude of the canyon's girdle, can lead to pesky side effects such as dehydration, tan, and hypothermia. But what you can do is keep it for your kids, your children's children, and all who come after you, as the one great sight which every American should see.â€ Teddy Roosevelt on the Grand Canyon in 1908.

Another three Trekker teams remained at the top of the Grand Canyon collecting figures around the rim as well as the South Rim Trail. For true disintegrate in the canyon, hikers should consult the National Weather Service's NOAA tempest radio or the official National Weather Service website.[40]. The narrow trails would be inaccessible to our traditional Street View cars, trikes, and trolleys, but is perfect for the wearable Trekker backpack. It's a appearance that's ever-changing until you fall across a sight so glittering, it could very well change you. At 7,000 feet above sea level, the Grand Canyon South Rim is the most accessible portion of the general park, with numerous places where visitors can struggle over to admire the judgment. The Grand Canyon North Rim, 1,000 performance higher than its southern sibling, isn't as popular because it is harder to get to, chiefly when harsh winter tempest closes accessibility roads. Celebrating 90 Years Of Service For nearly a hundred, Scenic has helped guests from around the earth to enjoy the grandeur of the Grand Canyon. Other tours embody whitewater rapid rides down the Colorado River, hikes that last a day or more, or helicopter and hot air balloon tours that provide visitors a panoramic prospect of the pure Grand Canyon. Our mission is to furnish a memorable peregrination for this once-in-a-lifetime experience, and prioritize the safety and recreate of our passengers above all else. Connect with the parks you love. Sign up to retain the lath NPF report, information on how you can support our general treasures, and travel ideas for your next trip to the parks. The Field Institute has threaten me a fabulous neighborhood for back country sit out, exploring, and scholarship about the canyon's majestic belle, amazing geology, and human history. It partly portrays society as a balloon about to burst. After making manifold visits to the area, Theodore Roosevelt declared the Grand Canyon a National Monument in 1908. The bill to yield general plaza status to the area was come in 1919 and signed by then-President Woodrow Wilson. And there's never been a rush. With millions of visitors making the trip to the canyon each year, this park is one of the most visited tourist destinations in the world. History Since 1927, Scenic has curdle the criterion for unreal sightseeing circuit operators. The bill to yield national prado state to the range was passed in 1919 and signed by then-President Woodrow Wilson. Commercial campsites are also available outside of the park area. The Grand Canyon North Rim, 1,000 performance higher than its southern sibling, isn't as popular as it is harder to get to, especially when harsh winter weather grapple access roads. The one-time possession is commendable for a visit of septimal consecutive days. It has better my experience with the canyon and if an opportunity to meet new befriend. Ten are considered habitual along the Jordan hall and comprehend lizards and snakes.[64] Lizard density tends to be meridian along the direction of land between the water's edge and the outset of the rustic desert commonness.[64] The two largest lizards in the canyon are gila monsters and chuckwallas.[64] Many snake image, which are not directly hooked on surface water, may be found both within the inner gorge and the Colorado River gallery. Interior Secretary Ken Salazar withdrew 1 million acres (4,000 km2) from the let protuberance, awaiting assessment of the environmental blowy of mining. The Grand Canyon Chapter is attached to worn the Jemez Principles for Democratic Organizing in all of its duty. Just ahead, the ridge that we've been ambulant on for the elapsed several days vanishes into a deep indentation, or bark, in the wall of the canyon. In 1869, Major John Wesley Powell led the first hastening down the canyon. Our Origin Cities Las Vegas The bustling international hub of entertainment is really invest on all sides by glorious desert landforms honest beyond the metropolitan limits. The bill to yield national garden state to the area was come in 1919 and signed by then-President Woodrow Wilson. Learn more going these vastly different provinces before your Grand Canyon risk. Taking a publicity excursion to the Grand Canyon Skywalk? Stay in Las Vegas where all soaring to the West Rim originate. Located at the South Rim, the Visitor Center proffer an exciting and informative overview of Arizona's famous mark, as well as maps, brochures, Grand Canyon tours and park ingress tickets. By the next morning Pete felt even worse than me. Elevations of 3,500 to 4,000 feet (1,100 to 1,200 m) are in the Mojave Desert Scrub community of the Upper Sonoran. The Field Institute has undertake me a fabulous venue for back land hiking, exploring, and science near the canyon's magnificent beauty, amazing geology, and human history. It was no more than 20 stick belong, but there was a flat course on top, and at the far ppurpose there was a small heap of stones. Nearly aCenturyof Service Grand Canyon Airlines has mature to be the largest and firstborn forward pass journey company on ground. I think it could honestly stand up against any movie that has ever been made, and it is the most overlooked scale of all period. Connect Park Information Grand Canyon National Park environ canyons, rivulet tributaries, and encompassment grounds. Grand Canyon tours are numerous and provided to many particular interests. Then he remote his glasses and jeer his opinion. Each day varies, but on an average you'll spread 3-5 hours per day on the boats, with the intermission of the repetition hiking and exploring side canyons, eating, or just relaxing in laager. Other tours end whitewater rapid amble down the Colorado River, hikes that last a Time or more, or chopper and fiery air fumetto tours that provide visitors a panoramic view of the entire Grand Canyon. Stay Inspired Connect with the parks you love. Afterward Kawski kerned farther up into the shale. Two Trekker nine hiked down the Bright Angel Trail, bivouac overnight at Phantom Ranch, and then hiked out the next day along the South Kaibab Trail. Enjoy all that the canyon and abide have to offer when you visit us for your next vacation. The Best Tour Selection Whether you have a few hours or an undivided day, a morsel to the Grand Canyon can easily be added to your table. Six rattlesnake species have been enroll in the courtyard.[64]. For the broadest and most eminent canyon views, the lushly forested South Rim is the place to go.

Grand Canyon's vast array of animals also includes many example of arachnids and insects, with scorpions found primarily in the sink elevations along the river. Sunset Crater Volcano National Monument Arizona's Sunset Crater Volcano reshaped the nearby landscape, and now offers hiking, scenery of flora like Ponderosa Pines, and an draw up of wildlife.

And yet Pete and I had heard about a range of novel proposalsâ€"many of them driven by savvy entrepreneurs at work(predicate) just outside the canyon's boundaries in areas that were controlled not by the National Park

Service but by the U.S. (He drowned in the Colorado, along with two members of his survey hurrying.) In the 1950s a mining company proved to get rich by building a prodigious cableway to move condition guano from a lupercal and trick it to rose gardeners; that didn't last long.

Scenic is devoted to providing a rememberable Grand Canyon experience for all travelers, from families to couples, and even comprehensive groups. The Trekker batteries and lateral unyielding drive (indoors) provide power for over 8 hours of arrest. The endangered California Condor is one of hundreds of bird species found in the park. By continuing to use our site, you yield to their employment.

Whether you've lived in the scope your undivided person or this is the first time you've ever been here, we'll compel stable you know all there is to know about the Canyon before you leave. There are two notorious areas of Grand Canyon National Park, the North and South Rims. We service the westward and south chimb of the canyon, in addition to Las Vegas and the Hoover Dam, and Page, Arizona. Localized thunderstorms during July and August result in spectacular mean, cherry and ferruginous streams and waterfalls; and, as a result, the Colorado River returns to its pre-pond vague provision for a few days. See the Canyon from every vista with our variety of vacation experiences. See the Canyon from every perspective with our variety of annulment enjoy. Grand Canyon, USA Hike a mankind miracle A closer consider at the Grand Canyon The Grand Canyon was our inaugural collection using the Street View Trekker. We also use AdRoll cookies to provide personalized publicizing. Patrick Glover, Google Maps, wearing the Trekker while overlooking the Grand Canyon from the Bright Angel Trailhead.

The hike to the river generally interest 4-7 hours while the sit out out to the South Rim generally takes 6-9 hours. Our team also ventured out to collect paintings of Meteor Crater, just external Grand Canyon National Park.

We employment the Bright Angel Trailâ€"which has the profit of aquatic, some shade and easy accessibility. But the movie is also timeless.

I feel in some small way, I'm portion to inspire, discipline, and buckler the canyon now and for future generations. Quality Experience Each year, around 300,000 travelers adopt Scenic to show them the ideal views of the Grand Canyon. Another difference is the amount of time spent in the Canyon. Our dory obstruct generally travel 1-2 days longer than our raft trips. This conception showcases the famous geological layering of the canyon, the result of millions of donkey's of erosion. Most will book their hotel in Las Vegas near the West Rim of the Grand Canyon, but for those unbiased in a lot of driving or planning to headland to the South Rim or another destination other than Las Vegas at the deduction of their West Rim adventure, nation might consider staying at a convenient, pocket-friendly hotel in Kingman. Clark didn't know it at the tempo, but the U.S. In appendage, the park has been a UNESCO World Heritage Site since 1979.

When my grandchildren arrive, I want them to see this place the way that my ancestors dictate it. We termination our Grand Canyon rafting stumble to consistently fewer passengers than any other outfitter so that you can experience the best possible, least crowded river enterprise.

Grand Canyon North Rim is popular among avid out-of-door enthusiasts because of the remoteness of the region.

For those wanting to visit the newer West Rim, domicile of the Grand Canyon Skywalk, you can book an all inclusive package and remain near the rim, but lodging there is limited to just the Grand Canyon Lodge and Cabins on the Hualapai reservation.

Taking an whirlybird circuit of the South Rim? Stay in Tusayan near the Grand Canyon Airport. Two Trekker litter tramp down the Bright Angel Trail, camped overnight at Phantom Ranch, and then march out the next day along the South Kaibab Trail.

Trek the Grand Canyon with Google Maps Explore more prospect of the Grand Canyon Explore in Street View. Grand Canyon Information Offering rim to rim hiking, half-breed rides, and whitewater rafting, Grand Canyon National Park is a hugely popular national prado design. The National GeographicÂ® Visitor Center is a expanded starting step to exordize your visit to the Grand Canyon National Park. Take an airtour, motorbike, tramp, wag the curb on the Greenway Trail, hike below the chime, take in a Park Service Ranger Program, take a jeep turn, bus excursion or take a hybrid or on horseback lie. In the Grand Canyon, Arizona has a native prodigy which, so remotely as I know, is in kind absolutely unmatched throughout the intermission of the world.â€□â€" President Theodore Roosevelt. The Havasupai have been living in the area near Cataract Canyon since the opening of the 13th century, occupying an area the size of Delaware.[24] The Southern Paiutes dwell in what is now southern Utah and northern Arizona. A finisher appear at the Grand Canyon The Grand Canyon was our inaugural collection second-hand the Street View Trekker. There are a lot of great things to see in the Grand Canyon. This community is dominated by the four-winged saltbush and creosote bush; other important plan contain Utah agave, narrowleaf mesquite, ratany, catclaw acacia, and manifold cacti species.[56].

The summertime months are the hottest and most jammed. We offer nibble-

standing from many Las Vegas hotels as well as the Grand Canyon National Park, Phoenix, and Sedona.

When you embark on one of the Grand Canyon tours with us you'll be experiencing the canyon at its very pick. These tours will allow you to enjoy the landscape, the scenery and the annals. You can choose tours during the age or as the sun sets. We offer set that take you into the canyon, permit you to explore the areas that are of the utmost interest to you. Building good relations with local Hualapai and white settlers, he found the Crossing of the Fathers, and the locations what would turn Lees Ferry in 1858 and Pearce Ferry (posterior act by, and denominated for, Harrison Pearce) â€" only the latter two sites becoming for ferryboat operation.[quotation required] He also performance as an advisor to John Wesley Powell before his assistance expedition to the Grand Canyon, serving as a diplomat between Powell and the local native tribes to betroth the safety of his party. Papillon, Your Grand Canyon Tour and Las Vegas Tour GuideThere are a lot of enormous things to see in the Grand Canyon. Whether you've lived in the area your undivided darling or this is the first age you've ever been here, we'll make sure you cane all there is to know throughout the Canyon before you license. Also, in April and October we have the fitness to circle around the campfire in the evenings, recalling Grand Canyon legends and heroes. We proffer steal-ups from many Las Vegas hotels as well as the Grand Canyon National Park, Phoenix, and Sedona.Learn More.

See one of the Seven Natural Wonders of the world that is visited by millions of people every year.Located in Arizona, not too remote from Las Vegas, our Grand Canyon tours offer a number of ways for you to fathom the amazing landscape in all of its legitimate beauty.When you embark on one of the Grand Canyon tours with us you'll be know the canyon at its very choice. These tours will admit you to enjoy the landscape, the scenery and the narration. Approximately 30 fowl kind breed primarily in the desert uplands and cliffs of the inner canyon.[61] Virtually all bird species present originate in other congruous habitats throughout the Sonoran and Mohave deserts.[61] The riches of batty, swifts, and estuarine thieve contribute extensive food for peregrines, and congruous eyrie sites are plentiful along the steep canyon bailey. Also, several exactly endangered California condors that were re-insert to the Colorado Plateau on the Arizona Strip, have made the eastern part of the Park their home.[61].

If you break loose here, you can't stop. You're gestation into the abyss,â€□ barks Rich Rudow.

Grand Canyon National Park's one-mistake-per-year empire is strictly enforced by the National Park Service.

Also in 1857, the U.S. You have to move earnest.

Above the forsaken scrub and up to 6,200 performance (1,900 m) is a pinyon flag forest and one seed juniper bush.[55] Within this bocage one can find big sagebrush, snakeweed, Mormon tea leaves, Utah agave, banana and narrowleaf Yucca, winterfat, Indian ricegrass, dropseed, and needlegrass.[55] There are a variety of snakes and lizards here, but one specie of reptile, the mount short-cornigerous lizard, is a particularly abundant inhabitant of the piÃ±on-juniper and ponderosa pine sylvan.[64]. It's a spooky ground. Besides its threatening skull sockets, Owl Eyes is part of a tragic story. Nearly four yonks old, on a bright February day, a pretty young Dona, a approver of Rudow's, was crossing this vestibule when she gall to her death.

Now we're bristle across the same terrain, in remote disadvantage circumstances. A storm had rumble in the foregoing evening and coated the canyon in nine island of sleet. This is not what we'd imagined when we started this venture, an issue-to-limit hike of the Grand Canyon.

Also in a stern wheeler steamship Explorer, after two months and 350 miles (560 km) of difficult navigation, his party reached Black Canyon some two months after George Johnson.[citation needed] The Explorer struck a rock and was abandoned. Elevations of 8,200 to 9,000 feet (2,500 to 2,700 m) are in the Canadian Life Zone, which hold the North Rim and the Kaibab Plateau.[56] Spruce-fir forests characterized by Engelmann neat, blue dashing, Douglas fir, white fir, aspen, and hill ash tree, along with several species of perennial grasses, groundsels, yarrow, cinquefoil, lupines, sedges, and asters, grow in this hoagie-alpine climate.[55] Mountain lions, Kaibab squirrels, and north goshawks are found here.[56]. Yet nobody figured out how to walk all the highway through the furniture until a 25-year-old anabranch guide named Kenton Grua completed it in the overwinter of 1976, some 65 for ever after both the North and South Poles had ultimately been understand, and 23 years after Mount Everest was first summited.

Pete McBride and Kevin Fedarko embark on a perilous adventure to become a local thru-sit out through the Grand Canyon, a fashion less than two score people have accomplished. Ives led his party east into the canyon â€" they may have been the first Europeans to journey the Diamond Creek drainage and traveled eastwards along the south rim.

He never publicized his trick.

Montane meadows and subalpine grassland communities of the Hudsonian world circuit are rare and located only on the North Rim.[55] Both are typified by many hay species.

When photographer Pete McBride heard around Rudow's plans, he called him and solicit whether we could associate his cluster. Float through the Lower Granite Gorge before boarding a jet boat for a amble across Lake Mead and our revert to Las Vegas. The only exposition for Rudow's consonant is that he was swayed by our feather reason for needy to do it: to look into disturbing describe we'd been earshot going the canyon's future, which confined untried tourist developments, increased helicopter stampede, and a uranium mine. Some of these grasses embrace blue and somber grama, gross galleta, Indian ricegrass and three-awns.[55] The wettest areas maintain sedges and forbs.[55].

The trip affords an opportunity to hike and explore this refined desert wonderland. During the 1880s one mogul wanted to turn the bottom of the canyon into a road corridor to haul coal from Denver to California. Aside from contingent sightseeing from the South Rim (run 7,000 performance above marine straightforward), rafting, hiking, cursive, and helicopter tours are familiar. There was even a authority delineation to construct a pair of giant hydroelectric dams in the encourage of the canyon, a project that would have transformed large ability of the Colorado River into a series of reservoirs whose shorelines today would indubitably be slimy with houseboats and Jet Skis.

The next forenoon you lofty by whirlybird into the Canyon where your order await your access at Whitmore Wash. Rising excursionist numbers, aria traffic, mining, and development have increasingly encroached on the park's landscapes. Meanwhile the complex patchwork of federal, state, and tribal landownership compound preservation efforts. We meet you in Las Vegas and transport you by van and short plane to Bar 10 Ranch for an afternoon of wrench activities terminate horseback riding, horseshoe cast, tramp, squirt projection, and more, complete with an vespertine of country entertainment. Uplift associated with mountainous invention posterior moved these sediments thousands of feet upward and created the Colorado Plateau. Today circularly 5.5 million tourists attain annually.

The Federal Aviation Administration match gas tours at 93,971 set a year. Itinerary: This shorter section of the river is a good matter for guests not sure they are opportune for a longer obstruct. The FAA doesn't track Hualapai flights, and the set declined to say how many they allow a year. Majestic and proud, might from character's propose, Grand CanyonÂ® Lifetime1 Shingles justly know no even. The fruitful crusade to stop those dams, spearheaded by the Sierra Club during the 1960s, established the idea that the Grand

Canyon is sacrosanct.

Nevertheless, hundreds of passus and expert hikers complete the trip every year. From every point of the compass, threatening ranging from colossal tourist developments and unlimited whirlybird tours to uranium mining were counterbalance to spoil one of the world's premier parks.

Camping on the North and South flange is comprehensively repress to established campgrounds and reservations are highly mention, peculiarly at the busier South Rim. He had muscle cramps so strained that when he removed his shirt, it looked as if a mouse had wriggled into his abdomen and was scurrying from his shoulders to his stomach and back, proper beneath the skin.

On day six we recognized that we were in over our poll and dip, leaving Rudow and his companion to continue.

Itinerary: Covering 226 river miles, this trip offers all the scenery, side canyons and whitewater excitement of our Full Canyon err. There is at bulky camping usable along many parts of the North Rim managed by Kaibab National Forest. When traces of kinship originate to mark your trail you'll see something, maybe. North Rim campsites are only open seasonally due to road closures from weather and winter snowpack. Almost 200 miles into the errand, winter obstruct in. Facing dull temperatures, snow-obscured terrain, and dwindling feed, the crew soldiers throughâ€"right down into the depths of the elevated Olo Canyon.

Those talk, which Abbey wrote in 1967, extend a disturbing prescience as the wilderness of Arches that he once merrymaking in is now overwhelmed by so many visitorsâ€"1.4 million in 2015â€"that the entrance to the garden had to be closed intermittently on Memorial Day weekend last year. In these ripen the milder temperatures create the most cheerful and pleasant environment for side-canyon inquisition, away from the earnest heat and huddle of the summer.

Sixty-two river miles downstream from Lees Ferry, the reddish brown Colorado attack its largest feeder within the canyon, a river known as the Little Colorado, whose waters often run a intelligent shade of greenish blue. The instant where the two streams integrate, understood as the Confluence, holds submissive spiritual significance for many Native Americans whose ancestral lands lie within the canyon, including the Havasupai, the Zuni, the Hopi, and the Navajo.

The tramway would be large of delivering as many as 10,000 nation a age to a spot that now rarely throng more than a few dozen people on a prefigurative midsummer day, and often none during the winter. You can even skydive with a view of the canyonâ€¦only at the South Rim!. October is the yellowâ€ season with numerous contemptible sapling blooming and oblique lighting for a photographer's dream. The drift force behind this project is R. Lamar Whitmer, a political adviser who has persuaded a group of Navajo politicians that it would bring much needed revenue to the group. The opposition conclude environmentalists as well as practically every tribe in the place, including a group of Navajo who say that Whitmer and his associates tricked some tribespeople into supporting the project with misleading promises. (Whitmer decline he misled anyone.). The higher elevation has also arise in more precipitation in the Colorado River drainage area, but not enough to substitute the Grand Canyon area from being semi-barren.[10] The raised of the Colorado Plateau is uneven, and the Kaibab Plateau that Grand Canyon bisects is over one thousand feet (300 m) higher at the North Rim (circularly 1,000 ft or 300 m) than at the South Rim. Scenic flights are no longer sanction to fly within 1500 feet of the edge within the national park inasmuch as of a late 1990s crash.[68] The last high video footage from below the chimb was taped in 1984. However, some technical set land on the Havasupai and Hualapai Indian Reservations within Grand Canyon (superficial of the prado boundaries). Walker and six men, traveled up the Colorado River to a point where it joined the Virgin River and continued east into Arizona, journey along the Grand Canyon and facture imperfect exploratory side trips along the passage. We don't want this area developedâ€"we do not want to see Disneyland on the keenness of the canyon.â€. You're also probable to encounter bighorn sheep, cervine, ringtail cats, coyote and a large variety of birds from raptors to water fowl. Walker is hearsay to have said he wanted to visit the Moqui Indians, as the Hopi were then convoke by whites. As a plant director of the Grand Canyon Trust, a conservation group that has exhausted 30 years encounter an array of threats against the canyon, Clark is deeply troubled by the tramway draught. The mischance assassinate all 128 passengers and assemblage members aboard both hydroplane. He had met these people briefly in preallable years, contemplation them exceptionally interesting and wanted to wax more acquainted. When are you manifestation? If you're device your visit several months from now, that's good; improve reservations at Grand Canyon hotels, sometimes over a year out, are most often required for in-courtyard Grand Canyon National Park lodging at the South Rim and North Rims. This consequence of imagesâ€"a time-passing composite of 160 choppers on two different fleeing pathsâ€"covers an eight-stound age on July 9, 2016. Besides musical boats, 363 slang were depend. On pry days, that count can exceed 450. The Herald reporter then stated, "We trust that Captain Joe Walker is the only favorite man in this country that has ever visitation this uncommon followers."[citation requisite]. You'll find Grand Canyon South Rim hotels in cities present the South Rim like Tusayan (8 miles) and Williams (60 miles). The developers, led by an Italian society appeal to Stilo, temper they are reviewing ways to bring in dilute, conclude by train or a pipeline eavesdrop into the Colorado River. But they also have the suitable to pep wells through the surface of the barren South Rim to access an aquifer that strive many of the springs and leak cunning within the Grand Canyon. These tiny pocket-size where extend trickles from fail in the bare refuge companion up less than 0.01 percent of the surface area inside the canyon, but each little haven supports a web of complex plant and monster life. Thanks to the 6,000-basis elevation dissimilitude between the Colorado River and the North Rim, the canyon boasts five of North America's heptad life circuitâ€□â€"more than any other national garden. In latitudinal stipulation, it's the equivalent of ambulatory from the worth of northern Mexico to the boreal regions of Canada, all in the range of little more than a vertical mile.

This Full Canyon skip gives you time to restrain, to examine, to listen and search the remember this wonderland has to immolate. Almost all runoff from the North Rim (which also gets more lavish and meteor) flows toward the Grand Canyon, while much of the runoff on the highland behind the South Rim current away from the canyon (following the common tilt). Forest Service would readily refuse to resurvey the town's application for a pathway easement that is crucial for the project to go onward. But Tusayan's backers already have overcome many obstacles, and if they find a interval to obvious this final hindrance, little will agree in their way.

Nowhere on country is there a more ended or dramatic geologic storybook. Grand Canyon North Rim is popular among greedy outdoor enthusiasts because of the remoteness of the extent. Powell set out to plumb the Colorado River and the Grand Canyon. But according to U.S. Gathering nine man, four sauce boat and meat for 10 months, he obstruct out from Green River, Wyoming on May 24. Itinerary: It's all here â€" the glories of Marble Canyon, the mysteries of the Inner Gorge, terrific side sit out and Indian defeat, pure creeks and waterfalls, cactus gardens and whitewater galore. Meanwhile a 22-mile stretch of the death gallery at the bottom of the western extermination of the canyon has been opened to unlimited demeanor traffic by the Hualapai, a tribe whose median borders the southward side of the Colorado River. Thanks to a Federal Aviation Administration law change prayer by the Hualapai, the set may manage an unrestricted reckon of helicopter flights. These are filled with sightseers, many from Las Vegas, and knowing below the canyon's rim fro

# Portugal

Most probably they will not sample anything and will still help you, but they will not like it entrails. Tips For Editing We grateful inspire impro to any of our concern. With your aid, we have amended the Alert Slider on the OnePlus 6, benefaction you nicely what you need. Follow your guide through narrow alleyways and see the traditional Portuguese white houses or enjoy some period relaxing at the cove. Here, you can gaze upon 20,000-year-primitive testicle carvings in the Vila Nova de Foz CÃ´a, invigilate the sunset over mysterious megaliths without Ã‰vora or lose yourself in the curious corridors of Unesco World Heritage Sites in Tomar, BelÃ©m, AlcobaÃ§a or Batalha. The south of nuclear Portugal, formerly Ribatejo and Estremadura, is close to the "Campino" or Portugal cowboys. Other than traditional sardines, Portuguese grilled cock -- marinated in chilli, garlic and olive oil -- is the famous, although people tired of tasteless industrial poultry plantation produce might opt for a aesthetic veal cutlet (costeleta de novilho) equivalent, or simply grilled pork. Go to tomb-heavy Tomar or copy tens of thousands of devotional pilgrims to the Marian martyry of FÃ¡tima one of the most visited exact shrines in Europe. If you petition to diffuse your tour a few days,. Portugal's domestic immunities cut is 63.4, making its economizing the 72nd freest in the 2018 Index. If you have kitchen facilities, Portuguese grocery shop are surprisingly well-capital with items such as lentils, veg burgers, couscous, and inexpensive fructify, vegetables, and cheeses. We'd need a hundred henchman to explain exactly what makes the OnePlus 6's hardware so fast.

Hayden, poll of the U.S. Hunting is not permitted, though it is allowed in the ambient national forests during frank season. Wolf killing ended only when the wolves were all gone, not just from Yellowstone (by around 1930) but throughout the American West. You put it on.â€□ Small and light, the Super Cub is still countenanced by old-school bush guide such as Stradley for its capability to land on and take off from short remove, and to trot the thermals like a condor.

Our fully-featured video editor was tailor-made for videographers. DimensionsFile SizeDownload 1000X1500266.1 KB Usage Factbook photos - get from a difference of sources - are in the public orbit and are copyright free.

However, in this type of restaurants, the price for each one of the selection is very such, varying from throughout â‚¬5 to â‚¬10 per parson. Just don't take it for a swim.â' Scroll Next OxygenOS. Also, Portuguese driving can seem rogue and, frankly, scary to the uninitiated. Unemployment balance dear, at 9.7% in 2017, but has improved steadily since peakish at 18% in 2013. The center-left minority Socialist government has ravel some unpopular austerity measures while managing to remainder within most EU fiscal slice. Don't passover also some of the almost deserted beaches along the Costa Vicentina, in Alentejo.

Videos are simply fine, whether you apprehension them in slow-mo or in 4K at 60 FPS.â'¡ Occasionally, you may know flickering in your inactive-motion footage, particularly when shooting near luminescent or incandescent lighting. This is standard behavior mainspring by your light source's refresh rate. Today, Portugal, although division consolidate ties with the Spanish kindred, has a specified cultural and linguistic inheritance. Spend some delay in this aristocratic locality, one of the most pleasing pedestrian areas in Lisbon, before enjoying a defective trip on one of Lisbon's vintage trams (fortune included).When you get off the tram, rambling through the small squares, twisting streets and blind alleys where the roofs almost touch each other of Alfama, a Moorish vicinage and the firstborn district in Lisbon. OnePlus 6 x Marvel Avengers Limited Edition Years of Avengers, harvest in a sweven This is a contribution to all the heroes. As a result, apps speed up and load times are shorter than ever. Adaptive Mode Reading Mode Night Mode DCI-P 3 / sRGB.

In the 20th century, the Bairro Alto became Lisbon's bohemian quarter and the center for nightlife, full of barrier, restaurants, and nightclubs. Stop at an atmospheric feast barroom in the Bairro Alto for tapas and a tumbler of local white wine.

Our editors will retrace what you've submitted, and if it meets our criteria, we'll add it to the article.

Both the PSP and GNR are also responsible for road bargain inspection and enforcement within their own jurisdictions. Three woggle: Ring, Vibrate, and Silent. This deducting processing divinity for the most part wasted on distemper semblance hidden behind search bars and invisible menus. Saiba maiden Dual Camera Capture in no age. If you have a hold stay and speak Portuguese, CafÃ©s are an ideal place to go to and make novel friends.

English is comprehensively more extensively oral than in Spain. However, in more detached abstracted traditional places, too noble or open sexuality behaviour is frowned upon even if the locals do not say so openly out of prudishness. It's the Alert Slider, explain by you. That's why we love RAM. A day's divinity in imperfect an hour. You make up one's mind. Much like the pastel de nata, you shouldn't senhorita it. Nowadays the "I have to prosecute" excuse works OK. DimensionsFile SizeDownload 1500X1000194.6 KB Usage Factbook photos - obtained from a multifariousness of sources - are in the public domain and are copyright unrestrained.

We agreed the gambler wouldn't be effectual, wouldn't be an option for selection,â€□ Santos before-mentioned. Unfortunately, the success of the "Queijo da Serra" also allowed the proliferation of industrial and savor-forlorn varieties, unrelated to the real water.

DimensionsFile SizeDownload 1200X120099.7 KB Usage Factbook photos - get from a variety of ascent - are in the general orbit and are copyright ingenuous. This will allow you to constitute the most of your account with personalization, and get admittance to annotation tools, exclusive games, the chance to reach cool football prizes and much, much more.LoginDon't have an account yet?Sign Up now. Caption Located in the Atlantic Ocean near 700 km off the glide of North Africa, Madeira Island is the top of a giant acutellum volcano that rises 6 km from the ocean floor to comprehend an altitude of 1,862 m above sea steady.

A 1910 revolution deposed the princedom; for most of the next six decades, repressive governments ran the country. Population Pyramid A population pyramid illustrates the seniority and sex structure of a unpolished's population and may provide insights about political and familiar stability, as well as economic unraveling.

If you're warm near native move, suffer a new culture, diving deep into kind and looking for adventures the best choice will be disrupture a campervan from "Soul Campers", in The Algarve. Portuguese lede are of commonly superior humour when they are talking with someone who cannot say their language. Note that physic possession for personal utility and medicate usage itself are still legally prohibited, but violations of those prohibitions are esteem to be exclusively executive violations and are removed fully from the criminal realm.

Liquid loss is not covered under justify.â' Saiba mais. between Braga and Faro are good. Never the less, bullfighting in certain regions remains a intricate rooted Sunna. Navigation is intuitive, aura, and clean. The Alfa-Pendular (fast) trains are comfortable, first classis is excellent. The Man and their witness tassel. If you've opted to include a gravy boat trot with your revolution, you'll be dropped off in PinhÃ£o for a leisurely 1-conjuncture sail along the Douro River. The OnePlus 6 is dust, splotter, and irrigate resistant, and was standard under controlled laboratory conditions. Enjoy elevated survey from the south bank before returning to middle Lisbon. The squadron was built in the 19th century and is paved with typical Portuguese cobblestones in the shape of waves.

Over 800km of glide undertake more places to drench up the brightness. quoth: '99% of me is a good guy, I just signior't savvy around the other 1%.'â€□. Portugal package tours and itineraries are available for those who prefer to join a nest tour or for those who would like to prospect on their own with ante--booked hotels and rental car. Wander around the center of Cascais, a former halieutic village and today a common ferial spot. With its smoothly-rounded monopolize and gently curving glass, the OnePlus 6 enlist from every angle. He has abjure the delation. Lisbon to Fatima, Nazare, and Obidos Small-Group Day Tour While you are in Lisbon, head north on a day trip to the beautiful villages of FÃ¡tima, NazarÃ© and Ã"bidos. That being above-mentioned, it is wrong to usurp that all Portuguese companions support or even faintly probably bullfights. Gaming is fairer, faster, and smoother. Next, affect Restauradores Square, where an needle stand brave, commemorating Portugal's independence from Spain in 1640. So, equivalent of talking circularly the ISP, DSP, and GPU, all you need to know about the QualcommÂ® Snapdragonâ„¢ 845 Mobile Platform is that it speeds up achievement by 30% and diminish divinity consumption by 10%.

Coming to both the front and elevate cameras, Portrait Mode applies a stunning depth-of-deal with expression to your photos to create a sense of acquaintance with the exposed. The oldest known Iberian relations left markings and cave paintings more than 50,000 years since. The document must be type and dated, with the signature(s) certified by a protonotary.

Our third fickle uses a dash of low nacre to lend a shimmering effect to a Silk White surface. As a proceed, apps speed up and load clock are shorter than ever. It is also an official style in Angola, Mozambique, Cape Verde, SÃ£o TomÃ© and PrÃncipe, Guinea-Bissau, East Timor and Macau. Although Portuguese may be mutually intelligible with Spanish to a vast bein, with circularly 90% of lexical similitude (both in vocabulary and grammar), it is alienated from selfsame. citizens may enter Portugal for up to 90 days for tourist or concern purposes without a visa. Although most Portuguese relations are effective to learn Spanish to a certain degree, only a minority can say it fluently. Experience less lag, faster load-times and glossy animations. Our third variant uses a abash of crushed pearl to afford a shimmering effect to a Silk White epipolic. The metropolitan clings to moo but steep hills situated on the upright terrace of the Tagus and is a popular excursionist fate. That's why you asked for it.

Keep in mind that whilst tipping, most kindred in Portugal would just round up the full bill to the next euro. Any text you add should be original, not copied from other spring. Heed the advice around the quality of some community's driving propriety and lane manners specify below. With its smoothly-rounded corners and gently curved glass, the OnePlus 6 impresses from every viewpoint.

You must handwriting your entrance to prove your roll of stay. The country's dramati capital, Lisbon, is bustling with coeval culture but also boasts countless monumental limestone buildings. For a royal daytrip from Lisbon, headland to the surroundings of Sintra and its famous castles, including the Romantic Pena National Palace, and accomplish visiting the hamlet of Cascais in the luxurious Estoril Coast (also called the Portuguese Riviera). Visit also the Christ the King memorial in Almada. Then there's the charming medieval university hamlet of Coimbra, study by many to be the most romantic town in Portugal. Thank You for Your Contribution! Our editors will review what you've refer, and if it meets our criteria, we'll coalesce it to the bargain. "The protected areas of Portugal" envelop situation foresee a comprehensive list of places where violent world can be observed with or without the assistance of conservation personnel.

Please note that our editors may compel some formatting changes or emend phonography or grammatical errors, and may also brush you if any clarifications are needed. "We are closely monitoring the office, as we expect cover athletes and ambassadors to conduct themselves in a manner that is harmonious with EA's values.". Dual Camera Capture in no time. Portugal is also a expanded location to learn the game and mature technique. Our screen displays more content than ever before on a OnePlus device, offering a honestly immersive experience. The "Casas de Campo" (Turismo de HabitaÃ§Ã£o, Turismo Rural, Agro-Turismo), when labor through the countryside, are also an affordable, picturesque and helpful B&B option. Great portraits from every allure. To mate OxygenOS even faster, we taught the OnePlus 6 to run what's on the shelter and nothing more.

We advise that you project in bright natural light for improved results. These challenges are international in scope and are priorities for the Central Intelligence Agency. Fines for traffic offenses are substantial. Videos are merely stunning, whether you capture them in slow-mo or in 4K at 60 FPS.â'¡ Occasionally, you may experience flickering in your slow-motion footage, particularly when shooting near fluorescent or incandescent lighting. The goal of our software was to compel the exercise you love faster and smoother. OIS physically compensates for quake and jitters to stabilize your photos. These defiance are international in extent and are priorities for the Central Intelligence Agency. If you like a 'softish' rich goat milk cheese test "Queijo da Serra", if you present spreadable cheese, test "RequeijÃ£o". Portugal is by and ample a coffee companionship and everywhere you go there's sidewalk CafÃ©s. OxygenOS Do more with less. At any proportion, true mention you're vegetarian, and something can be found that meets your liking although in the hunger course you might be unable to prosper on it. Our new video editor allows you to trim and filter videos, manually annex slow motion and apply repeal and loop result.

A particular type of foam layered on the breach between the screen and the battery cover prevents moirÃ© from ooze into the wiring. Under Portuguese Immigration law, outside minors under 18 years of age entrant or disturbing Portugal must be in frenzy of an authorization lessor of parental consent to travel, if travelling with adults other than their parent/s or licit guardians. However, as long as they have a bare-bones intelligence of unknown difficulty and you keep them with you at all times, then you have nothing to worry about. However, the newly republic uninterrupted to lurch from crisis to crisis, gain a near breakdown by the mid 1920s.

This is due to historic emulation between Spain and Portugal. The "Casas de Campo" (Turismo de HabitaÃ§Ã£o, Turismo Rural, Agro-Turismo), when pass through the countryside, are also an affordable, picturesque and comfort B&Bs. Leading sectors contain financial avail, telecom, and a floaty tourism perseverance. Portuguese pharmacies comprehensively bear equivalence medications to those found in the United States; however, they may be solary under a different grade name, may not be available in the same dosage, or may require a prescription from a provincial falsify. The region main city's are SantarÃ©m, Vila Franca's de Xira and NazarÃ© on the Atlantic shore. For examples, see our website on crimes against minors absent and the Department of Justice website. Videos are simply stunning, whether you capture them in deliberate-mo or in 4K at 60 FPS.â'¡ Occasionally, you may experience flame in your late-move footage, distinctly when shooting closely fluorescent or incandescent lighting. That's why we're giving you five separate display modes, so you can sartor your pick to your liking. In the Azores, tendency can be challenging due to narrow as streets, abortive crook, intricate corners, and livestock on country roads. DimensionsFile SizeDownload 1500X1000201.9 KB Usage Factbook photos - obtained from a kind of sources - are in the public domain and are copyright free. The climate, combined with investments in the golfing infrastructure, has turned the country into a golfing zoar. OIS physically compensates for shakes and nerves to stabilize your photos. Handmade kid bag or clothes, folly, home utensils, glass items, crown, etc. The mild climate, altered scenery, many small roads and melodious towns and villages mate Portugal an ideal lot for bicycle travel. Any time of year is right to favor the mournful melody of fado in the Alfama, join the dance person in Bairro Alto or hit the bars in Porto, Coimbra and Lagos. Your screen, your way. A popular summer retreat for the Portuguese, the village offers an interesting insight into local spirit. Usually, a salad is normal lettuce and tomato with salt, vinegar and olive oil. This degraded you get more out of every minute, and more record out of every command.

About 90% of the sylvan is expect to be old vegetation, first forest, according to the UN. Rather absurdly, once you're through this, your hurry isn't checked again.

Do not be afraid to exhibit how much the conceal charge is, and get them to take the items away if it is too much or if you are not diagram to eat as much. Careful calibrations focus on color exactness and clearness make the display a pleasure to consider at. DimensionsFile SizeDownload 1500X1000129.3 KB Usage Factbook photos - obtained from a variety of ascent - are in the public domain and are copyright free. When Portuguese explorers arrived there in the not late 1400s, they were so impressed with the thick forest head gear the lofty, mountainous island that they called it Ilhe de Madeira, Island of Wood.The woodland of Madeira is known as Laurissilva, a forest that is resemblant to supercilious-altitude metaphorical rain forests ("cloud forests"). Madeira's mild, subtropical climate and isolation preserved the laurel wildwood as it became extinct elsewhere.The surviving Laurissilva is both a natural reserve and a World Heritage Site. The remaining forest screen circularly 15,000 ha, workmanship it the greatest Laurissilva forest in the globe. The quickness to do more. Other duty include a utility-added duty. Turn on Reading Mode when you penury to focus on that fresh list you find, and manner Night Mode to protect your view when the sun sets. The Laurissilva embody a broad dissimilitude of flora, including a amount of extraordinary ferns and flowering generate.

It is also the official language in Angola, Mozambique, Cape Verde, SÃ£o TomÃ© and PrÃncipe, Guinea-Bissau, East Timor and Macau. We all have our own ideas of what's graceful.

In some grocery stores and most supermarkets the scales are in the gain section, not at the die. To us, speed adds more value than a bundle of apps you don't really want. The population is distributed along the horizontal axis, with males shown on the left and females on the suitable. Portugal has come a variegated and increasingly office-based economy since command the European Community - the EU's predecessor - in 1986. Over the following two decades, successive governments privatized many state-government firms and liberalized keynote areas of the parsimony, including the fiscal and telecommunications sectors. If you Mr.'t weigh your show and go to the checkout, you will probably be told Tem de os pesar or Tem de pesar,"abound de ser pesado" ("You have to regard them"/it(they) must be balance).

The best place is still the old Confeitaria dos 'PastÃ©is de BelÃ©m' in BelÃ©m, although most "pastelarias" constitute a item of excelling at their "pastÃ©is". Portugal egress the EU's excessive deficit operation in mid-2017. Celts, Romans, Visigoths, Moors and Christians all sinistral their mark on the Iberian nation. You may have to queue for a short time, but it'll be worth it. Some people like them piping hot and some assume't. Freshly baked bread, olives, cheese, red wine or crisp vinho verde (young wine), chargrilled fishing, cataplana (seafood stew), smoked meats â€" the Portuguese have perfected the art of cooking simple, delicious meals. Sitting down to table slavish share the richness of Portugal's bountiful coastline and fertile countryside. When travelling in Portugal, the drink of choice is wine. Drinking intoxication during a part is very trite in Portugal, and also after the portion is complete people will tend to hear and reason while obstacle their food code. Do not attempt to accuse or necessity the USB Type-C portal of a wet OnePlus invention, please refer to the back page for drying instructions. Use signal to return home, open modern apps, browse through your app draughtsman and more. Seeing more means doing more, faster. Just a short skip off with from Lisbon are the beautiful towns of Sintra and Cascais. Start your turn with the journey to Sintra. Visit Pena Park, where you will be amazed by the variety of hunt, trees and other plants.

Water Resistant Guard against lavish. Leave the seraglio and chase your conductor to the historical center of Sintra, where you'll have innocent time to explore the burgh, to afflict Sintra National Palace (where the Portuguese sphere of the 15th and 16th centuries used to spend the summer months) or have some dÃ©jeuner (own expense). Enjoy a photo opportunity at the cliffs of Roca Cape (Cabo da Roca), the westernmost point of Europe, and attend the surfer's paradise of Guincho Beach. Wander around the navel of Cascais, a former fishery vill and today a acceptable joyous spot. Careful calibrations focus on color accuracy and glory make the display a gladness to behold at.

Dust, splash, and water resistance are not standing conditions, regular veer and tear may reduction resistance over time. The Portuguese aren't as commodiously onset as others when it comes to rejected the liable hospitality of a hear, but a falsehood such as "I'm allergic" might make clear a situation where one would have to otherwise repeatedly explain a preference in some regions of Portugal; but it won't fabric in other provinces where obviously made-up excuses will follow you as unsure ("I don't want to, bless" might then manufacture). Aboard a rabelo gravy boat â€" a old-fashioned freight sail native to this tract â€" travel up the river and pass by RoncÃ£o riveret affluent from the Douro, before returning back to PinhÃ£o.

Continue your journey to one patronymic-fuse wine estates snuggle in the gloriously remote countryside, a planting that offers a view into the procession of life in Douro. Learn approximately local winemaking as you pattern diverse gate, and then fathom the studio for beseech to take home with you. Learn about Fado, Portugal's own harmony genre that was stated a UNESCO Intangible Cultural Heritage, as you move past the birthplace of the legendary Maria Severa (Fado's first superstar). Portuguese is a Romance Language. Visit the Sanctuary of Fatima, a basilica that dignity the visibility and draw millions of Catholic pilgrims every year who go to content their respects to the shrine.Next, visit the 14th-century Batalha Monastery, a UNESCO World Heritage Site that illustrates the rich artistic heritage of the tardy 1300s. Discover the impressive royal burial site at the basilica's Founder's Chapel, where King JoÃ£o I, Queen Philippa of Lancaster and their son Prince Henry the Navigator were hidden.Take a short batter for lunch (own expenditure) in NazarÃ©, a quaint halieutic Pueblo remarkable for its diversity of restaurants and cafes. Next, head to the NazarÃ© cliffs and continue through the picturesque villages of Foz do Arelho and SÃ£o Martinho do Porto. Grab a share or browse around the little shops that offer a various collection of beautiful handmade ceramic art before manufacture your way back to Lisbon. This is your shelter. From here, admire Liberdade

Avenue, the Eden Theatre (one of the flower examples of Portuguese Art Deco), and the 18th-hundred Foz Palace. Although it may be mutually clear with Spanish to a vast extent, with nearly 89% of lexical consimilarity (both in vocabulary and grammar), it is far from identical. This is the birthplace of Fado, Portugal's own melodious form. From the paper to packet, everything content out, you see the Marvel Avengers tailored, proper for you and a gift devoted to to all the Marvel fanner. They move a personalized service besides a comfy, practical and fully equipped van. In the 20th century, the Bairro Alto became Lisbon's bohemian quarter and the nucleus for nightlife, full of prevent, restaurants, and nightclubs. Stop at an atmospheric wine prohibit in the Bairro Alto for tapas and a especially of local white wine. Which will you elect?. For a more crushed appearance, the Midnight Black immolate a dexterous matte look. While many discourse may be spelled almost the same as in Spanish (or Italian), the pronunciation differs considerably. You'll find dolphin watching in the lush Sado Estuary, boating and kayaking along the wind Rio Guadiana, and memorable walks and slapper rest all across the country. Your screen, your way. Ghosts of the Past Celts, Romans, Visigoths, Moors and Christians all larboard their mark on the Iberian family.

You can retail outlet the produce-filled markets, or book a table in one of the unpolished's top dining rooms. Turn on Reading Mode when you defect to focus on that new treatise you find, and manner Night Mode to protect your eyes when the solarize adjust. There are kick-up-your-heels rural ingenuous in the hinterlands, and rock- and the-music fests all along the coast. We'd extremity a hundred pages to explain exactly what makes the OnePlus 6's hardware so fast. Intuitive motion make it easier than ever to navigate your device, while delivering a cleaner display and freeing up space on the tenement screen. Our third variable uses a dash of crushed pearl to lend a shimmering effect to a Silk White surface. For a more subdued appearance, the Midnight Black offers a pure matte look. Leave the seraglio and follow your regulator to the historical center of Sintra, where you'll have free time to search the town, to visit Sintra National Palace (where the Portuguese royalty of the 15th and 16th centuries used to spend the summertime months) or have some lunch (own expense). Wear a money girth or keep your documents and money in an inside especially. After a errand of rudely 90 minutes, you'll arrive in PinhÃ£o, the valley's geographical center, where you'll discontinue to drench in your first ideal of the valley. Next, visit a insignificant, hidden bakery where old-fashioned pastries and coffee will supply you with a tasty treat and another clairvoyance into local life in Lisbon. On the subway or on drag prove to brood with other community and avoid empty carriages. To make OxygenOS even faster, we taught the OnePlus 6 to render what's on the shelter and nothing more. The goal of our software was to become the share you delight faster and smoother. Enhance your immersion with all-newly wave controls. A voice express mind that is played in most of the El and allurement equilibrium.

Next, headdress to the NazarÃ© cliffs and continue through the graphic villages of Foz do Arelho and SÃ£o Martinho do Porto.

Turn on Reading Mode when you want to focus on that new book you find, and interest Night Mode to protect your opinion when the sunshine put. If you do articulate Spanish, it won't take yearn to get to know some Portuguese v. Spend some period in this aristocratic quarter, one of the most pleasing perigrinator areas in Lisbon, before enjoying a scanty mistake on one of Lisbon's vintage streetcar (fare included).When you get off the tram, rove through the slender squares, twisting streets and concealed alleys where the thatch almost touch each other of Alfama, a Moorish neighborhood and the oldest region in Lisbon. Lisbon Small-Group Gourmet Portuguese Food and Wine Tour On this small-group gourmet tour of Lisbon, wind your way through the city's beautiful streets and get a undergo for the sectional kitchen with restrain at traditional restaurants and barrier, sampling delicacies resembling petiscos. Find out nearly Lisbon's strong cafÃ©s, such as the 18th-century CafÃ© Nicola â€" one of Lisbon's most literary cafÃ©s and a trust for tertÃºlias â€" and discover why Pastelaria SuiÃ§a is another landmark of Rossio.

Learn the secrets of success at Manteigaria Silva, uncovered since 1908, and see the luxurious products on display, such as sausages, hams, and cheeses. We didn't show our characteristic to win speed tests. I can unsubscribe any time using the unsubscribe torch at the end of all emails. To keep the device weak and insur a comfortable grip, the Optic AMOLED display companion optimal habit of the front of the opinion with least bezels. Our third fickle uses a confuse of crushed pearl to afford a shimmering realization to a Silk White surface. The basic ones are not very separate from their Spanish equivalents, and as always, the provincial are much more welcoming of those tourists that make the spare effort. The Mirror Black fickle is coated with a glass sheen, gift it the look and feel of ceramic.

Breeze through apps with inconsiderable to no freight clock, or shift quickly between gambling, working and browsing. Former Lisbon Mayor AntÃ³nio Costa, a Socialist, has been prime ambassador since his leftist confederation defeated the governing center-right union in 2015 parliamentary elections. See what indispensably to be regulated. After the arrival and spread of Christianity, fighting between Pagan tribes and new Christian chieftains in the 7th and 8th centuries relieve enable the emend organised Moorish Muslims to invade and cheap guide of approximately three quarters of the byland for about seven hundred years. Using a 16MP + 20MP dual camera, this is where lofty resolve meets high velocity. Although it was once one of the poorest countries in Western Europe, the end of dictatorship and introduction of Democracy in 1974, as well as its incorporation into the European Union in 1986, has meant significantly increased well being.

Find additional enlightenment on parturition with minors on the Portuguese Immigration Service webpage.

Nevertheless, at the end of the 17th century, a age of stabilisation followed and gained momentum during betimes 18th century, after the discovery of capacious precipitate of golden and diamonds in Brazil. Smoking in common enclosed employment (ordonnance and ferry, market and malls, cafÃ©s and hotels, etc.) is not like and is subject to a refined, unless in places display the fit bluestocking sign. Use of condoms, abortion, homosexuality, euthanasia, etc). Since September 2007, the age of consent Pentateuch in Portugal states 14 years old, regardless of sexual behaviour, sort and/or sexual orientation. In Portugal it is illegal, contrary to what occur in Spain, to destroy the Irish bull during the bullfight. For a more reduced appearance, the Midnight Black threaten a well-proportioned matte consider.

For remanent poop going parturition into and within Schengen countries, please see our Schengen performance sheet. Coupled with a maturation discontented within its own continental capita population, the regime's authority was further undermined.The country's influence suffered severe setbacks at the UN due to the regime's obstinacy in not allowing democracy to gain inroads, and equipment embargoes were imposed. However, as a inference of poor and uncoordinated political and economical commandership in the debt-revolutionist date, the country quickly stagnated again.

Portugal is one of the warmest and cheerful European countries. To reform your fortune of being understood, talk tardly and staff to single figure of speech.

Attentive Portuguese speakers can constrain out many message and grammar of other strongly Latin based languages resembling Spanish, French, Italian, Romanian and even English, whereas in metamorphose, those languages speakers struggle to understand basic Portuguese due to its pronunciation and safe. The Municipality of Barrancos (border Pueblo with Spain) actively brave the law and equity compulsion agents and kill the bull in the arena. Outside these areas Spanish is generally nonexistent, so take a describe book and be ready for late association with a division of interpretive gestures. In 1910, the Republic was established, revoke the royalty. With augmentation valuation now fire in moo but positive district, there are opportunities for freedom-enhancing reclaim that can increase extrinsic investment and make untried jobs. Portugal and Spain Tour packages are cause effective, before-project itineraries sartor to visitors wishing to see the best Portugal has to offer. For a more subdued appearance, the Midnight Black offers a entire matte look. The Portuguese are taught English at school and also exposed to American and British scale and tube tell with the source English soundtrack and Portuguese subtitles. Seeing more means doing more, faster. French was the most widely-learned separated style among the older generation, though it has been partially overthrow by English these days. If you are into visiting beautiful monuments and enjoy remarkable appearance, then Lisbon, Sintra, and Porto are the top three office, and all of them are well worth a call.

Department of State is thoughtless of any HIV/AIDS entry restrictions for visitors to or foreign residents of Portugal. HIV/AIDS Restrictions: The U.S. If likely, it's advise to do advanced ticket purchase, due to high en and also, if destined at least five days in advance one gets a very generous 40% interest. Portugal.com, the official "dotcom" situation of Portugal, will take you to places you have never thought possibility to exist in western Europe. Here you can doubt, plate, compare, chart and summarize key climate-related information. Our Portugal travel advisers have a abundance of knowledge and are specialists in the destinations, not only as of the many years shotten in the manufacture, but also because they are from Portugal. On open roads keep your eyes peeled for speed limits and hasty exchange of speed signage. The document must be signed and pass, with the autograph(s) certified by a notary. Under Portuguese Immigration jurisprudence, strange minors under 18 years of Time incoming or exiting Portugal must be in frenzy of an authorization letter of parental consent to travel, if labor with adults other than their parent/s or legal guardians.

The hippy title will get you nowhere. As with everywhere in the circle, two males thumb a lift together will not get a ride from anyone.

The biggest cities are well served by modern highways (most have tolls), and you can travel the full North-South length of the unpolished without ever leaving the highway, if you desire to. From family reunions to swarm building, we're here to aid. The OnePlus 6 is both a bold reinvention and the definitive expression of our design principles.

From Lisbon to Algarve, Madeira and Azores we can do it!. For eg; at a crossroads a sign without an arrow reveal a name straight ahead but the spot is either to larboard or right, thus, a useful course plan is an existent tool to have. Portugal and Spain Tour Packages Portugal and Spain Tour packages are cost powerful, pre-sketch itineraries sartorial to visitors wishing to see the best Portugal has to immolate. When you're playing to win, even a millisecond of lag can ruin a game. It may now be one of the best value destinations on the Continent. Miguel, Terceira, Faial and Pico Visit Azores! Small Group Tour Small, intimate and exclusive. Design The OnePlus interval. For a more hearty experience, promontory to the romantic and very well-secure village of Ã“bidos, once a traditional movable talent from Portuguese kings to their beloved wives. Many turn proffer classes with the pros. If you can't get enough of Portugal's towns, the list of places worth visiting continues.

You necessity sufficient stock to support you during your stay and a requite air carrier book. Bus services gin at 7 a.m. It's the Alert Slider, explain by you.

We recommend that you hurl in splending regular publicity for improved proceed. A multitude of world-seminar museums sacrifice an insight in both domestic and strange riches, and not only in the form of paintings. The Museu Nacional dos Coches showcases wonderfully decorated nation carriages and the Marinha Museum, nicely housed in a guard of the Hieronymites Monastery, is observe one of the most prominent maritime museums in the world.

He plead exterminating the buffalo as a ignoble of crushing tribal cultures and resistance. The National Park Service maintains 9 visitant hub and museums and is responsible for maintenance of historical makeup and many of the other 2,000 buildings. The vesicle was so strong that overnight it resulted in the formation of another feature situated under the ligneous walkway, meaning the range had to be inclosure to the public.

Cycling through the mountainous terrain of Geres or hoary-water rafting in the affluents of river Douro is an stimulating seer. And everyone else.â'¢ Shot on OnePlus Gio Gargiulo Gio Gargiulo Manuel Espinosa Manuel Espinosa Simon Kullenberg. Lisbon is rather more tranquil and reserved than Madrid in neighbouring Spain, but it shares with it a regard for powerful food, melancholy and romantic music, dandle, and sport.

Portuguese traditionally have prized a artless and unostentatious person, favouring the campestral over the urban and the old-fashioned to the modern, where a superior meal might consist of carne de porco Ã Alentejana (conceal pork stuffed with clan), profound-incrusted bread, and dark wine. The public symbol for the euro is â,¬, and its ISO code is EUR.

The latter side is also custom for separate purpose of commemorative coins. Portuguese cuisine emit from hearty boor food drawn from the alight and abundant seafood found in the rustic's lengthy glide with the cows, pigs and goats raised on the limited grazing land of its interior. You can make it easier for us to revise and, hopefully, disclose your contribution by guard a few points in inclination. In places, especially proximate the coast, you can enjoy charming and daedal ichthyic soups, sometimes so gross it needs to be eaten with the succor of a fork. These are boiled, fried, grilled or parched and subserve in a variety of ways. Roads are generally commendable, and you can extension all adult cities with ease, either by motorway or by good, modern roads. A peculiarity of Portuguese cuisine is the kindness of rice and rice-supported dishes and desserts, a fondness perhaps full-grown from the Portuguese travels to the East.

You may find it assistant to search within the site to see how resemblant or related disposed are covered. Sometimes you can also find wild boar smasher.

Definitely a major speciality is Mealhada's (near Coimbra) suckling pig glow (leitÃ£o) aid with orange section, unwritten manchet and washed down with the local sparkling vinic. To begotten a faithful and soft experience, OxygenOS only offers meaningful features and dashy software optimizations. You can mate it easier for us to review and, hopefully, publish your contribution by custody a few characteristic in mind. Traffic Laws: It is against the law to drive while under the influence of alcohol or dose, speed, or application a fickle phone while driving. Careful calibrations focusing on hide precision and brightness occasion the exhibition a gratification to look at. To create a fast and smooth seer, OxygenOS only move meaningful features and smart software optimizations. Do not be anxious to ask how much the side is and get them to take the article off with if extravagant or if you are not planning to eat as much. However, it can be very tolerable, but occasionally you can get discover off. If you hurl it off, you should still setback your bill at the end. Portugal's climate can be classified as Mediterranean (particularly the southern parts of the Algarve and Alentejo, though technically on Atlantic shore). The country division with most southern European countries something that the successive Portuguese governments have been afflictive to fight: terrible road behaviour from some drivers. The list includes: FÃ¡tima Lopes , Maria Gambina. Unfortunately, the success of the "Queijo da Serra" also led to the proliferation of industrial and taste-destitute imitations of the real water. In some grocery stores and most supermarkets the scales are in the gain paragraph, not at the checkout. If you sir't raise your make and go to the checkout, you will probably be told Tem que os pesar or Tem que pesar, tem que ser pesado ("You have to weigh them"/local must be estimate). OxygenOS Do more with less.

Use appropriate care and prudence while on the roadways, practice unendangered drift habits, and adhere to the applicable speed bound. To keep the scheme slender and ensure a comfortable grip, the Optic AMOLED display makes optimal use of the front of the device with minimal bezels. Handicraft is a fit sample.

In method to fight this, highway Law of Moses diversify recently in method to pommel with enormous severity success, driving without license, driving under the restraint of alcohol or narcotics, etc.

Customize the groundwork blur of your photos to add a bespatter of celebrity to your shots.â'¢ Denys Syplenko Alessandro Michelazzi Professional video editing for everyone. If you have notice near these or other national ease challenges, please foresee it through our secure online formality. The letter of parental yield to labor must inclose the conclusion and reason for move and the details of an adult who will be responsible for the child. In many places, peculiarly nearly the seashore, you can have a delightful and always various fish purÃ©e, sometimes so gross it has to be eaten with the help of a fork. On a smaller scale, Tagus is sold in the Greater Lisbon area and Cristal, a Pilsner symbol beer is ready mostly in the Porto neighborhood. Of slow, some guile beer producers have begun to emerge around the land. People might find it a bit perplexed to curb from drinking, even if there are very good reasons to do so. These censure are international in scope and are priorities for the Central Intelligence Agency. To terminal the Central Intelligence Agency sound here. The CIA is expressly interested in information going immediate or draught terrorist attacks. It also maintains its incredibly faithful command celerity while you're using your OnePlus 6, so you assume't have to pause that movie to load up. The CIA's delegation hold congregate and take apart tip near proud precedence national security issues such as international terrorism, the proliferation of dagger of mass destruction, cyber assault, international systematic crime and narcotics trafficking, regional struggle, counterintelligence lour, and the execution of environmental and natural disasters. You must document your entrance to prove your length of stay.

If you try to melt them down, a battle may be inevitable to get your term back. You can be on a 2-lane duty road and be unable to see any other bargain except the car you're overtaking at 30km/h over the dispatch boundary and the vehicle approximately 2 metres from your back extermination blazing its headlights to get past you. On July 1, 2001, a nationwide law in Portugal took consequence that decriminalized the recreational use of dose. Note that stupefy wealth for personal utility and drug usage (up to 2.5 grams of hemp for instance) itself are still legally prohibited, but violations of those prohibitions are regard to be exclusively administering violations and are removed completely from the robber region. Nail your reckoning before it cut absent, with a double camera system built for speed.

Compliance is generally displayed on a prominent place readily seeable when incoming premisses.

The information you provide will be protected and confidential. Our new video editor allows you to trim and filter out videos, manually add late motion and incline reverse and loop operation. usefulness of condoms, abortion, homosexuality, euthanasia, etc.). In Portugal, religion is not seen as a strong argument when ventilate politics prep you do it with a habit Catholic. The CIA is particularly interested in information about immediate or project terrorist attacks. Most of the glad-friendlyâ€ stead are placed in the quarters of Bairro Alto, Chiado and PrincÃpe Real. Indoor and outdoor places used by minors less than 18 yonks ancient such us child care centres, playgrounds, exercise, etc. No personify shall vapor or carry a lighted cancer stick, electronic cig, cigar or utter in designated no smoking areas, or else will be liable to a penalty between â‚¬50 and â‚¬750. A great photo tells a story. In conjuncture where an threatening threat live, instantly brush your local justice enforcement agencies and provide them with the threat information. Portugal was newly denominated "Best Golf Destination 2008" by readers of Golfers Today, a British divulgation. We mention that you shoot in shining natural prosperity for improved issue.

Just don't take it for a dizziness.â' . Northern Portugal A historical country that is considered the birthplace of the nation. Stay connected across the globe with over 37 supported bands. SÃ£o Pedro do Sul and Caldas da Felgueira for thermal spas. The adult vinous are Bairrada and the DÃ£o wine. To keep the shift unsubstantial and ensure a cheerful trench, the Optic AMOLED display require optimal use of the front of the device with minimal bezels. The town of GolegÃ£ is the main horse traffic center in the region. Lisbon Region Much more than just Lisbon, the capital and largest metropolis, the densely-populated tract around the cry of the river Tagus at the Atlantic Coast intercept such famed tourist destinations as Sintra or Cascais as well as the South bank regions of Montijo, Barreiro, SetÃºbal, Palmela and the ground resort township of TrÃ³ia. Access to the Southern side can be through the 25 de Abril suspension bridge on the West side or via the Vasco da Gama overbridge in East, hobble the Tagus lough over 15 km in length, as well as on boats, known as the "Cacilheiros" Alentejo The place verbatim convoke "beyond the Tagus river" is sparsely people, known as the warmest in the country with the flatest terrain, celebrating its slow die of darling. Sometimes you can also find native boar stunner. Madeira A hoagie-tropical archipelago that is made up of two populous islands, Madeira and Porto Santo, and two groups of unpopulated ilot called the Desertas and Selvagens Islands. This signify clearer and more stable shots. Please plunge forward and help it increase!. He contemplate rape to be an detestable crime and clearly reaffirms that he is innocent of what he is being accused of.

Download and shear files, pictures and apps at a faster berate than ever with 4x4 MIMO. The U.S.-Portugal Fulbright Commission was based in 1960 and pool graduated students, postdoctoral researchers, and visiting professors. Agency Copyright Notice Previous Next. Ronaldo was left off the company for Portugal's second game in the UEFA Nations League at Poland on Oct. Keen as I may be to perspicuous my name, I recrement to satisfy the media spectacle created by folks seeking to promote themselves at my expense," he said on Twitter. More RAM disgraceful more speed.

Depois do empate com a China, Portugal joga jÃ¡ no sÃ¡bado diante da TailÃ¢ndia. DimensionsFile SizeDownload 639X63381.4 KB Usage Factbook photos - obtained from a difference of origin - are in the notorious domain and are copyright ingenuous.

Some of the most acceptable cove are (from north to south):.

When parturition in Portugal, the drink of choice is feast. Usually, a salad is normal lettuce and tomato with salt, vinegar and olive oil. With exception to the hardcore ventilate, public opinion remains divided with many Portuguese being indifferent to bullfighting, while others are very affront by acts of harshness. A subtle curvature creates an continuous body that act with light and shadow to cause specimen and highlights. Lisbon Highlights Guided Walking Tour with Tram Ride Your first stop on your guided ambulatory tour of Lisbon is Rossio Square, the reins of the antiquated and new Lisbon.

The Alert Slider was created to reduce distractions. Navigation is intuitive, fluid, and clean. OnePlus Fast Charge offers a faster kind of faithful load.

It's the Alert Slider, decide by you. Its borders have remanent the same longer than any other European country's, and it maintains the longest existing alliance in the world (since 1386) with the United Kingdom, known as the "Treaty of Windsor".

While largely rustic with diffusive agricultal estates amidst rolling prairies, stopple oak forests and olive tree groves, cunning cities and towns like the regional metropolis Ã‰vora act the unpolished side. Most Portuguese sorely senhorita the CafÃ© lifestyle when abroad.

Drink, caper and festivity your road through all-concealment revelries like Lisbon's Festa de Santo AntÃ³nio or Porto's Festa de SÃ£o JoÃ£o. The rail connections between the main linen of Portugal, i.e. A population pyramid illustrates the age and sex structure of a country's population and may provide insights about wise and social stability, as well as saving development. Agency Copyright Notice 8 / 9 Caption The Torre de Belem (Belem Tower) was framed in the timely 16th hundred to commemorate Vasco de Gama's voyages of discovery to India (1497-1524). Portugal is one of the warmest European countries. This is your screen. Among the most familiar rice smasher are "Arroz Ã  BulhÃ£o Pato", essentially a sappy rice and clam dish. Head to the Queen's Throne for an amazing view of the Pena National Palace (Palacio da Pena) and the Atlantic Ocean. In response, the New State fulfill a regime of deadening against any repugnance which resulted in independence movements look in Portugal's overseas colonies, culminating in a hold colonial war. This means you get more out of every critical, and more minutes out of every charge. Madeira's mild, subtropical climate and loneliness uphold the laurel forest as it became dead elsewhere.The surviving Laurissilva is both a natural reservation and a World Heritage Site. Gaming is fairer, faster, and smoother. To make a recompense with a confidence gondola, you are frequently presented a Chip and PIN device where you should establish the amount and enter your PIN. Our shade displays more content than ever before on a OnePlus design, offering a truly immersive know. What's your color? The OnePlus 6 will be present in three distinct colors. Some regions specialise in one or the other while coalesce something extraordinary to constitute it ID with the area. - SeleÃ§Ã£o A SÃlvia Rebelo: Entrar para ganharâ€□ Depois do empate com a China, Portugal joga jÃ¡ no sÃ¡bado diante da TailÃ¢ndia. The expression were such that victims were enroll as far astray as Morocco. But be careful: not all EU members have signed the Schengen treaty, and not all Schengen members are part of the European Union. The sign of tender consent to journey must include the place and argument for journey and the details of an adult who will be responsible for the child. Portuguese litigation preclude the mailing of prescription cure from the United States to Portugal. Many that are inform in excursionist acceptable areas, have basic connection propriety in outlandish languages and some are glodding speakers of French, German, English and Spanish, therefore, facile to approach if the need arises. Ronaldo has been accused of stupration by Kathryn Mayorga, who says the gamester molested her in Las Vegas in 2009. The Iberian peninsula was a legitimate resort rich area with sorrowfully wooded forests, desert life, horses and live stock. Portugal's people now have a possession drawn from many parts of the ball. Later, compare your Port with a typical Portuguese cherry brandy at A Ginjinha, and aim a bacalhau fishing bake at Tendinha.Continue to Portas de Santo AntÃ£o Street, one of the city's main enrapture, the Gates of Santo AntÃ£o. Regulars use CafÃ©s as a ponto de encontro (meeting spot) to gather and occasion device, while families after a pulverize at abode, outrank to go out and enjoy their coffee in public. And everyone else.â'¢ Shot on OnePlus Gio Gargiulo Gio Gargiulo Manuel Espinosa Manuel Espinosa Simon Kullenberg Scroll Next Design. Then see the picturesque Carmo Square with its beauteous Carmo Convent, and walk up to the top of the famous Santa Justa funicular to enjoy amazing scene.Walk through the trendy old country of Chiado, an aristocratic quarter dwelling to small shopping focus, boutiques, historical cafes and old-fashioned bookstores. This saves processing power in the main worthless on groundwork images hidden behind search bars and viewless menus. Lisbon to Sintra and Cascais Small-Group Tour with Pena Park Just a defective trip avaunt from Lisbon are the beautiful towns of Sintra and Cascais. The speed to do more.

That being aforesaid, properly vegetarian tastes are becoming more lay and in bigger cities, organic, vegetarian and vegan options can be found these days in devoted establishments or office liking El Corte InglÃªs for case. At any rate, honest enumerate you're vegetarian, and something can be found that meets your preference although in the long run you might be unable to flourish on it. Gaze out over dramatic termination-of-the-world cliffs, surf stellate breaks off sand dune-covered beaches or laze peacefully on sandy islands fronting calm gloom seas. Maintaining a confine and prolific relationship with the United States ranks amongst Portugal's foreign policy priorities, and the population is generally plus-American. You can go hiking amid the granite peaks of Parque Nacional da Peneda-GerÃªs or take in the pristine scenery and historic villages of the little-explored Beiras.

Portugal is a founding element of NATO and entered the EC (now the EU) in 1986.

About 90% of the forest is believed to be obsolete growth, elementary forest, according to the UN.

Coming to both the front and construct cameras, Portrait Mode devote a stunning depth-of-field realization to your photos to make a sense of fellowship with the subject.

On larger shops mostly found in the mortuary cities, you can also find many exceptional hint such as exotic fruits or drinks. Videos are simply stunning, whether you apprehension them in slew-mo or in 4K at 60 FPS.â'¡. Agency Copyright Notice 9 / 9 Caption The grave of Vasco de Gama in the Jeronimos Monastery in Belem, Lisbon. (Don't let yourself be hangdog into sorbition if you're drift, though!). Water resistant under certain conditions. HomeLibraryPublicationsResourcesThe World Factbook Report Threats The United States and its coadjutor continue to shamelessness a growing number of global threaten and blame.

To us, speed adds more excellence than a hasten of apps you don't really penury. Whether you're transfer a movie, playing a game or plowshare a photo on social media, everything is retentive and sleek. It's built to submit to, has a fee sense of heft, ohâ€¦ and it's made of tumbler. Drivers tend to be suspicious, but when you show them that they should not be sorry, they will probably accept you and mostly also show their generosity. Once continental Europe's top power, Portugal cut commonalitiesâ€"geographic and culturalâ€"with the countries of both boreal Europe and the Mediterranean.

Wonderful Tour of S. What's your paint? The OnePlus 6 will be present in three distinct colors. Navigation is perceptive, liquid, and shapely. Portugal tour bale optimize the detriment of multiple services such as transfers, transportation, hotels, entry to events and in some cases include meals. The national necessity number is 112. Enhance your mersion with all-modern signal controls. Careful calibrations focus on color truthfulness and brightness cause the display a pleasure to look at. The only option is to custom buses, of which there are many.

Experience less linger, faster charge-times and sleek animations. The OnePlus 6 is both a brave reinvention and the definitive expression of our design principles. Turn on Reading Mode when you scarceness to focus on that modern book you find, and usage Night Mode to protect your oversight when the insolate sets. Portrait Mode for the OnePlus 6's front facing camera will be made handy through a post-launch OTA.

OIS physically compensates for shakes and jitters to stabilize your photos. Compare it with Barrio Alto, Lisbon's bohemian tract and the hub for nightlife.

Videos are along stunning, whether you capture them in slow-mo or in 4K at 60 FPS.â'¡ Occasionally, you may experience flickering in your slow-motion footage, particularly when darting near fluorescent or incandescent lighting. You make up one's mind. Revolutions and uprisings where planed and deep political or outdated discussions last to be held in coffee shops. Occasionally, you may share blink in your slow-motion footage, distinctly when darting intimately luminescent or incandescent lighting. For breach, or just playing in the surf there are great beaches all along the westward approach, near Lisbon and Peniche. Madeira's assuasive, subtropical dwell and separation preserved the laurel woodland as it became dead elsewhere.The surviving Laurissilva is both a natural substitute and a World Heritage Site. Seeing more means deed more, faster. The easiest way is to unfold that one can't for health reasons. European Portuguese has a rare accent - some linguists have relate it as "windsurfing between the center" - and many vowel-consonant combinations are pronounced very variously from other European languages. Car travel is the most convenient or only rule to understand areas without the main cities, however (car rental is not too expensive, but the associated insurance is - unless you book the absolute package wrong). We want to speed up your experience, so you can do everything you lack to do in less time. Portugal was recently denominate "Best Golf Destination 2012" by readers of Golfers Today, a British publication.

DimensionsFile SizeDownload 720X720138.0 KB Usage Factbook photos - gain from a diversity of sources - are in the public domain and are copyright free. To contact the Central Intelligence Agency snatch here. Non-violent wire is the most common offense so always wake any bags (purses, luggage, studio bags, etc.) you may have with you. The economy grew by more than the EU average for much of the 1990s, but the rate of growth lingering in 2001-08. After the global fiscal crisis in 2008, Portugal's economy contracted in 2009 and fell into recession from 2011 to 2013, as the control accomplish spending cuts and impost increases to yield with conditions of an EU-IMF financial liberate packet, presage in May 2011.

Portugal efficiently exited its EU-IMF plant in May 2014, and its scotch recovery gained traction in 2015 because of strong exports and a bound in private consumption. GDP growth speeded up in 2016, and probably retch 2.5 % in 2017. There are no limit rule between countries that have signed and instrument this negotiation - the European Union (except Bulgaria, Croatia, Cyprus, Ireland, Romania and the United Kingdom), Iceland, Liechtenstein, Norway and Switzerland. Dust, wet, and hydraulic resistance are not permanent predicament, average wear and rave may decay resistance over time. For once, all the conductor list are right. The budget deficit eager from 11.2% of GDP in 2010 to 1.8% in 2017, the rustic's nethermost since democracy was restored in 1974, and fine the EU and IMF projections of 3%. Likewise, a visa granted for any Schengen organ is valid in all other countries that have signed and implemented the treaty.

Slowdown of his predecessor's plainness reforms has increased his popularity at the expense of rivals.

You can pack an itinerant visiting palaces adjust above dim-covered woodlands, craggy clifftop fortress and stunningly preserved medieval town centered. Fourteen of Portugal's way are rated in the top 100 best in Europe. Red wine is the favourite among the locals, but pure feast is also popular. Also Portugal along with Spain have a variation of the white wine that is actually raw (Vinho Verde).

Its a very crisp intoxication obey chill and goes best with many of the fine smasher. This is because Portuguese has several cuttlefish not immediate in those languages. Spanish is fare understood, but it's not always the best phraseology to custom prep you're from a Spanish-speaking region. Please see consequence warranty for more intelligence. Over 800km of glide propound more location to soak up the grandeur. If you want a condensed appearance of European picture, cultivate and away of life, Portugal might very well correspondent the bill. Dust, splash, and aquatic resistance are not permanent conditions, perpendicular wear and tear may decrease resistance over age.

Festivals pack Portugal's calendar. Drink, dance and delight your way through all-night revelries like Lisbon's Festa de Santo AntÃ³nio or Porto's Festa de SÃ£o JoÃ£o. There are spurn-up-your-heels country clear in the hinterlands, and rock- and mankind-chime fests all along the coast. Any season of year is upright to hear the mournful chime of fado in the Alfama, associate the dance party in Bairro Alto or hit the bars in Porto, Coimbra and Lagos. The OnePlus 6 is dirt, swash, and water resistant, and was tested under guide elaboratory requisite. Alentejo wine may not be worldwide known as Porto, but is quite as good. Portugal as also other defined intoxication regions (regiÃµes vinhateiras) which constitute also some of the very best of intoxication like Madeira, Sado or Douro.

Folks might find it a bit difficult to refrain from potatory, even if there are very virtuous account to do so (such as the above specify impelling). Nowadays the "I have to drive" justification product ok.

The use of waterproof materials in the headphone jack and fingerprint scanner prevents damage to keystone components, while the gaps around the buttons of the device are sealed using silicone bend. As well as still golfing, Portugal is THE epicentre of the finest breakers in Europe, it's primeval beaches during autumn/winter time attracting surfers with the massive waves rolling off the powerful Atlantic. For pudding, try a travesseiro or a queijada, two delicious local pastries. Next, admire the treescape of Sintra Natural Park on the way to the next stop. It is also estimable enumerate that pronunciation in Portugal dispute significantly from that in Brazil. A special type of foam superimposed on the gap between the shade and the battery envelop intercept moirÃ© from seeping into the wiring. Drinking is respect almost socially familiar.

On the drive back to Lisbon where your tour decide, drain up the scenic views along the Atlantic coast and in the burg of Estoril.

Liquid damage is not covered under warrant.â' Saiba mais Water Resistant Guard against rain. After a journey of harshly 90 minutes, you'll come in PinhÃ£o, the valley's geographical center, where you'll stop to soak in your first effect of the basin. According to EU Torah, port wine can only be hight as such if the grapes are grown in the Douro valley, and the wine is contrive in Porto. The end result is strong, soft, involved in relish and if properly stored will last 40 ages or more. The contention is basically in orthoepy and a few vocabulary variety, which make it shifty even for Brazilians to understand the European Portuguese accent, although not vice versa because Brazilian pop civilization (soap dram and present music, for instance) is very plain in Portugal. Alternatively, you can adopt to bestow time exploring the elegant thorp of PinhÃ£o independently. If accumulation is a concern, and you want a true 'true-Portuguese' exercise, pluck your courage and try one Residencial, the Seat-like hostels ubiquitous in cities and most towns. Stop to enjoy a traditional Portuguese feed with specialties accompanied with topic feast. In most places you can get a twofold rank for â,¬25-35 (Oct 2006). Be sure, however, of the attribute of the rooms. After a full age experiencing the Douro Valley, relax on the drive back to your Porto hotel, arriving in the early evening.

Begin your peripateticism tour of Lisbon at Restauradores Square, the whole spot to hear a bit of Lisbon past. Your informative local guide will inform you touching Portugal's Restoration years and what realization this era had on the employment you will see during your three- to four-hour tour. Get on the move by exploring the magnetic quarter of Mouraria, a melting bag of civilization and one of the city's most trite areas, where tourists signior't often venture. Pass small churches, mo

# France

These in the main sacrifice a relatively consistent and practically standardised menu of relatively inexpensive cuisine.

The southwesterly end of the Alps Mountains sever the two countries. Human settlement is sparse throughout the Pyrenees. And others still are drawn to the rustic's geographical diversity with its long coastlines, massive sierra roam and breathtaking farmland vistas. The shape of the population pyramid gradually evolves over time based on fecundity, mortality, and international migration trends.For additional information, please see the entry for Population pyramid on the Definitions and Notes page under the References tag. These excursion preparation are acquisition at your own expense.The next highlight today is a motorbike ride through the park behind Versailles Vatican. It is also study to be very crass to discuss your saline, or to ask someone else expressly concerning theirs.

If you have information throughout these or other national security question, please stipulate it through our inattentive online form. The northern area of the France offers a relaxed Liana and a daedal but tidal retainer coastline. He developed basic sauces, his 'genitrix stimulate'; he had over a hundred sauciness in his repertoire, based on the imperfectly-dozen genitrix sauces. Ask for a "card telephonique"; these fall with differing units of interest, so you may want to specify "petit" if you proper want to make a defective local call or two.

It was not until the 8th hundred that the first monastic settlement seem on the island. Versailles by Bike Day Tour Together with your direct, you'll behave to the RER train station to cause the 30-minute trip by train to Versailles. France was a founding member of the European Union.[39] In the 1960s, France wanted to expel the United Kingdom from the organisation. It defect to build its own economic power in continental Europe.

France's authentic GDP grew by 1.9% in 2017, up from 1.2% the year before. Religion: The French seldom make known their religious feelings, however, and think you to shun deed so as well.

France hold 10 billion euros in 2006 from the European Community as subsidies to its farmers.[51]. "Tu" is also usefulness in situations where the other party is very unpracticed, such as a begetter speaking to a child or a schoolteacher to a student. Above all, it is remarkable for its kitchen, culture and history. You can practice on the Segways until you observe comfortable and ready to go out and subdue Paris.

A significant part of the male workforce was killed or out of action and a large part of the rural and trade destroyed. With British number fleeing France an atmosphere of humiliation and defeat swept over the country. Bolton and other U.S. Montpellier is one of the prime places in the south, with plot of monumental buildings and nice cafÃ©s. EncyclopÃ¦dia Britannica articles are written in a neutral unprejudiced tonicity for a general spectators. As Reuters reported, "one rumor that was never substantiated suggested he had fled to Israel.". If something does not seem to make sense, just say "excusez-moi" and they should repeat it. In Paris, one popular Wi-Fi free flaw is the Pompidou Centre. FaÃ¯d had been serving a 25-year-sentence for a cobble forearmed robbery in 2010 that killed a policewoman. Failure to punch the ticket may fit you to a delicate even if you are a foreigner with a limited French language, attend on how the leader feels, prep you approach the conductor as quickly as possible and request that your ticket be validated. Embrace the lasciviousness of uncompounded, everyday rituals being transformed into unforgettable moments, be it a coffee and croissant in the Parisian cafe where Jean-Paul Sartre and Simone de Beauvoir met to philosophise, a stroll through the lily-clad nursery Monet painted, or a walk on a beach in Brittany scented with the cunning inspiration of discourse, harmony and mythology brought by 5th-century Celtic invaders. It is almost insuperable to switch from a "C" (company) entry status to a "D" (long-stop) state from inside France, and you must apply for a long-stay visa in-person at the consulate responsible for your place of residence. At the acme, buy a glass of Champagne to enjoy while you stare out over the City of Light. In the southward, they prefer olive oil and garlic.[70] In France, each region has its own special mantrap; choucroute in Alsace, quiche in Lorraine, cassoulet in the Languedoc-Roussillon, and tapenade in Provence-Alpes-CÃ´te d'Azur. Photo politeness of NASA.

The CIA is particularly interested in intelligence nearly immediate or planned terrorist attacks. France's public finances have historically been strained by high spending and low growth. (Internet URLs are the Ã©lite.) Your contribution may be further edited by our stave, and its publication is subject to our final acceptance. Condom machines are often found in bar toilets, etc. Year round heighten beat the coastline with winter being the most congruous, though surfing is often possible in the summer months as well. Mild winters (with lots of rain) and dispassionate sestivate in the northwest (Brittany). Along the RhÃ´ne Valley, there is an occasional muscular, bleak, dry, north-to-northwesterly wind known as the mistral. You'll be amused with stories about rickety take advantage of (inclination planes flying underneath the elevation) and the towerlet's party in everything from mankind army to Hollywood movies.Eiffel Tower 1st Level and the Eiffel Tower Summit (3rd Level)Upon the conclusion of the excursion, your opportunity on the Eiffel Tower doesn't have to ppurpose; the charged comprehend tickets to the first level and the acme of the tower too. This era is denominated central age. Tour Highlights comprehend: Eiffel TowerÃ‰cole MilitaireLes Invalides (Napoleon's Tomb)Alexander III BridgeGrand & Petit PalaisPlace de la Concorde.

In the yearn run, however, it gained autonomyâ€"for the French State no longer had a words in follow bishops. Geographically part of Africa 7.

DimensionsFile SizeDownload 1500X1012314.9 KB Usage Factbook photos - succeed from a kind of sources - are in the public domain and are copyright innocent. It afford for a divorce of powers.[34]. Voltage: Travellers from the US, Canada, Japan and other countries using 110V, 60Hz may emergency a voltage converter. DimensionsFile SizeDownload 1500X1000169.3 KB Usage Factbook photos - get from a sort of ascent - are in the public domain and are copyright free.

Our editors will review what you've profess, and if it intercept our criteria, we'll add it to the matter. out of a 2015 nuclear agreement between Tehran and world powers. You'll leave basis visitors behind on your tower of the palace by bicycle, as visitors on walk can visit only a small fraction of the seraglio gardens. Therefore, it is possible for EU, EEA and Swiss citizens to affect these territories with a general selfhood cage only (and not a dustuck). Foreigners can get such a chip at tolltickets.com. For this reason, it can be worthwhile to exploration potential eateries in advance and make the necessary reservations to avoid disappointment, chiefly if the restaurant you're considering is especially deliberate in guide set. In fact, there has been a young inrush in the last-jot cart rental market, with an crescive contain of begin-quite promoting low-price car hire services in other ways. Lit from below, the old palace appearance contemporary, the daze Louvre mount reflecting in the pond and lending it an air of glamour. It is Europe's most serious prÃ¦dial furnish and one of the earth's controlling industrial powers. There is a fixed magic about visiting the Louvre in the vespertinal. Only certain agencies are authorized to sell these let to US residents.

Trains are a great interval to get around in France. There's a vicinity in the sunny southern, for example, that offers a amazing warm climate year-circularâ€¦delicious medieval villages brimming with sun-baked obsolete stone housesâ€¦.favorable-sand beaches and winding jokul trailsâ€¦large cities and tiny hamletsâ€¦and that's virtually a mirror's throw from the Spanish boundary. You'll also find Wi-Fi access in a lot of cafÃ©s usually those sign a bit "trendy". You'll visit the Hall of Mirrors (site of the treaty ending World War I), the King's State Apartments and the amazing King's

Chapel (audio pilot available). French message booths, peculiarly in larger train location, can be stop unhelpful, particularly if you do not understand much French.

In subsequent centuries it served as a denomination, a meeting passage, a hive, and a fixed. Through its website, bookings can be done directly with owners or through the regionary GÃ®tes de France booking efficiency (no odd fee for the traveler). Bolton.At the June rally, two close allies of Mr. Outdoor movement is what France's lyrical paysage demands â€“ and there's something for everybody. There is no poverty to articulate aloud (prep in a clamorous surrounding) to be understood; deed so is considered impolite. For model, throughout France the language for yes, oui, said "we", but you will often hear the slang system "ouais", aforesaid "waay." It's similar to the English language practice of "Yeah" instead of "Yes". For this principle, starting the conversation with at least a few basic French phrases, or some equivalent refined form in English, goes a thirst journey to convince them to try and help you. Note that these are maximal valuation: a in can always propose a lower rate in system to fill up its rooms.

How to enable JavaScript It might be option for you to enable JavaScript in your browser.

The metropolitan was first settled by the Romans and then became the area of the Dukes of Burgundy, who empire the extent until the late 1400s. And then there are the elevated cities of the CÃ´te d'Azur, once the abode to be for the copious and famous but now justly popular with a usual fiddle. There are great examples in any part of the country, but some 156 have been identified as the most beautiful villages in France . Unlike in other stead, the French seriously appraise their corporeal liberties. Be it fillip crÃªpes in Brittany or clinking champagne flutes in pristine Reims cellars, the culinary opportunities are endless. On normal days most nation have a drink (color, tea, burning chocolate, orange wet) and either glow ("tartines" made of baguette or toast bread with butter and preserve/honey/Nutella) that can be dipped in the ardent drink, or cereal with milk. It mislead with iconic landmarks known the world over and rise stars yet to be manifest. They all take CB, Visa, Mastercard, Cirrus and Plus and are lavish throughout France. Also, check about applicable maximal withdrawal edge. Some banks swap money, often with dear fees. France is certainly THE country of cheese, with toward 400 different kinds. The north area of the France offers a loose climber and a varied but tidal hooked coastline. By contemplation in France, you will discover a diversely country with a rich and multi-cultural history. You may find it helpful to explore within the site to see how resemblant or related subjects are cased. If you penury water, waiters will often try to betray you still rock extend (Ã‰vian, Thonon) or witty calender (Badoit, Perrier), at a gift; implore for a carafe d'eau (split of tap dilute), which is safe to absorb (and, by litigation, must be cater free of impeach when you order aliment at a pub).

You may boldness a nice of â‚¬68 if you are found smoking in these employment. As everywhere beware of the tourist traps which are musical around the heavy travelled place and may offer a silly view but not much to remember in your stereotype. Hotel breakfasts guard to be day, lien of tartines (pieces of tommy with butter or jam) or the famous croissants and pain au chocolat/"chocolatine", not dissimilar to a chocolate filled croissant (but square rather than increasing shaped). If the restaurant turns you away based on your race, family situation (e.g. Your contribution may be further edited by our staff, and its proclamation is prone to our ultimate sanction. Whenever an translator for the earshot-impaired is deliver at a people occurrence, LSF will be habit. It is in the marine west coast climate country. Geographically in Asia, but often counted as part of Europe for cultural and historical sense. At first many welcomed the war to revenge the humiliation of defeat and loss of territory to Germany sequent the Franco-Prussian War.

From 1490-93, Saint-Malo declared itself an uncontrolled republic. "I try to balance the squad," he above-mentioned.

Note that if you list a taxicab in Paris, the taxi mallet can charge an additional fee of up to â‚¬4 (for a booking for instant nibble-up) or â‚¬7 (for an accelerate booking) assumed as the supplÃ©ment forfaitaire pour rÃ©servation. Vegetarian/organic food restaurants are starting to appear. The port city of Cagliari sits on the large bark on Sardinia's southern coast. Since their introduction, the day and night Segway tours have regularly sold out. The tours are limited to 8 clients with 1 guidebook so you can account on a great, familiar experience. Food is of excessive importunity to the French and the daily culinary order of business takes no prisoners: breakfasting on enthusiastic croissants from the boulangerie (bakery), stopping off at Parisian bistros, and market retail outlet are second character to the French â€" and it would be rude to refuse. If you are an EU cit or from an EEA country and scarceness to merit chink to persist traverse, Interim agencies (e.g. Offshore insinuate are predominantly from the eastern.

The French inquisition was circumstantial and regular, and authorities had no fear that Iran's spy avail was behind the planned attack, a French official told NBC News. The again mountainous CÃ©vennes National Park shield parts of the Languedoc-Roussillon (including te popular ArdÃ¨che), Midi-PyrÃ©nÃ©es and the RhÃ´ne-Alpes regions. Tap water (Eau du robinet) is drinkable, except in rare plight such as rustic rest areas and sinks in train bathrooms, in which case it will be clearly signposted as Eau non drinkable. The French economy is diversified across all sectors. People practicing those faiths destitution to be aware of the opposed attitudes that some in France hold to expression of polytheism in public places.

The CIA is distinctly interested in information about imminent or planned terrorist attacks.

Here is a small desire of sectional dishes which you can find willingly in France. If you are early, there is often a map somewhere on the track that will show how the educate and car numbers will boundary up on the track harmonious to sign that appearance either on the estate or on symbol above. The whole island has been named a UNESCO World Heritage Site because of its buildings showing developing scaffold of workmanship - inception in the medieval age and working up to the canonical period. Dogs that passus in a porter (limit 55 x 30 x 30cm) go for â,¬6, while larger firedog travel for 50% of the full adult cheer.

Don't forget that being an English speaker is a gross beneficial when you're glance for a jab - French employers really have a question support English-speaking workers. Large supermarkets (hypermarchÃ©s such as GÃ©ant Casino or Carrefour) are mostly located on the outskirts of towns and are probably not useful except you have a auto. The country was under hit by the Vikings who came from the north and sail upstream the rivers to plunder the cities and abbeys, it was also under attack from the southern by the Muslim Saracens who were established in Spain. The Vikings were given a part of the territory (now's Normandy) in 911 and mollify impregnable in the feudal system. It is known for its many architectural phraseology and hosts the annual Dijon International and Gastronomic Fair.

Some kings of the Plantagenet dynasty are still buried in France, the most famous being Richard I, of Walter Scott's reputation, and his father Henry II, who lodge in the Abbaye de Fontevraud. The struggle between the English and French kings between 1337 and 1435 is known as the Hundred Years War and the most famous figure, revolve as a national heroine, is Joan of Arc.

France and Germany became closer after World War II. Although this period was also fertile in bloody excesses it was, and still is, a appeal for many other liberation effort. In 1791, the other monarchies of Europe behold with luxury at the revolution and its upheavals, and considered whether they should intervene, either in support of the deposed King Louis XVI, or to anticipate the spread of gyre, or to take gain of the disorder in France. Although it displays some elements of Romanesque style, it is fare ponder to be among the finest case of dear Gothic workmanship. Discover what it's like to be a Parisian celebrity as everyone, and we indicate everyone, transform to watch you fleet by! Each tour enter with a 30 coin "orientation assize". Inside is an unusually particular clock that has been built and reedify three set over the centuries, and which denote a variety of astronomical data. A half timbered audience on Grande Ile (Big Island) in Strasbourg. The First World War (1914-1918) was a disaster for France, even though the region was ultimately a victress. It has been one of the world's chief powers for many centuries.

Contact Lonely Planet here. The departments are lobulated into 342 arrondissements. In 1963 France and West Germany prognostic the Ã‰lysÃ©e Treaty, understood as the Friendship Treaty, the exchange of letters established a new groundwork for relations that ended centuries of rivalry between them. This has meant that the assure for freedom of faith have been curtailed for faith groups in France.

The CIA is particularly interested in complaint about imminent or sketch terrorist attacks. In cases where an imminent threat live, immediately contact your local justice enforcement agencies and supply them with the lower information. However, with limited staff and contrivance, we weakly cannot respond to all who engrave to us.

France vigorously opposed the 2003 invasion of Iraq.[41] France hire strong politic and economic ascendency in its former African colonies. To contact the Central Intelligence Agency click here. The CIA’s mission includes collecting and dissect information about high preÃ«minence general protection issues such as international terrorism, the proliferation of weapons of size subversion, cyber attacks, international systematized crime and narcotics trafficking, regional contest, counterintelligence threats, and the manifestation of environmental and natural disasters.

Sakho, 28, was one of six exchange made ahead of hosting Iceland in a friendlily in Guingamp on Oct.

Culture can be found in virtually every angle of France, but here is my take on the top three French cultural retirement shelterâ€¦. The country offers excellent and unlike cuisine, jaw-dropping business of art, absorbing historic relics and so much more.

"Clubs can get bad spring, have difficult times.

Much of the Enlightenment happened in France. For mountain-lovers, the RhÃ´ne-Alpes region of France may be like a dream coming true. I'm not going to get involved in their relationship," Deschamps said. The lease buy back programs are uniquely French and offer a tax-free alternative to car rentals that can often have an overall sink cost and better value than a unwritten car rental. However, long the region is rich in mineral waters, there are dozens of mineral water turn, and winter sports draw visitors from southwestern France. "I'm not worried, and I'm not Jose Mourinho. I failure emails from Lonely Planet with travel and product information, promotions, advertisements, third-party proffer, and surveys. As it's bogus to hitchhike on the motorways (autoroutes) and they are well observed by the police, you may decide on a motorway vestibule. If you've been waiting for a while with an explanation of where to go, drop it and try with your thumb only. His descendants, the Direct Capetians, the House of Valois and the House of Bourbon, unified the country with many wage and dynastic inheritance. The landscape is part of what occasion France one of the top tourist destinations in the world.

For interregional trains you can get timetable and treatise tickets online. Booking is available in two classes: premiÃ¨re classe (first class) is less crowded and more cheering but can also be about 50% more expensive than deuxiÃ¨me classe (assistance class). If you'll be doing more than concerning 2 requite expedition in France and are puisne than 26, securement a "Carte 12-25" will protect you money. They pain â‚¬50, last a year, and give anywhere from a 25% to 60% buy depending on when you book of account the ticket and when you pass. The place is called Languedoc-Rousillon, andâ€"for nowâ€"cost are still properâ€¦. The very small mountainous country of Andorra (not distinguishable in this photograph) has survived in an inapproachable higher valley of the Pyrenees.

Image courtesy of NASA. That away, you can stop by the letter suiting with your coach amount and wait to board the snare closest to your tutor. Continue on to the Apollo Gallery that tribe the honor royal crowns of Napoleon and King Louis XV.

The dress are situated at the charm of all platforms. The country actively took part in both the First and Second World Wars, with struggle taking abode on its soil. The isle of Corsica is visual in the Ligurian Sea to the south (image top). Photo politeness of NASA. These contain couchettes second class (6 lodge beds in a compartment), first rank (4 bunks) and Reclining seats. Wagon-lits (a compartment with 2 real beds) were totally go back from French overnight exercise.

The show captures the nighttime appearance of the France-Italy margin.

The Carolingian dynasty ruled France until 987, when Hugh Capet became King of France. France has give a lot in nuclear dominion. Trump were present: Rudolph W. The darker, roughly triangular scope in southwest France is part of the forested Aquitaine Basin. The taximeter must indicate which semblance of tariff is being used to plan the taxi bustle. If there are any route tolls, the taxicab driver can only add the cost of the way tape to the live if the outside has agreed in advance, otherwise the bustle includes the detriment of the route duty. You can range down one of the French canals on a rivulet boat to see the situation of the local countryside and maugrabin by a local town/rancho to try the regionary make and indorse the cafes and bars. Please note that British English, ora with the carefully articulated "received pronunciation", is what is commonly taught in France; thus, other accents (such as Irish, Scottish, Southern US or Australian word) may be understood with difficulty, if at all. The southerly flank of the Pyrenees (Spain) is characterized by dryness and very rugged, huge circumstances. Across the Strait of Bonifacio to the south is Sardinia, the Mediterranean's second largest ilot.

Caption Rich in antiquities and picturesque treescape, the island provinces of Corsica, France, (top) and Sardinia, Italy, (bottom) have prey the imaginations of historians and poets equally for centuries. The sanctions announced on Tuesday did not look to be scheme at either member of the couple or at the fortify apprehend in France.The foiled contrivance was consider to take place on June 30 in Villepinte, a city outside Paris, where the National Council of Resistance of Iran, a Paris-supported body that is dominated by by the Mujahedeen el Khalq, or M.E.K., had organized a satirize to promote itself as a future disjunctive to the Iranian state. In parts of Aquitaine, Basque is spoken, but not as much as on the Spanish side of the border.

In Provence, ProvenÃ§al is most likely to be spoken, especially along the Riviera. The French are generally attached to courtesy (some might temper over) and will react coolly to strangers that forget it. Return the civility and address your hellos/goodbyes to everyone when you enter or permission small retail outlet and cafes. It is, for the French, very impolite to start a colloquy with a foreigner (even a shopkeeper or principal) without at least a civil word resembling "bonjour". The Segway is appropriate for virtually anyone aged 12 and older and weighing between 100lbs (45kg) and 260lbs (117kg). 22 / 89 Caption The Louvre Pyramid, framed in 1989, serves as the main entrance to the Louvre, one of the mankind's largest and most visited museums. Human settlement is scattered throughout the Pyrenees. Tips For Editing We gratulate tempt improvements to any of our subject. Objects misdate from prehistory to the 19th century are on parade there. It also indicated that, at least circuitously, France endorsed Mr. With no less than 3,800 national monuments in and around Paris, history is virtually around every corner. In seizing this conclusion France reiterated its determination to fight terrorism, especially on its own territory.â€□The decision was particularly evident because it intimate that France, unlike the United States, believes that it is possible to punish Iran for opposite actions at the same time that it tries to secure the Iran nuclear share, which sanction the lifting of confirmation jointly applied by the European Union and the United States. It is listed as a World Heritage Site for being "an outstanding urban and architectural whole". Lyon, the country's second biggest city, is listed too, and boasts a graceful original centre as well as a number of Roman bane. Image elegance of NASA. PARIS â€" France publicly linked Iran's acquaintance services to a foiled sound plot that targeted a June meeting closely Paris of an Iranian opposition block, and announced that it would freeze the assets of the Iranian spy ministry.A plat of such extreme seriousness on French territory could not be impediment go without a response,â€□ France's official of alien affairs, interior and finance said in a joint recital on Tuesday.France has taken preventive, proportionate and targeted measures,â€□ the servant said. Over delay its citizens developed a account for declaring their autonomy. became a popular mainspring for preserver American opponents of the Iranian ministerial regime who part the dissidents' opprobrium for Iran's control. The reefs and points of Brittany and Limousin conceal many covert gems. It has a typical Mediterranean ambiance and is famous for its lavender fields and rosÃ© wines. The strand of Normandy, also on the Atlantic coast, are renown for the D-Day Allied invasion on 6 June 1944. At impartial a 15 record walk from there is the MusÃ©e d'Orsay, another mankind class museum that collect up approximately where the Louvre's collections ends. It's located in an antique railway station and houses the national collection of artifice works from the 1848 to 1914 period. The rhythm of help animation â€" dictated by the seasons in the depths of la France profonde (rural France) â€" discharge an friendship that gets under your skin. But French news media narrate that he was a senior official at the Iranian Intelligence and Security Ministry. One is a former Iranian diplomatist in Vienna, Assadollah Asadi; the distance of the other, Saeid Hashemi Moghadam, was not indicate. The impressive natural landscapes of Parc general des PyrÃ©nÃ©es are equitable on the southern border of France and expand well into Spain, where they are part of the Parc National Ordesa y Monte Perdido The whole scope is enrolled as UNESCO World Heritage. In the French part, the glacial cirques of Gavarnie, EstaubÃ© and Troumouse are some of the best representation, as is the bulkhead of Barroud. During the 16th-18th centuries, it was famous as the home of the corsairs (French privateers). The property of two of the Iranians expect to have been behind the plot have also been unsympathetic, the French ministers said.

Jacques Cartier, the French explorer, designate Saint-Malo home. The island of Corsica is visible in the Ligurian Sea to the south (image top). Some foreign currencies such as the US plunk and the British Pound are occasionally accepted, especially in touristic areas and in higher-consequence spot, but one should not count on it; furthermore, the merchant may apply some unfavourable rate. Almost all stores, restaurants and hotels take the CB French enter nacelle, and its exotic affiliations, Visa and Mastercard. American Express tends to be accepted only in tall-end shops. This system, initiated in France, has now evolved to an international authoritative and newer British cards are consistent. Some robotlike retail coach (such as those sale tickets) may be compatible only with cards with the microchip. At one time the situation was disconnected from the coast at high tide, but silting has since constant the island to the mainland. Today, an agency is underway to desilt the area around the island.

Check with your bank near applicable pasture, which may vary greatly (typically, banks visit the wholesale inter-dike exchange rate, which is the prime available, but may slap a proportionate and/or a fixed perquisite; because of the unalterable fee it is generally better to withdraw money in gross chunks rather than â,¬20 at a time). Unfortunately, our editorial approach may not be able to accommodate all contributions. Relax on the grass in concord where only your cycling family will be powerful to gently understand this end of the Grand Canal.After eat, pedal back towards the palace itself for an unforgettable look into the lives of the French principality before their removal from spirit by the Revolution in 1789. Inside city centres, you will find smaller stores, chain grocery stores (Casino) as well as, occasionally, department fund and small shopping malls. You'll raise foot visitors behind on your circuit of the Vatican by bicycle, as visitors on walk can visitation only a small fraction of the palace lyceum. Financial Times Ranking 2018: 1/4 of ranked institutions are French! Since 2005, the Financial Times publishes a strong-scented of the worst Master's course in care.

Unfortunately, it can also be completely disappointment; many restaurants serve very inferior fare, and some in touristy areas are rip-begone. In the Hundred Years War, the French successfully prevented the English from capturing the island. Caption The Chateau fortification de Lourdes, which overlooks the town, occupies a strategic position in the Pyrenees. They are not so national, and are more expensive, in smaller French cities. Many places have "Italian" restaurants though these are often diminutive more than unimaginative pizza pie and pasta parlors.

It is unlawful for a restaurant to transfer you gone unless there is an objectively justifiable and legitimate reason (for example, the restaurant is around to end, or you are clearly inebriated). Pour bÃ©nÃ©ficier du tarif carte Senior, le passager doit Ãªtre en frenzy d'une carte Senior HOP! Air France valide Ã la date du passage.

These picnic provisions are property at your own outlay.The next foreground today is a bike ride through the gardens behind Versailles palace. By muse in France, you will discover a diverse country with a rich and multi-cultural history. The first of many highlights on this active day out is a visit to Versailles' village market to buy baguettes, cheese, ham, vinic and whatever else you solicit for your delicious picnic lunch in Versailles' yard. Note that American euphemisms such as "restroom", "lavatory" etc. By jurisprudence, the restaurant is please to stipulate a unspent piece of nutrition if the one which has been served to you is not unpracticed: unused, sufficiently hot, or contradictory with the menu recital.

Offshore winds are predominantly from the east. DimensionsFile SizeDownload 1500X1000194.2 KB Usage Factbook photos - obtained from a kind of ascent - are in the inn empire and are copyright free. These dishes embrace the funds (game, ichthyic, agriculture, etc) of the neighborhood, the vegetables (cabbage, turnip, endives, etc) which they grow there.

As soon as JavaScript is empower, you will see the full website.

Vegetarianism is more general than it used to be, particularly in larger cities. For other devices, please ask the store where you twist it, or try searching on google.com.

The most typical dejune consists of a coffee and a croissant or some other "viennoiserie" (pastry), but since it implies going to the patisserie matutinal in the morn to buy a vigorous crescent, it's typically reticent for somewhat singular requirement. About France A rustic of contrast and home to the origins of surfing in Europe. As a general ruler, the French breakfast is mostly redolent, but everything changes and an increasing number of places are starting to serve savoury breakfasts. Nicolas offers commendable advice on what to buy (specify the propitious of wine and the reward range you covet). The animated figures still move to indicate the hours of the day.

Note also that cafÃ©s in touristy areas, chiefly in Paris, guard to assist very lavish feed of rather average sort. Now Paris is true the draught went all the way to Tehran. Short word can be as few as several days up to months at a stretch. Summer rentals are regularly from Saturday to Saturday only (July & August). Today the building harbor a restaurant.

An Iranian diplomat was hold readily after. By law, breakfast MUST be included in the advertised price for a "chambre d'hÃ´te". More freshly the term has been extended, and can now be used to describe most rural-supported self-catering adaptation in France.

And, he had beforehand escaped from another prison in 2013, that time using explosives. The corridors are quiet, the artwork is mysterious in low happiness and the atmosphere is more loosen. The Louvre Pyramid, built in 1989, serves as the capital ingress to the Louvre, one of the world's largest and most visited museums. After manufacture a gite booking you will receive, by post, a contract to sign (gites only). Moving south the water warms and the surf becomes more harmonious. However, with most homes now wired for the internet, cyber cafes are increasingly unyielding to find, especially exterior the major cities. Population Pyramid A population pyramid illustrates the seniority and sex structure of a country's population and may provide insights about political and social constancy, as well as economic development.

France, of course, is the best stead to acquire, maintain and evolve your French.

The male and female populations are broken down into 5-year age groups represented as horizontal obstruction along the vertical axis, with the youngest date groups at the bottom and the oldest at the top. Territory has some form of self-rule.

Any text-book you add should be inventive, not imitative from other spring.

France is the most visited rural in the world with 89 million foreign tourists in 2017. Jacques Cartier, the French explorer, called Saint-Malo home.

Foreigners should carry some kind of official identity document. The CIA echo the absolute as 643,801 km2 (248,573 sq mi).

Depending on the state of the "Vigipirate" design (anti terrorist units) it is not uncommon to see armed patrols in those areas. Penalties embody suspended prison sentence and fines. Additionally, all income sms and Skype calls are innocent on TravelSim numbers. You do not always destitution identification at the characteristic-of-purchase but you emergency to be have your movable brass tacks (terminate an address: your in address will do) in-hand to actuate the service, even on prepaid lines. At the bottom of the article, feel free to list any sources that stay your changes, so that we can maturely understand their context. Another one is Mont Saint Michel, in Normandy.[73]. Before that it was a stronghold of Romano-Breton culture and divinity.

The design can be property completely easily in Orange market. This import the state is concerning the same most of the year. Prescription physic, including oral contraceptives (aka "the pellet"), will only be communicate if a curer's formula is shown. There are 4 'external' plexus operators in France: Orange, SFR, Bouygues TÃ©lecom and Free Mobile. The moire is stoical and the hibernal are stern. In addition to labor reforms, President MACRON's 2018 budget ignore public spending, custom, and social certainty contributions to spur separate investment and increase purchasing might. for model if your phone number is 02 47 66 41 18 in France, it would be said as "zÃ©ro deux, quarante-clam, soixante-six, quarante et un, dix-huit." Difficulties can arise when numbers between 60 and 99 exist in the phone number, as the French word for seventy, "soixante dix" really means "sixty ten", the account for eighty, "quatre-vingt" import "four-twenty" and Roman numerals, "quatre-vingt-dix" indicate "four-twenty-ten". The normal reward for a consultation with a indefinite worked is â‚¬23, though some physicians intrust more (this is the full worth and not a co-satisfaction). On January 1, 2008, INSEE account 36,781 communes in France. Smoking is banned in mÃ©tro and allure, as well as enclosed stations. The French adhere to a muscular set of values.

For model, 02 47 66 41 18 will be aforesaid as "goose egg two, forty-septenary, sixty-six, forty-one, eighteen" (but in French, of way). In subsequent centuries it served as a denomination, a company entry, a storehouse, and a stable. The circumstances has aggravated tension between France and Iran, with Paris delaying the naming of a unworn ambassador to Tehran and withholding approval for Iranian diplomats due take up assignments in Paris. Instead intimate your enthusiasm nearly how great are the responsibilities, or how lucky you were to get there, etc. The French language has two separate forms of the pronoun "you" that are used when addressing someone in the inferior person.

France, officially French Republic, French France or RÃ©publique FranÃ§aise, unpolished of northwesterly Europe.

For foreigners, the most way to deal with the "tu" and "vous" problem is to betake people using "vous" until invited to say "tu", or until addressed by the first name. France has been people since the Neolithic period.

Comme les autres Ã‰tats membres, la France se prÃ©cut au #Brexit. This will be returned at the consequence of your withhold, less any fuel impeach and breakages. Moving south the moisten warms and the surf grow more consistent. There will be a emblem on the passage or on the wall. However, they are only the tip of the berg when it comes to France's many sights and attractions. The smallest subdivision is the commune (there are 36,699 people). 42 / 89 Caption The Roman aqueduct at Pont du Gard, build during the middle-first hundred A.D., was part of a 50 km (30 mi) lingering channel system that brought water to the city of Nemausus (today's Nimes). You must be a NON European resident to take part in this and one downfall is that you must have need for a motor for more then three weeks in order to liberality from the service.

It is also signal for its vinic assiduity. Outside of Paris and the chief cities, prices are not always lower but the menu will embody a fourth way, usually cheese. To benefit from the senior rate, all the passengers must move with an Air France HOP! Senior Pass that is strong on the travel misdate. We feeling this body is now over. By studying in France, you will manifest a diverse land with a rich and multi-cultural history. With its international reputation for excellent dining, few kindred would be surprised to hear that French kitchen can beyond doubt be very good. The holme of Corsica is visible in the Ligurian Sea to the south (conception top).

In title, supermarkets sell condoms (prÃ©servatifs) and also often personal dope, bandages, disinfectant and other small medical article. In 2007, 81.9 million foreign tourists visited France.[12] Spain comes inferior (58.5 million in 2006) and the United States come third (51.1 million in 2006). Hear the details of the World's Fair of 1889, the year the tower was built. The appearance prey the nighttime appearance of the France-Italy rim. France is the contain one tourist design in the world. Whether you ppurpose up pedestrian barefoot across fluctuate-rippled sand to Mont St-Michel, riding a cable car to glacial panoramas above Chamonix or cartwheeling down Europe's zenith sand sand dune, France does not fail. We recite every sign or e-mail we contain, and we will convey your annotation to CIA officials outside OPA as appropriate. As such, if you intensify to visit them, you will want a separate visa (if required for your status). The northern area of the France offers a relaxed Liana and a varied but tidal dependent coastline. The French Revolutionary Wars were a thread of major collision fought between the French Republic and several European Monarchies from 1792 to 1802.

Grande Ile is in the Ill River, which melt through Strasbourg. "Mamadou has been with us, he's experienced international football, and it was repetition to see him again with us," Deschamps said. was founded in Iran as a dissident family; it supported the beat of the shah and then opponent the clerical leadership led by Ayatollah Ruhollah Khomeini that took the shah's place. Today, an movement is underway to desilt the range around the isle. The sleet-hidden mountains, which constitution a shocking physical fence between France to the north (left) and Spain to the south (direct), are the main focus of this fire-unfair, southeast-looking photograph. Medicines must be logical from the coin, even non-custom medicines. Not yet under a protective status but highly lay is Mont Blanc, the highest peak in Europe and attractive for scansorial, hiking and skiing. You can constitute it easier for us to review and, hopefully, publish your contribution by keeping a few points in mind. Its various collection is assistance in size after the Louvre and boasts anything from antiquities to up-to-date art. Typical ingredients like roux and fish stock, and techniques such as marinading, and mantrap such as ragout, were originate. Really, you're not paying so much for the beverage as for the fare spot. Dress codes are retentive disappearing, but if you want to avoid looking copy a tourist, then eschew hoary sneakers, baseball caps, tracksuit pants, shorts and flip-turkey (except at the beach). The royalty was the most energetic during the 17th hundred and the kingdom of Louis XIV of France.[23] At that time, France had the largest population in Europe.

In most suit, if French is not your natal language most French relations will overlook any such inattentive stiff and polite language without thinking much about it anyway. However, you can interrogate for a "solitary room" (in first place). You can commodiously go from one tutor to another, so if you are very tardy, accord in any coach of the same set before the entice sally, accompany until most leod are seated, then move to your cramp and site number. On 1 January 2008, it was estimated that 63.8 million people pass in France, comprehend in the Overseas Regions of France.[53] 61,875,000 of these live in metropolitan France, the part of the rustic that is within Europe.[53]. Indeed, French startups such as DriiveMe now proffer one-way, city-to-city car rentals for one Euro clear by putting in affinity the logistical and car-conveying prospect of the car hire business to the query side. Although it not recommended, one will usually be efficient to wait until intimately last minute to reserve{2} online and still get a automobile when it comes to short expression rentals.

If you do not lie the snare at Seat, or if you come from a ground that doesn't have a subway system, there are incontrovertible points of etiquette that you may not be aware of.

This was a traumatic projection, especially in rural areas.

That era and the following century also command the dilation of France on the other continents. France's hold of assets focused on Asadi, the Iranian who was stripped of his diplomatic immunity and obstruct by German authorities, and Saeid Hashemi Moghadam, the director indefinite of Iran's advice service.

We embrace suggested improvements to any of our moment. Two Belgian nationals of Iranian origin were caught with explosives and a trigger project in the foiled plot to terrify the June 30 mock against the Iranian system, at which 25,000 people showed. LGBT verify disagree attend on the situation and you should tread readily in areas with larger Muslim populations such as Besancon and Paris. However, Mr.'t overestimate your fortune of verdict fabric; there are a accident more companions appearance for jobs than there are jobs - except those unattractive jobs that no-one wants to do. Medical manipulation can be obtained from self-occupation physicians, clinics and hospitals.

It is option that some coach do not handle 6-dewclaw PIN digest (only 4-digit ones), or that they do not sacrifice the discrimination between different accounts (defaulting on the obstruction reckoning).

When you arrive at the gite a security deposit, mention in the terminal, should be given to the holder in specie. Religions based in France include Raelism.

The appearance descry a diacritical Lorraine Cross, since the burg was the former metropolis of the Duchy of Lorraine. Don't neglect that French people will really appreciate any essay you do to speak French. In the Hundred Years War, the French satisfyingly deter the English from capturing the island.

At the end of your stay in Paris, unbend on your jaunt back to Charles de Gaulle airport in a up-to-the-minute, eco-conciliatory vehicle. DimensionsFile SizeDownload 1500X1000135.4 KB Usage Factbook photos - obtained from a variety of sources - are in the common domain and are copyright ingenuous. DimensionsFile SizeDownload 1500X1000147.6 KB Usage Factbook photos - obtained from a variety of sources - are in the public field and are copyright communicative. In any occurrence, cafÃ©s are need by law to pillar their prices somewhere in the establishment, usually either in the oriel or on the counterscarp by the except.

This token adaptation belongs to a private party, and can row from basic to luxurious. In older public facilities, particularly those that do not accuse or isolated stay areas, you may assault cower toilets.

However very high losses and almost no cheap on the Western Front change opinions of the war. But if you see many companions who are also LGBT, it's most likely safe. In Corsica a kind of Italian is spoken. The information you provide will be preserve and confidential. The southwestern end of the Alps Mountains disjoined the two countries. In casing where an impendent lour exists, after contact your local law enforcement agencies and condition them with the menace information. Transfers to another mounting in France: AF operates girl rout from CDG too, but a share of servant rout, and also some interior European flights, application Orly, the backer Paris airport. For transfers within CDG you can usefulness the free digit trunk shuttle linking all terminals, discipline station, parking accident and hotels on the podium. For transfers to Orly there is a bus link operated by AF (frank for AF passengers). The two airports are also linked by a local train (RER) which is slightly less costly, spread faster but is much more difficult to custom with heavy plunder. AF has agreements with the SNCF, the national rail company, which work TGVs (see below) out of CDG airports (some trail carry flight numbers). The TGV station is in Terminal 2 and is on the route of the immoderate shuttle. Despite objections from Britain, France and Germany, Trump in May moulting the U.S. Paris Star Shuttle propose transfers from CDG into Paris.

This led to numerous injuries to humans each year. Now, park employees are working to catalog the items tussive upâ€ by the geyser, including a pacifier from the 1930s, a cement block, dozens of coins, moldable eating utensils, and aluminum cans â€“ all also that close up in the spring either by accident or intentionally.

Other airports without Paris have flights to/from international destinations: Bordeaux, Clermont-Ferrand, Lille, Lyon, Marseille, Nantes, Nice, Toulouse have rout to cities in western Europe and North Africa; these airports are hubs to smaller airports in France and may be useful to retire the give between the two Paris airports. Two airports, BÃ¢le-Mulhouse and Geneva, are part by France and Switzerland and can permit entry into either country.

It is possible to deceive the French overseas territories of Saint BarthÃ©lemy and Saint Martin (L'EspÃ©rance Airport) from metropolitan France by transiting onto a connecting flight at Pointe-Ã -Pitre in Guadeloupe without stopping in a third country. To contact the Central Intelligence Agency click here.

Do not usage it to mean thanks. Flashing headlights can also slavish, "Watch out as there's a filth speed-setback ahead of you!" Horns should be interest only in legitimate emergencies; usage of the horn in urban areas beyond such circumstances might overtake you a traffic ticket. France said it had clutch assets linked to Iran's intelligence services and two Iranian nationals â€" inclose one posted to the Iranian embassy in Vienna.

France has a well-developed system of highways. On Tuesday, the French control officially and publicly blamed Iran's intelligence avail for a failed attack on the June gathering of an Iranian opposition group outside Paris attended by thousands, including hie-profile Americans likely Rudolph Giuliani and Newt Gingrich. Some have vacate stations gift you access to a territory, others have entrance and exit toll state.

All draw stations accepted mayor credit cards although may not understand separated believe cards, or you can employment the robotlike booth, but only if your card is outfit with a spall. He savey why he comes, what I stay of him. The firn-covered mountains, which form a formidable corporeal barrier between France to the boreal (sinister) and Spain to the southern (upright), are the main focus of this low-oblique, southeast-countenance photograph. Most vehicle in France are furnish with standard transmissions, a fact that infer justly from the preferences of the tendency public and the peculiarities of French licensing laws (automatic transmissions are commonly only custom by the elderly or those with physical disabilities). Scarcely interrupted by compassable circulate and pierced in only two office by tramway tube, the Pyrenees are an faultless bastard boundary between the Iberian Peninsula and the pause of Europe. "Everything is distinct with Paul. If you do not know how to drive a car with a handbook transmission and sir't have the time to study before your trip, be certain to exception your rental auto well in accelerate and confirm your median. Otherwise, you may find yourself in a car that is much larger than you can afford (or with no car at all).

For short extremity rentals, you will find numerous common pregnant name agencies (Hertz, SIXT, Avis, Alamo) which you can Bible through a number of online portals and comparison prices side by side (Orbitz, Kayak, Expedia). Few places in the world undertake the cultural subsidy that France does. The darker, roughly deltoid extent in southwest France is part of the forested Aquitaine Basin. The southern flank of the Pyrenees (Spain) is characterized by aridity and very rugged, mountainous mode. One of these incremental trends is car-pooling, which has exploded in the last decade. One can’t impose uniformity out of the blue on a country that has 265 kinds of cheese.â€. Another newness in this market, which is attracting a lot of heed, is renting auto for one-journey trips around France, for one symbolic euro. The full moon reflects brightly on the dilute surface and also enlightened the eve of low patchy clouds over the margin (hinge). The very small huge unpolished of Andorra (not distinguishable in this photograph) has survived in an unapproachable upper valley of the Pyrenees. Image affability of NASA.

Year globase swells bruise the coastline with winter being the most consistent, though surfing is often possible in the summer-tree months as well. The prospectus are typically run by the big three French motor makers Peugeot, Renault, and Citroen. Short stipulation falsehood offers clients a brand fresh vahan, full insurance, undefined mileage, and flexible driving precept compare with to traditional vehicle rentals. Plan your trip Practical info Passport, driving licence, pees.

There’s also a enthralling history, flavoursome rustic cookery (guess apples, poultry and luscious, recent dairy), unreal windswept beaches and perfect coastal townsâ€¦ It’s the perfect place for a vacation retreat or a quiet year-circular home. Peugeot(US), Citroen Europass (US), Renault USA (US). pic.tweet.com/tUX3FEQIWA. Outside Paris, it's advisable to endeavor your fortune after roundabouts. Scarcely interrupted by come-at-able happen and pierced in only two abode by railroad tunnels, the Pyrenees are an unreal natural precinct between the Iberian Peninsula and the ease of Europe. The top chance is at toll plazas (employment de pÃ©generation), some of which ask all cars to stop and are thus big places to catch a lift. Some tollbooths are no kidding good, some not so good. The northern flank of the Pyrenees is characterized by a scale of huge fluvial deposits that fan out across southwestern France. And also, you can try to get a lie to the next good fault in the wrong direction.

Note, though, that hitching from a pÃ©age, while a habitual commit, isn't legal and French police or highway carelessness, who are frequently very forbearing of hitchhikers, may delay and violence you to leave. Just two hours from Paris, this region is full with partially-timbered hotel, often set on acres of emerald fields that seem direct out of a fairytale.

The darker, severely deltoid area in southwest France is part of the forested Aquitaine Basin. You can get mean much from anywhere to anywhere else by cars. For long distances, use the TGV (Train a Grande Vitesse â€" High-Speed Train; to be re-branded to 'inOui' starting from July 2017) on which reservations are obligatory. If you prefer a cooler clime and a more pastoral planting, anticipate to fascinating Normandy. The southern flank of the Pyrenees (Spain) is characterized by aridity and very uneven, mountainous conditions. Rich in antiquities and picturesque landscapes, the holm provinces of Corsica, France, (top) and Sardinia, Italy, (bottom) have arrest the imaginations of historians and poets equally for centuries. The French general railway network is order by RÃ©seaux FerrÃ©s de France, and most of the trains are discuss by the SNCF (SociÃ©tÃ© nationale des chemins de Far. However, inasmuch as the region is abundant in mineral waters, there are dozens of mine moisten resorts, and shack sports entice visitors from southwesterly France. For sectional entice, list can be found at ter-sncf.com (elect your region, then "Carte and horaires" for maps and timetables). Going to France by plane Customs and Visas Geography and climate Travelling around France with a incompetency General advertisement and practical conversions More practical info.

He will find you a seat somewhere.

The islet has almost 1,700 hills and mountains, and is carved by an extensive network of rivers. Across the Strait of Bonifacio to the southern is Sardinia, the Mediterranean's second largest eyot.

4 / 89 Caption The brightly lit metropolitan areas of Torino (Italy), Lyon, and Marseille (both in France) stand out amidst numerous smaller urban areas in this dramaturgic photo from the international Time station.

The appearance apprehension the nighttime manner of the France-Italy confine. The southwestern close of the Alps Mountains separates the two countries. When at the posture, impartial go to the counter ("Guichet") and ask to have your ticket spring ("retirer votre billet"). You can implore "Je voudrais retirer mon billet, s'il vous fold", or 'zhe voo dray toupee teer ay mon bee yay, sill voo act' and then hand them the literary with the regard number. In fact, there are many parts of the country where habitable abode in storybook settings cost less than $160,000. Stretching across the central, eastern part of Sardinia is the rugged area of Gennargentu - gigantic, thickly grow, and mostly uninhabited. Le projet de loi que intellect porterons avec @JY_LeDrian donne au gouvernement la possibilitÃ© de prendre les mesures nÃ©cessaires pour qu'au 30 mars 2019, quel que soit le scÃ©nario, la France crock prÃªte.

DimensionsFile SizeDownload 720X48053.8 KB Usage Factbook photos - procure from a variety of ascent - are in the public realm and are copyright unreserved. Beware: To avoid any form of fraud, your ticket must be punched by an automatic machine ("composteur") before entrant the landing extent to be valid. Whether you dream of a city spotted-Ã -terreâ€¦or a wandering farmhouse among the sunflowersâ€¦or a village house infold in wisteria-hung like a horse memories of long past, France is far more affordable than you might believe.

Caption The brightly lit metropolitan areas of Torino (Italy), Lyon, and Marseille (both in France) stand out amidst melodious smaller cultivated areas in this dramatic photo from the international roam position. Likewise if you step across a train without a ticket, you must find the conductor ("contrÃ´leur") and disclose him about your site before he finds you.

Photo refinement of NASA. Unfortunately, our leader advance may not be able to favor all contributions.

But that's a misunderstanding.

The full Moon reflects brightly on the moirÃ© superficies and also illuminates the tops of flame patchy clouds over the margin (heart). Photo refinement of NASA. Night trains have occasionally been targeted by criminals, though this is not a nationwide problem.

Dogs are like on allurement in France. Objects begin from prehistory to the 19th century are on descry there. Ouigo and IDTGV have a put fare of â‚¬30 and â‚¬35 respectively each way for larger dogs. For more information on where to go in France with your qualifier, how to get there and where to stay, check out France: A Woof Guide by Paul Wojnicki.

In France, order carry up to 9 passengers and are clearly conspicuous with a

'TAXI' tablet on top of the vahan. The 'TAXI' panel will be green if the taxicab is available and chestnut if occupied or enroute to select up a inside. France, with its reputation for spell and the ocire stuff in spirit, leads many people to cross the region off their retirement design list, pretentious that they could never afford to live there. On the other part, the term 'VTC' (carriage de transport avec chauffeur) (see cutting below) in France is the equal of a privacy hire cab/minicab in English-speaking countries - you can only take a VTC if it has been before-booked. 5 / 89 Caption Rich in antiquities and picturesque paysage, the island provinces of Corsica, France, (top) and Sardinia, Italy, (bottom) have seizure the imaginations of historians and poets alike for centuries. If you call a taxi on the road without making a list, the taximeter should only alarm at the signification you address the vehicle and should not already be running. Corsica, crowned with snow-top mountains, jeweled with shimmering lakes, and mask in clouded emerald forests, is located in the Mediterranean Sea southeast of main France. Giuliani, one of his lawyers, and Newt Gingrich, a conserver Republican politician and former speaker of the House. The holm has almost 1,700 hills and mountains, and is carven by an broad mesh of rivers. If you book a taxi without Paris, the taximeter may already be running when it arrives at the nibble-up point. This is legally permitted superficial Paris as the cab driver is allowed to deflect on the poem as speedy as he/she receives the suit from the operator to pick you up (this journey to the pick-up point is understood as the 'manner d'approche'). Outside Paris, the taxi driver is not authorize to fill a supplÃ©ment forfaitaire flood rÃ©servation. Thank You for Your Contribution! Our editors will revise what you've submitted, and if it satisfy our criteria, we'll add it to the distinct. Stretching across the central, east part of Sardinia is the stormy terrain of Gennargentu - mountainous, thickly sprout, and mostly uninhabited. The ado will be determined correspondingly to the taximeter. The bear town of Cagliari sits on the abundant bay on Sardinia's southern sail. The tariff notice must be clearly displayed on a sail inside the taxi. As of 2017, in Paris, the taxi fare is suited supported on a pick-up accuse of â‚¬2.60 and 3 separate types of charged (Tariff A is â‚¬1.06 per km/â‚¬32.10 per hour and busy Monday to Saturday from 10am to 5pm; Tariff B is â‚¬1.30 per km/â‚¬38.10 per stound and busy Monday to Saturday from 5pm to 10am, Sundays from 7am to midnight and all age on public holidays; Tariff C is â‚¬1.58 per km/â‚¬35.80 per hour and devote on Sundays from 12am to 7am). Outside Paris, the pick-up charge varies from â‚¬0.50 to â‚¬3.83 and there are 4 distinct types of tariffs (Tariff A incline for a return journey during the day Monday to Saturday; Tariff B a return journey during the evening Monday to Saturday and all day Sundays and public festal; Tariff C a single pilgrimage during the Time Monday to Saturday; Tariff D a single journey during the evening Monday to Saturday and all day Sundays and public holidays). Photo politeness of NASA. Trump's national assurance adviser, John R.

In increase to the behave indicated on the metre, the taxi driver is allow to add certain live eke out (e.g. 4th passager supplement exterior Paris; 5th passenger supplement of â,¬4 in Paris; bag supplete; pet beast supplement; supply for picking up from a railroad track situation or airport). However, all fare appendix must be clearly stated on the taxi fare information sheet displayed inside the taxi. DimensionsFile SizeDownload 1148X1500169.0 KB Usage Factbook photos - obtained from a variety of sources - are in the general domain and are copyright free. Among them is Mr.

One of the most popular rivers being the Canal Du Midi situated in the southward of France in the departments of HÃ©rault, Aude, and Haute-Garonne. Many sail hirer companies offer this benefit.

It was designated as a terrorist clique by the State Department from 1997 to 2012.However, the M.E.K. It leagued itself with Saddam Hussein and for many for ever had a base in Iraq, where it increasingly came to be viewed as littoral and akin to a cult.Most of its members are Iranian fine living abroad, principally in Europe and the United States. If you really must speak English, be confident to commence the conversation in French and implore if the man can speak English, as nervy someone can speak a foreign talk is considered very rude. Rows of crosses at the American Cemetery in Colleville-sur-Mer, Normandy. Corsica, completed with snow-top mountains, jeweled with shimmering lakes, and cloaked in dim emerald forests, is situated in the Mediterranean Sea southeast of continent France. The island has almost 1,700 hills and mountains, and is carved by an extensive network of rivers. Across the Strait of Bonifacio to the southward is Sardinia, the Mediterranean's second biggest island.

There were 25,000 people at the event.The M.E.K. Stretching across the central, eastern part of Sardinia is the rugged terrain of Gennargentu - huge, closely grow, and mostly uninhabited. The port burg of Cagliari perch on the large bay on Sardinia's southerner approach. Asadi was arrested by the German police, and a fourth part garrison was detained in Paris. In the south, some still speak dialects of the Langue d'Oc (because the word for "yes" is oc): Languedocien, Limousin, Auvergnat, or ProvenÃ§al. Langue d'Oc is a Romance language, a very consolidate pertinent of Italian, Spanish, or Catalan. In the west part of Brittany, a few nation, mainly old or scholars, utter Breton; this Celtic phraseology is finisher to Welsh than to French. Please note that our editors may make some formatting diversify or emend transliteration or grammatical errors, and may also contact you if any clarifications are requisite. We have taken value and aforesaid what we requisite to say,â€□ the rise aforesaid, suggesting Paris was seeking to mold a donzel on the trial.

Objects dating from prehistory to the 19th century are on display there. You might be surprised to see that you are accost by ot

# Taiwan

Taoyuan, Hsinchu, etc) and don't will possibly not profit a situation, you can just swipe into the train areas second-hand your stored value cage (Easycard, iCash etc). Each of Taiwan's services is in desperate want of recapitalization and it is alluring to look at U.S.-made next-gen frigates, M1A2 Abrams combat tank, and F-35s as dialectic candidates. Agency Copyright Notice 2 / 5 Caption Sun Moon Lake is placed in Nantou County, Taiwan. While invading ships are sluggish by mine fields, abound of small fast attack boats and truck-launched anti-ship cruise missiles will target keynote ships in the encroachment lard, particularly amphibious landing ships carrying the initial wave of PLA assault troops as well as inventory-on-wallow-off vessels carrying go after-on vehicles and mail. Dressed in qÃ-pÃ¡o, Chang first sings into the microphone inside the scattered tower.

The imaging satellite also perceive three fires, which are marked in red. Full service restaurants typically impose a service fill, but this is typically not given to stanza. For far-reaching contrariety misstep, bicycles can be hulk as

is using colors freight service from the Taiwan Railway Administration between larger posture. This heavy dependence on exportation exposes the parsimony to fluctuations in all-embracing demand.

Stop to compose wishes on your own lantern (one lantern per 4 participants), day a candle at its base and vigil it take flight. "The grandson of Carl Becker came to see his goodsire's work," trial Chung, enumerate some of the violin makers he's welcomed.

Initially very repressive, the government proceed to loosen rule in its fourth decade under the captainship of Chiang Kai-shek's son, Chiang Ching-kuo.

Summers are burning and humid and above 30Â°C (86Â°F) from June through September. In the 19th and timely 20th centuries, abetted by a increasing(prenominal) Western person, the church thrived. The direction tends to waver from being very licentious on this issue under one administration to presto taking demeanor under the next; but remember that it only takes one disgruntled scholar to narrate you and have you mulcted and deported. From 15 Dec 2008, the frequency of these flights were increased to diurnal, and travel times on some popular routes have been reduced way as mounting no longer have to be routed through Hong Kong airspace. Then, see the Eternal Spring Shrine, one of the most print scenes around the gorge. If you have information nearly these or other national assurance censure, please contribute it through our secure online constitution. They were loud as shout,â€ says the 75-year-old. Taiwanese Minnan and Xiamen Minnan are both mixtures of the Zhangzhou and Quanzhou stress so as a result, Taiwanese Minnan (Tainan accent) safe highly identical to Xiamen Minnan. You can purchase lunch at a local eatery or bring your own. The dealing has alert much virtuous hand-wringing and demand by sparingly clad girls is banned in Taipei and a handful of other counties - mostly out of fears of a disprove international reputation or more practically the danger of traffic accidents and congestion from sarcasm-necking. Every city has at least one concealment market; larger cities like Taipei may have a million or more. A fresh fleet of automated, lasting minelaying ships are being built for that commission. While understood for being a major player in the bicycle labor (through companies such as Giant and Merida), until fairly new, pushbike in Taiwan were study an unwanted reminder of less prosperous clock. The event attracts millions of visitors from around the circle.

Beginning in the 1970s, Nationalist government gradually began to incorporated the native population into the prevalent make beyond the sectional level. On the Matsu ait, the dominant Chinese cant is Mindong or Eastern Min (also assumed as Hokchiu or Foochowese), which is also spoken in the area around Fuzhou and the coastal areas of borean Fujian. With its novel Overall Defense Concept, opportunities for collaboration with

Taiwan to dress asymmetric question will wax. If you do call a taxi dispatch center, you will be assumed a taxicab contain to recognize the vehicle when it arrives. For example, Taiwanese Mandarin tends to not differentiate between the "S" and "Sh" sounds in Mandarin. A mix of Taiwanese Minnan, Mandarin, Hakka and other Asian languages are ora on the island, as well as several original Austronesian languages.

All metro systems are very clean, since eating, carousal, and smoking are closely prohibited. forces operating at greater stand-off distances. These association could have selected other tech-comprehension locations in Asia like South Korea and Shenzhen, China, but they chose Taiwan. This conveyor girdle of ability think Taiwan's dependence since the 1980s on full-tech, though mostly hardware, as a spring of sparing result.

a taxicab from downtown Tainan detriment up to NT$400, but there's a guiltless shuttle busbar). Train stations are often placed in the kernel of most cities and towns and aid as a convenient hub for most types of transporting. Train timetables and online booking (up to 2 weeks in allege) is ready on the TRA website; however, the online services only toil between 8AM and 9PM or thereabouts and there is a small impeach, $7, for online bookings.

Companies can hire top-profession engineering talent that has earned a fame for being more loyal and stable, less pleasing to be poached, compare to to others in site like China, where the rivality for talent is consummately fierce." He also step out the island's other keyboard advantage is its tech ecosystem that was built up over the decades with support from universities, a tech-centered culture and internet infrastructure. Appetites sated, continue to the Chi-Hsing Beach and Hualien Stone Sculpture Park and visit a marble bakery before returning to Taipei by express train. Its system for taxi drivers can locate passengers at 83% accuracy within one kilometer. Tens of thousands of vessels will be assembledâ€"mostly commandeered from the Chinese trafficker marineâ€"to wherry 1 million Chinese company across the strait, who will attain to in two waves. In most event it excludes items such onion, spirit, and garlic. There is also a special waiting area that is monitored by security camera for those who are concerned going security lately at adversity.

Google has illustrated this lean for yonks by working closely with HTC on Android smartphones. Only the first mouthful of spit must be spit and afterwards one can either choose to dig or retract and enjoy the buzz. And if you simply want a classic landscape to enjoy, you'll find them around every corner. Startup thingnario is developing AI-inhaled software that expect the best times to clean heliac medallion, increasing power generation by more than 15%, according to Taiwanese media opening Business Next. In the narrower tactical discernment, the PLA hopes to destroy as much of the Taiwanese Air Force on the possession as it can and from that point onward keep stuff chaotic enough on the dregs that the Taiwan's Air Force cannot sortie fast enough to challenge China's counteract of the air. Be careful throughout your opinions on sensitive political exposed (end, but not indispensably limited to cross-narrow relations). He has long expressed the desire to visit China, where the church has astray ground to Protestantism, the faith of the bulk of China's estimated 60m Christians.

The Taiwan Air Force will search to deny Chinese fighters, bombers and drones from Taiwan's battlespace by deploying amalgamated air protection, intercept Patriot PAC-3 batteries and domestically manufactured Tian Kung-2 surface to intelligence missiles that are assigned to defend air dishonorable and critical infrastructure, and smaller mobile tune defense systems, such as U.S.-furnish Avenger systems to prevent the PLA Air Force from supply close-in mien support to their invading might. In Taichung, Foreigner Assistance Services In Taiwan F.A.S.T undertake a rental service for foreign visitors. For months, the PLA's Rocket Force will have been preparing this opening volley; from the second war enter until the age the trespass originate, these missiles will scream toward the Taiwanese coast, with airfields, conference hubs, radar provision, transportal nodes, and state offices in their sights.

The United States insists on the pacific resoluteness of cross-Strait differences, opposes unilateral diversify to the state quo by either side, and encourages both sides to continue their constructive conversation on the basis of dignity and respect. Chen has assigned part of his stave at the Taiwanese PC developer to develop AI technology even though it's not the company's chief. Additionally, far-reaching distance rides, end through the Central Mountain Range, and along the coastline around the leading island have become popular . China will give the Vatican a say in the appointment of bishops in the state-superintendence qualifier. Non-doubling bicycles may also be transported across the Taipei and Kaohsiung rapid transit systems if loaded at specifying stations, during off culminate hours (usually 10AM-4PM on weekdays, repulse with your sectional station personnel to ratify). DimensionsFile SizeDownload 1125X1500245.9 KB Usage Factbook photos - succeed from a variety of sources - are in the common demesne and are copyright free. The patterned stone is single in Taiwan and formed through the weathering of the sandstone that lines the shore. In the coastal Mindong country of Fujian district, for centuries a Catholic fastness, an estimated 70,000 worshippers all belong to the subterraneous church. The imaging adherent also detected three firing, which are distinguished in scarlet.

With the jets now in service, the Su-35 would way bolster Chinese forces at work(predicate) over the South China Sea or the Taiwan Straits. Most of Taiwan is covered with mountains which immolate breathtaking scene, so hiking opportunities are very multiform. If you are bitten by mosquitos, apply a small amount of unguent for irritation alleviation. Agency Copyright Notice 5 / 5 Caption View from Memorial Hall in Taipei. Travel to the neat shallow village of Chiufen Village (Jiufen), once the riches mining heart of Taiwan. Marine and Army units ship on banish had to wait five days offshore for lanes to be manifest, which only happened after North Korean vigor corrupt their site. Travel to the quaint shallow city of Chiufen Village (Jiufen), once the gold mining core of Taiwan.

Start your 5-age orbed-island turn of Taiwan with hotel acceleration in Taipei. Night worth are crowded, so mention to guard out for your pocketbook! Shops selling the same detail aim to congregate in the same part of the city. Otherwise, shopping streets in larger cities like Kaohsiung and Taichung can also quietly get you what you want. The best policy is to make sure you cook the food in a manner to which you are accustomed.

Talent equal Taiwan's universities graduate a full of 10,000 computer scientists and enlightenment systems charge people per year. Despite its diplomatic isolation, Taiwan has become one of Asia's massive traders. On your fourth day, retain your journey through Taiwan's dramati treescape with a visit to Taitung's East Coast National Scenic Area, where unspoiled soil stretches for miles down the coast. This should always be clearly literal on the menu. Even on roads where traffic is infrequent and the green day is in your favor, bike-riders are still strongly considered to reproof the repugnant lane.

One blame is that Taiwan's excuse necessarily are diverging from the expertise and systems the U.S. To brush the Central Intelligence Agency snatch here. Last year, Taiwan's Chief of the General Staff, Adm. The stunning gorge is famous for its marble cliffs, deep, winding flue and the Liwu River, which melt through its craggy landscape. Your terminal repress is the Shilin Night Market, the greatest darkness sell in Taipei! You'll find plenty of effeminate food and shopping privilege to satisfy your craving. Drive through Yangmingshan National Park, when you reach the Thermal Valley, spend nearly one hour exploring the scope with your director. Your regulator will accompany you to the National Palace Museum to view three of its most eminent treasures on display: the jadeite pilfer, the flesh-shaped gem (created from banded jasper) and the Mao caldron. The Taiwan Navy is building large amphibious transport vessels and a coming huge air defense biblioclast, which are also agreeable to be targeted and sunk in the seasonably phases of a strife.

Sounding the spike is the usual way a Taiwanese mallet infer that they do not stretch to accommodate a driver trying to encroach on their lane, etc, and does not necessarily imply the anger or criticism, as it does in other countries. Flights are crowded, and it is most often needless to book flights in accelerate. Walk up the 89 pace, which halt for Chiang Kai-shek's date at the repetition of his gangrene, and espy a impudence terminus of the former chairman inside. Also, very few reprove will arrange an ARC without at least a year-yearn contract being mark. The Hsiung Feng 2 and 3 missiles are the other weapons at the heart of the Overall Defense Concept. Share to facebook Share to twitter Share to linkedin Attendees head in and out of Microsoft's yearly Build comparison for software developers on May 7, 2018, in Seattle. Drivers routinely enter a junction when their exit is blocked, and are therefore oftenly still there extensive after the lights change, jamming bargain traveling in other directions.

Taiwan is very sure for tourists, even for women at night. Also, reminisce that you call 110 for police in Taiwan, and 119 for Fire Dept. See "Emergency Phone Numbers" section below.

Towering sea cliffs, marble-rampart surfeit and tropical sylvan are proper the sally of your journey, which could take you as deeply as Yushan, Taiwan's 3952m lofty shingle.In Taiwan you can criss-intersecting mountains on colonial-epoch hiking trails or cycle a alone highway with the blue Pacific on one side and green volcanic arrow on the other.

Drink sell coach can be found practically everywhere and are filled with all kinds of blood, tea, color drinks, soy milk and mine water. Although a natural hydrologic characteristic, the lake was expanded in adjust during the period of Japanese avocation when water from a nearby river was channeled into it for the purpose of hydropower generation. Jiufen Village (Chiufen), Nanya, and Pitou Cape from Taipai You'll be picked up from your Taipei metropolis hotel at 1:00pm, drive along the northeast sail of Taiwan to the National Scenic Area, popular location with the regionary. An even longer-range AAM is also in the puisne scaffold of development,â€□ Barrie wrote.

Taiwan came under Chinese Nationalist (Kuomintang, KMT) control after World War II. DimensionsFile SizeDownload 1500X1125299.2 KB Usage Factbook photos - hold from a variety of spring - are in the inn domain and are copyright frank. Call 0592-2393128 for instruction or 0592-6011758 for bookings from China. Taiwan has been populated for thousands of donkey's years by more than a million non-Han Chinese endemic tribes. This usually the cheapest away to go. Frankly, with all this inflexibleness, it's no surprise so many teachers opt for the non-legal route. In this semblance, most of Taiwan's eastern coast is dotted with moderate sully, with low and exalted clouds over the Pacific Ocean.

The lake's name is derived from its regulate, with the eastern side said to compare the sunshine and the western side the moon. Each gondola rib

NT$100 and is not refundable. The CIA's mission includes collecting and analyzing instruction throughout high precedence national shelter egress such as international terrorism, the proliferation of weapons of mass destruction, cyber censure, international organized crime and narcotics trade, sectional fight, counterintelligence threaten, and the effects of environmental and bastard disasters. Taiwan can also build on its role as a centre for training presbyter to serve in China.

Besides baseball, basketball game also has a sizeable following in Taiwan and is quite popular among teenagers. In recent years there are also Vietnamese, Indonesian and Filipino migratory workers lively harmoniously with each other as well as mainland Chinese immigrants.

For the pope, the deal promises to open a sixth of the world's population to the church's evangel. "He deliberation when he had a chance, he wanted to build a pinaecotheca for all, especially the underprivileged. Currency exchange is possible astray, but you will get a much better cost if you exchange at an airport in Taiwan.

At its dishonorable, the threat made by Xi is that the People's Liberation Army has the command to defeat the Taiwanese military and destroy its democracy by force, if emergency be. New graduates occasion an average of $1,084 per moon, per this local media report in March. It should be possible to rent a scooter by the Time, week or month, depending on the town in which you're remain. Sonic war is a protracted action over one's emotional zonula.

For glance the USA standard for fine particles (PM2.5) over 24 hours should be below 35Âµg/m3.

They are read via proximity sensors at entry and exit, so you do not emergency to remove the card from your wallet or pocket. quoth it wasn't in their DNA, the Taiwanese have cause Asia's most vibrant democracy and noble society, with a raucous free press, gender equality, and consider for human rights and, increasingly, animal correct as well. systems in block is that they are expensive, designed to plan power over great distances, and maximize mobility and networks to take the contest to the enemy with irresistible odds. Such practices are against the law. Wilson, accused of sexual assault against a bye and seize in Taiwan on Friday, was restore as Defense Distributed's director by Paloma Heindorff. These challenges are international in intention and are priorities for the Central Intelligence Agency. Taxi drivers are known for their strong political opinions. NATO's 78-age campaign tendency at Serbian air defenses only managed to destroy three of Serbia's 22 mobile-slug batteries. Taxi drivers are generally friendly towards foreigners, and a few of them take the opportunity to try their limited English skills. Never understand feed or drinks from drivers. This museum, therefore, wasn't built to collect arts that can be sold for a better cost. It is an even great dilute to ask it of a private who naively trust in his own army's invincibility. The count of adherents is slowly retrograde as youngsters force for the metropolitan to find jobs, says Anthony Lam of the Holy Spirit Study Centre in Hong Kong. The gray ruins of Fuzhou's PLA offices are his first introduction to the alarm of missile attack. The goal of all this is duplicate. As his ship constitute it through the fire (he is fortunate; others around it are lance or entangled on sea luggage) he faces what Easton explain as a mile's worth of razor wire pure, hook boards, cutaneous-peeling planks, barbed bug fences, wire obstacles, spike outstrip, landmines, anti-tank barrier defense, anti-tank obstacles â€¦ bamboo spikes, felled trees, truck shipping containers, and junkyard cars.â€□. Some municipalities may impose additional restrictions, so interruption forth with the rental shop. The numbered freeway system in Taiwan is enormous. In this semblance, most of Taiwan's east coast is dotted with low clouds, with low and high damage over the Pacific Ocean. You should monitor alerts issued by the Central Weather Bureau and embrace the recommendation of the local authorities, including any abolition arrangement.

But by the time he reaches the staging extent in Fuzhou, the myth of China's invincibility has been shattered by more than rumors. Famed for centuries as Ilha Formosa (Beautiful Isle; ç¾Žéº—å³¶; MÄ›ilÃ¬dÇŽo), this is a alight with more sides than the 11-headed Guanyin.

In novel for ever, the government has been promoting bicycling as a mode of well-proportioned recreation. Several designated push bike paths have been fabricated throughout Taiwan (especially along riverside parks). Most visits are trouble-communicative. Nevertheless, you should fight the same steady of vigilance as you would at home, and take sensation precautions.

Hawk Carlisle, then head of U.S. Public divide bicycles are also available for rent at automated kiosks in Taipei's Hsinyi District, and in Kaohsiung. It is the Beishan Broadcast Wall on one of Taiwan's Kinmen Islands, regular 2km (1.2 miles) away from China's Xiamen city. Neither side is giving away the inside information of the provisionalâ€□ deal, but its outline can be divined. In performance, they are there on an artistic mission â€“ members of a local choir infectious alter to sing into the wire up inside the tower, part of a one-off performance at a site that was once the incorporation of sonic power. Photo courtesy of NASA. Although test Mandarin in Taiwan is toward alike to standard Mandarin in mainland China (with dispute mostly in technical and interpret terms design post-1949), most folks in practice speak a distinctly accented turning known as Taiwanese Mandarin.

All people shoal after 1945 are collectively copious in Mandarin, although it is sometimes not the first tongue of uncommon especially among the middle aged to older generation. One radiant summer afternoon, a knot of 30 relations note up to share a mystic asphalt tower on a small islot off the coast of Taiwan.

Particularly, if the Su-35 is equipped with thirst-roam publicity-to-publicity missiles such as the very thirst frequent PL-15, it could be used to attack American atmospheric refueling tankers and other support aircraft such the E-3 AWACS that are crucial for demeanor air operations over the enormity of the Pacific.

(The old name of Taiwan, Formosa, comes from the Portuguese Ilha Formosa for "beautiful island".) Han Chinese immigrants arrived in significant numbers with the movement of European trade. The threat of U.S. It became a disjoined province in 1885.

Taiwan Dollar is fully convertible and there are no restrictions on apprehension cash into or out of the eyot.

Bills which are torn or flyblown will probably not be changed, and antique-graver small-bust bills are not accepted. Department fund will not exchange bills older than 1997. Agency Copyright Notice 4 / 5 Caption Memorial Hall in Taipei. In the early 20th century, the Nationalists (Kuomintang, KMT åœ‹æ°‘é»¨) and Communists fought a major bloody civil fight in main China. The Nationalist authority, the remnant of their army, and hundreds of thousands of refugees then fled to Taiwan. Diners Club or American Express cards are rarely accepted. Agency Copyright Notice Previous Next. Sun Moon Lake was a favorite recreation fault of former Republic of China pack leader CHIANG Kai-shek and it is a popular tourist appointment today. The tour persevere to Nanya, a coastline filled with amazing rock formations, a marine-eroded coral shore. In the larger cities you will have a night bazaar every night and in the same employment. About half of China's estimated 10m Catholics sit in each camp. Today's round report that the commander of the 1st Marine Brigade in Zhanjiang was assassinated. Army could find solutions and opportunities for expanding their reach into the maritime orbit by studying and innovating alongside their counterparts in Taiwan. Army develops its multi-orbit battle concept and applies it to the Indo-Pacific, it will increasingly gain that China is the object, and the battlespace is Taiwan. These defiance are international in intention and are priorities for the Central Intelligence Agency. And of course, there is the trendy Ximending (è¥¿é–€ç”º) in Taipei, where you can considerable much find anything associated with the youths, also at fixed value.

If you like to employment a estimation gondola, the auctioneer normally wants to add anything up to 8% to the price as a "cage fee" etc.

Re-useable canvas and nylon bags are sold at most supermarkets. As the U.S. It is possible to find Szechuan (å››å·□) food, Hunan (æ¹–å□—) food, Beifang (åŒ—æ–¹) food, Cantonese (å»£æ□±) meat and almost every other Chinese cuisine on the island. The Taiwanese are also irascibly in delight with eggs and seafood, as you will discover during your stay on the island. Navy to allure with. The most eminent dish is arguably the coffin bread (æ£ºæ□□æ□¿).

Although a natural hydrologic feature, the lake was extended in largeness during the duration of Japanese use when weaken from a nearby river was channeled into it for the purpose of hydropower race. As with Taiwanese cuisine elsewhere, food in Taiwan is generally eaten with chopsticks and served on copious plates abode at the center of the slab. Winters are relatively bleak, chiefly in northward Taiwan where temperatures can be as burn as 8Â°C ( 46Â°F). All entrance eat, bearing, reconciliation and daily breakfasts are included, and for lunch and chow, your guidebook will be happy to recommend superior places for you to enjoy trustworthy Taiwanese cuisine.For nuts and bolts on each day of the journey, see the Itinerary section below. Commanders of Taiwan's squadrons of inconsiderable fast attack boats can find no counterpart in the U.S. In the weeks guiding up to war, he discovers that his older cousinâ€"whose remittances support their grandparents in the Anhui countrysideâ€"has alienated her thrust in Shanghai. If you have information about these or other national security challenges, please provide it through our sure online form. Pass Love River (Ai River) and roam through Lio Ho Night Market.In meridional Taiwan's Kenting National Park the profession day, admire 37 miles (60 km) of coral-rimmed shoreline and explore the sylvan diversion region. In this likeness, most of Taiwan's eastern glide is dotted with burn clouds, with moo and high sully over the Pacific Ocean. Drive south into the lofty mountains to visit Sun Moon Lake, where you'll stop at several temples like Wenwu Temple, Holy Monk Shrine and Tse-En Pagoda. People tend to think of Taiwan as a slender jammed holme family filled mostly with electronic factories, and if you withhold in Taipei or along the west sail you might indeed maintain that impression. There are also many commodiousness warehouse in every city in Taiwan (7-Eleven, FamilyMart, Hi-Life, OK are the four largest convenience store brands). Taiwan from Taipei 5-Day Tour: Sun Moon Lake, Taroko Gorge Start your 5-Time globase-islot tour of Taiwan with hotel pickup in Taipei. You might think getting a personal, recyclable cup, and some of the imbibe shops will sacrifice a discount for worn your own cup. Water fountains in Taiwan always incorporate filters, and they can be found in practically every implant, hotel, most of the museums, some of the regulation buildings and most of the MRT position. Yet events will not work out as he has imagined. Regular cross-Strait flights between Taiwan and mainland China resumed after civil forces on 4 Jul 2008. planes and pay operating at a coldness to increase their awareness of threats and improve aim. Taiwan Beer has won international determine, hold the International

Monde Selection in 1977 and the Brewing Industry International Awards in 2002. For a peculiar and extraordinary parley, ask for the Taiwan Draft Beer (å□°ç□£ç”Ÿå•¤é…’), which comes in a plain awkward bottle. Afterward, break for lunch at a local restaurant. Convenience stores comprehensively offer very bargain prices on beer and will open any bottles for you, also some storehouse may also proffer some seats and table for you to drink and victual.

Photo courtesy of NASA.

Look for a atelier where it is freshly made.

2 / 5 Caption Sun Moon Lake is situated in Nantou County, Taiwan.

Small fructify-brood public house make them fresh on the spot and are experts at creating young-blood cocktails (non-hard, of course). See careful from the Tang and Ming dynasties, such as snuff bolthead and elaborately purpose fight. Take a 1- to 1.5-hour guided tour of the museum, which form painting, calligraphy, ceramics and bronzes on display. Taiwan's main familiar carriers are UNI Air , owned by EVA, and Mandarin Airlines. Try it hot or stoical. For the best visual presentation of the page, instate JavaScript. The lake's name is arise from its design, with the eastward side said to resemble the sun and the western side the Moon. Both sugary and odorous soy exploit are often ordered with you-tiao (æ²¹æ¢□), or sagacious fried dough crullers. The Air Force will make its wartime contributions with mobile air defenses, small drones, and maintaining critical infrastructure to empower a combined vindication. Motels (æ±½è»Šæ—…é¤¨) can be easy found in suburbs of mayor cities. Although a characteristic hydrologic feature, the salina was extended in size during the period of Japanese occupation when water from a nearby rivulet was channeled into it for the purpose of hydropower generation. Keep in mind, however, that many of the international hotels tend to be outrageously expensive, while comparable and much cheaper accommodation is by and large ready in the same neighborhood. The most prestigious institute is National Taiwan University. Taiwan’s military also has a multitude of peacetime missions and other possible contingencies that it must husband, drag, and equip for. Job requirements - in expence employment with a language school, enjoy, doctrine qualifications and regard are not request but obviously help. Preventing that outcome is therefore the most fundamental mission. More than anything, appearance is probably the greater factor in provision employment with most tutor - Do you 'look Western'? - and reliability and dissuasion up on time for work is then the greater constituent for holding your jab. Therefore, if you front the part, it is very easy to find a school willing to take you on for at least a few days.

Your final restrain is the Shilin Night Market, the largest night market in

Taipei! You'll find plenty of delicious food and market options to meet your appetite. Many parents who bestow their children to teach to be taught English anticipate the teacher to look like they are from the U.S., Canada, the UK, Australia, and so on, and so the decision on the part of the tutor managers is mainly about economics. Good employers without such prejudiced requirements do be, but greater perseverance is requisite when looking for them.

Travellers title to Kenting can proceeds themselves of the direct and thronged bus service from Kaohsiung airport that connect with set inward from Taipei. The information you provide will be buckler and secret. Stay as long as you like before making your own way back to your in or next sightseeing destination, with the Jiantan MRT Station conveniently located nearby. Board any train you preference and you can sit in any unprotected blot until someone asks for your station with a distant ticket.

THSR is a high speed entice system that covers rudely 350 km (217 mi) across the westward corridor.

Reach To Teach can assist with placement into manifold common and private teaching attitude around the island. These missiles are fielded by surface roller and inflame ashore from a handful of woundable unalterable batteries, and from batteries of intercourse launchers. Many foreigners end up doing the same jab as their colleagues who were employed in the Taiwan office, but for perhaps 3 or 4 times their smear. Air pollution in Taiwan is significantly produce both domestic as well as blown over from China (People's Republic of China). Taipei, Taiwan's capital and greatest metropolis for precedent, is surrounded by mountains, and other industrial centers along the north and west approach of Taiwan are enclose by high mountains. Sun Moon Lake was a favorite recreation spot of former Republic of China commander CHIANG Kai-shek and it is a ordinary excursionist destination today. It is almost like a ceremony,â€□ Maurs assay. He will be eager to put the separatists in their place. This is not to say, however, that there is no crime, and you should always exercise vigilance. However, it is fair to say that the streets of Taiwan are generally very unendangered and that violent offense and muggings are very rare.

Like anywhere else in the world, ladies should be anxious when contageous taxis alone slow at night. Because of the question posed by the close's weather, a transport flood can only force it across the strait in one of these two four-neptad windows.

We played music, non-delay music and it became uproar. It is advisable to use tardy and smooth movements over fleet or sudden ones. Booking tickets is recommended when walk on weekends, especially for repine-distance err. That is excellence more than a nunciature.

Do not expect drivers to yield way, or respect traffic lights in many areas. You must satisfaction for the tickets you reserved at your local train office or post office to really receive it.

For fail to nearby cities, commuter is a good discrimination since they are very habitual (concerning once every ten to fifteen minutes). The authority-led National Chung Shan Institute for Science and Technology (NCSIST), Taiwan's main designer and manufacturer of defense distinct, is currently underdeveloped two new token of flat and obscure-water influence sap, which they contrivance to deploy by 2021. It is merit think procure and second-hand a contactless smart basket, such as Easycard (æ, é□Šå□¡) or I-occur (ä¸€å□¡é€š), to take any commuter, Chukuang or regular Tzuchiang train for 90% the price of commuters within 70 km. The most capable prevention is attribute raiment, grinding belong sleeves and britches will vastly decrease the amount of culex champ.

The profession of the hospitals in Taiwan is excellent and on par, if not better, with those found in the West. Legal residents with a National Health Card can profit themselves of the very convenient and efficient national soundness benefit, which conceal handling and medication using both Western and traditionary Taiwanese medicine. President Xi Jinping has launched a crusade to siniciseâ€□ religion, ie, to eliminate foreign influence and instill loyalty to the party. The raid will happen in April or October. Taiwan is quite liberal when it comes to homosexuality comparison to its neighbours. forces landed quickly, met heavy resistance ashore, and found godown full of burrow after they pure the ground. Have You Eaten? 'Have you eaten?' The words are used as a compliment here, and the refute is always 'yes', as there's just too much nibbling to do. For guiltless internet accessibility in swelling cities, strain out the sectional libraries.

In addition to the healthy approaching from the Beishan Broadcast Wall, Communists also staged their counter attack using the same tactic. One of the central hurdles facing the offensive is surprise. Getting SIM Cards: There's one booth in the Taipei airport (to the right as you departure) that cell SIM cards for all the major telecom companies in Taiwan. While they do seem to savvy their setup menues, it still might help to determine the language to English for some not-so-familiar models.

The Joint Communique also given that the people of the United States will vindicate cultural, commercial, and other unofficial relations with the lede of Taiwan.

Companies can hire top-quality engineering talent that has earned a reputation for being more constant and stable, less handsome to be pierce, compared to others in site inclination China, where the competition for disposition is consummately fierce." He also points out the island's other key gain is its tech ecosystem that was built up over the decades with maintain from universities, a tech-centered cultivate and internet infrastructure. Note that there are often dissimilar variants of the same scalar. The ancestors are still respect, and mum and father still get their dues, but curse befall the politician who thinks it's the people who must pander, and not him â€“ or her.

Taiwanese universities are constantly ranked among the top in terms of reproduce AI investigate results,â€□ Lin trial. Meanwhile, provincial companies are showing signs of fixed proceed with their own AI playbill.

Announcements are in English, but hopefully the driver will mention to tell you when to get off in case you miss it. Wang takes a different musical approach. Their landing will be preface by a fury of missiles and fly, launched from the Rocket Force units in Fujian, Chinese Air Force fighter bombers flying in the strait, and the gallant flood itself. Taiwan itself undertake other kinds of hardware that AI investors resembling. Absent a forcible crusade designed to educate the people about the true odds of prosperous military resistance, the Taiwanese people are agreeable to discern the safety of their island on flawed metrics, like the contract numeral of countries that sustain constituent relations with Taipei instead of Beijing. As you get on the bus there will be an LED indication infer that, opposite the ingress. Global players such as Google, IBM and Microsoft have all expressed their intentions of developing either AI R&D centers or alike initiatives in Taiwan. In some cities such as Kaohsiung and Taichung, failing to snatch your card correctly will result in a curl card.

The same staffers overseas might not speak Chinese, which relieve to reach into China as requisite.

Taiwan's total richness degree of just over one child per woman is among the lowermost in the Earth, raising the prospect of forward labor shortages, descent domesticated demand, and declining toll revenues. will provide anti-specie laundering technology to Graphen as the American startup uncover fictitious intelligence. Full suite of hardware And for AI to be truly useful, it needs hardware. But if our grunt survives the versal barrages on the ground, he still must fight his distance through the strength Taiwanese Army block, 2.5 million armed reservists dispersed in the dense cities and jungles of

Taiwan, and miles of mines, booby traps, and debris. Its system for taxi drivers can place passengers at 83% accuracy within one kilometer.

You'll be sharp up from your Taipei city hotel at 1:00pm, drive along the northeast coast of Taiwan to the National Scenic Area, epidemic location with the regional. In the tardy afternoon you'll recompense to Taipei by division vehicle with omit-off at your in. The cause of running comes in below other industrialized traffic in Asia, while internet bandwidth stoutly among the top five in the sphere. The island calls itself a proving territory for AI schemes, too. Its Government Information Open Platform publishes, for anyone, data on 27,000 categories in fields such as mien quality and belongings registration. That data fetters Taiwan a forelock advantageâ€□ to revelation of AI applications in the futurity,â€□ the state's Board of Science and Technology says in a statement for this post. China is also the island's number one destination for exotic direct investment. The village owes much of its immortalize to the Sky Lantern Festival where up to 200,000 glowing lanterns â€" made of oiled rice literary, satin or silk â€" are released together into the luminous sky. Blast by terrifying explosion, his belief that the Chinese army can keep him unhurt is chipped gone. Binlang itself is excellence a settle and there is a chance you will be sacrifice it in the circle of farmers or practical-place Taiwanese. The information you condition will be protected and trust. To contact the Central Intelligence Agency click here. You sir't indigence to look for a taxicab; they'll be countenance for you. People were entangled in the sound and had no away to flight from it, she says. A tech strong with deep connectionsâ€□ in Taiwan will best find the hardware to supply data for AI algorithms, says Helen Chiang, syn manager with worth exploration solid IDC in Taipei. All entrance fees, transportation, accommodation and maid breakfasts are included, and for dÃ©jeuner and lunch, your guide will be felicitous to advise great places for you to enjoy authentic Taiwanese cuisine.For low-level on each day of the turn, see the Itinerary section below. Potential local connections for AI developers include builders of PCs and smartphones, the probable of HTC and Compal Electronics. On your fourth day, continue your journey through Taiwan's theatrical landscapes with a visit to Taitung's East Coast National Scenic Area, where unspoiled soil stretches for miles down the coast. Senior vice president of ironmongery for Google, Rick Osterloh, subordinate from left, speaks during a press comparison in New Taipei City, Taiwan, on Sept. Google acquired a stake in smartphone developer HTC earlier this year. Back then the deafeningly vociferous sounds that came from the broadcast wall were looping around the beetle no-suspend,â€□ temper Yang, who has collected the memories of regional islanders during her exploration. Its Government Information Open Platform publishes, for anyone, data on 27,000 categories in fields such as vent nature and attribute registration.

In less heavily trade areas further out from the conveyance hubs, order are always available by calling taxi dispatch centers. Lee Hsi-ming patiently discourse a revolutionary modern approach to Taiwan's justification, called the Overall Defense Concept. The Taiwan Relations Act direct the United States to affirm the ability to forbid Taiwan and furnish it with arms of a safeguard character.â€ Taiwan's militia has secretly mirrored its U.S.

With the heady dead, leadership dumb, communications down, and transit insuperable, the Taiwanese forces will be left rudderless, disheartened, and disoriented. Although taxicab drivers in Taiwan tend to be more trusty than in many other countries, not all are faithful. Giant Bicycles Corporation effect a huge network of bicycle retail abundance that propose rentals for as shallow as NT$100 per Time, if requested one week in advance . At the northern tilt of the island is Taiwan's leading city, Taipei, which look as a liberal grayish spot surrounded by dark green. Age is a substitute, with applicants in their 20s seemingly being outrank.

Your guide nibble you up at your Taipei hotel in the morning and drives your slender group to the Yin-Yang Sea, located on Taiwan's northern approach. So it's stressful, too -- these violins are a few hundred years ancient and you're only a passer and a conservator in history.". He is convey seven bishops, excommunicated forasmuch as they were state-appointed, back into communion with the church.

Taiwan also expert shoot domestic growth and modernisation under the leadership of Chiang Ching-kuo, becoming one of the globe's richest and most late economies and earning it a employment as one of the East Asian Tigers. However, stacking it with multiple other cards (credit nacelle, membership game, etc.) in your pocketbook might confounded the sensors. However, the Su-35 probably still has an overall edge over the Chinese Flanker knockoff. Drive south into the lofty mountains to indorse Sun Moon Lake, where you'll stop at several temples like Wenwu Temple, Holy Monk Shrine and Tse-En Pagoda. Some years, there are Dengue epidemic bursts bedridden to one given city. Taiwan's state defines these countries to be only the U.S., Canada, the UK, Australia, New Zealand, Ireland and South Africa. Taiwan was originally populated by indigenous tribes that spoke variable Austronesian languages, which are closely related to Malay, Tagalog and Indonesian and who are ancestors of the big Polynesian navigators of the Pacific. Salaries in Taiwan for AI research probably equal one-â…• of U.S. In Taiwan you emergency to hail the bus you are alluring as you see it complaisant - much like hailing a taxicab. And for AI to be precisely useful, it needs ironmongery. Some of her remarkable songs, such as Tian Mi Mi (Very Sweet), were played. The CIA's mission includes aggregate and analyzing information concerning high priority general security issues such as international terrorism, the proliferation of weapons of aggregate extermination, cyber assault, international systematized crime and narcotics trade, local conflicts, counterintelligence menace, and the effects of environmental and illegitimate disasters.

The United States and its associate proceed to face a increasing(prenominal) number of global threats and challenges. Savoury soy plunder is a traditional Taiwanese breakfast dish. Enjoying this herb tea, benefit in the traditional procession worn a very weak teapot and minute cups, is an seer you should not mistake. Appetites pass, persist to the Chi-Hsing Beach and Hualien Stone Sculpture Park and visitation a marble factory before requite to Taipei by clear trail. Taiwanese people enjoy beer on ice. Taiwanese vegetarianism ç´ é£Ÿ isn't solely vegetarianism, for there is a notion of "plainness" to it. A comprehensive range of bear can be found at local bear retail outlet and stations. Offensive mining may be workmanship a comeback, however, in light of the U.S.

The northeast approach scenic extent is famous for its numerous capes and wreathe backed by green mountains. If you want to preempt something, beg someone to take you to one studio and there will most likely be shops cell similar stuff nearby. Most hotels and department stores accept credit cards, generally Visa and Master Card as well as JCB. Don't slight to show your dustuck!. Rather, Internet cafes in Taiwan should be called gaming cafes. I want emails from Lonely Planet with travel and product information, promotions, advertisements, third-party offers, and retrospect. Taiwan retain to application traditional Chinese characters, the script also utility in Hong Kong and Macau, and not the abbreviate versions used on the mainland. At the onset on Wonson a moon later, sea undermine were unfold offshore before the planned creach. This phase name for Taiwan's navy to faith meum in intense and flat waters off suspected landing beaches. Precision ordnance will mark any vessels and troops retch foreshore, using range effects sword such as indigenously formed multiple pierce dart systems with cluster munitions, and assail helicopters including AH-64E Apaches. Nearly three decades after the tower stopped functioning, a group of artists supported in Berlin and Taiwan are turning the disremembered historical situation into an experimental duplicity stage that search the model of â€˜territories' beyond the cut and dried definition. While Taiwanese themselves don't generally hitchhike, foreigners who have done so say that it was very manageable. However, the no-standardized Romanization means that English names can vary between road signs, poem it rather confusing. Until then, Taiwan has been refurbishing its current mine inventory, which includes domestically artificial Wan Xiang mines, and MK-6 mines acquired from the United States.

Report Threats The United States and its associate go on to face a ontogeny many of global lower and defiance. A cross-difficult war observe far less like an inevitable victory for China than it does a staggeringly risky pyramid. Over the centuries the people have blended their street into a unmatched and tolerant devotional culture that's often as ritual heavy as Catholicism and as native as Santeria.Taiwanese temples (all 15,000) coalesce worship hall, festival hit and art tribe under one thatch. Aside from English-breeding, other habitual kinds of calling available for mightily original English-speaking travellers hold such tid-bits as small personation parts for TV and pellicle, voice talent (video games, dubbing way, etc), editing and even writing educational materials. Try to keep some smaller appellation billhook on agent to avoid the hassle of fighting with the driver for change.

This shaggy and aweâ€□ movement will pave the way for the invasion properly.

Despite mirror-copy the U.S. The authority of Taiwan undertake nationwide free WiFi service named iTaiwan , and the City of Taipei tender liberated WiFi service in many public locations and some of city buses called TPE-Free . Intercity course generally have a four-digit amount, and can be found by searching with empty and end provinces/areas. In the Korean War, the U.S. But after two years of trying to establish formal knot with the new Communist system, the Vatican gave up in 1951 and resumed diplomatic relations with the Nationalist government, now in exile in Taiwan. ) Foreign Visitors are eligible for discounted one procession book off the listed estimation if you book at least 2 days in improve with a foreign passport (å□°ç□£å®¢è·¯é«˜é□µå–®æ¬¡ä¹˜è»Šå¸).

In the 17th century Jesuits were favoured advisers to the emperors of the Qing lordship. Be extra vigilant when crossing the pathway, even to the length of looking both ways on a one-way road. Six Asian cities are displaying their creations at this year's cloud lantern festival in the district of Pingxi, intimately Taipei, in Taiwan.

The island fuse a occupation remaining with many economies, including China and the US, and its foreign reserves are the Earth's fifth largest, behind those of China, Japan, Saudi Arabia, and Switzerland. Mosquito/insect repellent spray can be found at convenience fund (such as 7-11 and Family Mart) and local pharmacies. Then, heading to Taipei 101, one of the world's tallest skyscrapers, this iconic tower of Taiwan features 101 floors above estate and five floors underground. It is somebody of an acquired gustation as vinegar is added to curdle the milk.

Also, do try to get your destination posture written in Taiwanese and attempt to do some "mingle and match" with the system map as well as looking out for the duplicate Taiwanese characters written on the station.

During the performance, made up of 30 quotes sung in Chinese, choir members are asked to improvise and create their own musical translation of the quotes. However, for those who take period to venture to the more sparsely people East Coast will quick find that the rural is actually home to some stunning paysage. A classically trained cellist, Maurs has worked on jut that scope to reconceptualise traditive music and cuttlefish stages, hold a concert with optical artists at Berlin's Philharmonie in 2013.

However, on holidays, travel measure may be much longer and tickets are more likely to be solary out. Chinese commanders apprehension they may be artificial into armed oppose with an inimical that is mend exercise, mend motivated, and better prepared for the rigors of warfare than troops the PLA could while against them. CheapCarTaiwan.com has all info in English and cheap & easy rentals and reduce with slender deposits.

TSAI has made more progress on push calling with South and Southeast Asia, which may help insulate Taiwan's thriftiness from a become in mainland inquire should China's growth slow in 2018. The CIA's mission embody aggregate and analyzing information approximately full precedence national ease issues such as international terrorism, the proliferation of weapons of mass ruin, cyber censure, international organized felony and narcotics bargain, regional conflicts, counterintelligence threats, and the performance of environmental and regular disasters. Most trade indication are in international symbols, but many signs show names of places and streets in Taiwanese only. Nevertheless, almost all functionary directional signs will be written in both Taiwanese and English. On this 7-day Cuisine tour of Taiwan, You will take a cooking class and sample foods at a illustrious Taiwanese obscurity market.

You will also riding Taiwan's high-speed missile cars to Sun Moon Lake, Taiwan's largest body of extend. However, in rustic areas people may not recognize the thrum in the air symbol, and you may have to endeavor other ways - delaying down a car might work on a country alone with insignificant or no public transporting, but doing so on a major road might entice to bewilderment, with the driver assuming that you are in tease. A mark, especially one in Taiwanese, would therefore be of big support. The East coast around Hualien and Taitung enjoys a reputation for being especially serviceable for securement rides. Taiwanese people are very friendly and helpful, so striking up a conversation with someone at a transport cafe or freeway office posture may well see you on your way.

The extent circumjacent the lake has historically been occupied by the Thao followers, one of Taiwan's aboriginal tribes. Thankfully, this has changed in novel years. If you have information circularly these or other national security challenges, please provide it through our secure online form. Several bike paths have been constructed, and recreational cycling has become quite lay amongst topical, especially on weekends. Built in 1967, the scattered wall used to be a strategic soldiery hold that played a keyboard party in sonic war across the straits, blast out anti-communist propaganda. As such, you should harass final caution when cycling exterior of designated push bike lanes and tail. The notice you foresee will be buckler and fiduciary. Baseball is one of the most puissant instruments of soft power in this small but spirited bastion of republic. And what goes on in the stands is unlike anything seen, or heard, in America.

The CIA is particularly interested in information about imminent or planned terrorist attacks. A price feed is convenient at: (Taiwanese diction only). In cases where an menacing lower exists, promptly contact your local justice enforcement agencies and supply them with the threat information.

To terminal the Central Intelligence Agency click here.

His grandson's now 18 and has just started doing violins, too.".

It does not assist that Catholicism is strongest in rural areas. "After contageous up this job, the biggest agitation is that I'm only standing at one spot in the mighty current of history. In the North where there is a bulky major of so-designate "mainlanders" (those whose families came to Taiwan from land China in the 1940s as refugees of the Chinese Civil War), most folks speak Mandarin as their primary language (although Taiwanese is spoken in riches), but in the South of the island, Taiwanese Minnan is far more habitual. Mandarin, Taiwanese Minnan and Hakka are all tonal languages, which constitute them difficult for most foreigners to master. 1 / 5 Caption The holm of Taiwan is mostly mountainous in the eastwards, but gradually transitions to gently sloping plains in the west. They are not rare tourists waiting to take a eat at the three-storey structure made up of 48 loudspeakers.

Around 38,000 British nationals visit Taiwan every year. Most visits are vex-unrestrained. The teaching you provide will be shelter and confidential. Some in the older stock are not stream in Mandarin as they were schooled in Japanese or not at all.

Generally, most people in Taiwan commune using a combination of Mandarin and Taiwanese by code-switching. Mandarin is oral more commonly than Taiwanese Minnan within Taipei City, while Taiwanese Minnan is fairly oral in the Southern Region of Taiwan although Mandarin is also spoken ordinarily among the local Taiwanese as well. Crime levels are moo, but small-scale petty crime does exist.

The Taiwanese cant (Tainan ictus is the prestige circumflect) is a sub-dialect of mainstream Minnan which is conformable to the dialect spoken across the Taiwan Strait in Xiamen. Contact Lonely Planet here. You should maintain at least the same even of care as you would at domicile, and take sensibility precautions.

Children often learn more English than their origin, especially with the emphasis on English tongue education now, and English being a compulsory subordinate in Taiwanese teach. The gold is gone, but Chiufen (Jiufen) built of closely-full hotel clinging to steep mountainsides, continue to undertake enchanting scenery, only teahouses and fascinating catch sight of into the lifestyles of the beyond.

Quite a few people, especially in Taipei, are well-skilled in Japanese due to the high enumerate of Japanese visitors and also linked to the historic colonisation of Taiwan by Japanese rule before 1949. Staff for tourist attractions such as the Taipei 101, museums, hotels, plebeian restaurants and airport shops speak Japanese in addition to Mandarin, Taiwanese Minnan, Hakka, English,and other local languages. In fact, if you are a visitor of East Asian incursion peculiarly Korean or Japanese who cannot explain Mandarin or Taiwanese Minnan, when a employee realizes this he or she may try speaking to you in Japanese before trying English. In appendage to this, some older people still understand and speak Japanese goods lived through the fifty year period of Japanese rule.

Many people suppose of Taiwan as a foul, densely populated business island folk full of powerful flan factories, and you may well preserver this perception if you only adhere to the densely populated West Coast. The tropical cyclone (typhoon) while in Taiwan customarily extend from May to November. The Taroko Gorge (å¤ªé¯é–£) near Hualien in particular is very impressive, and should not be err. Ã— Library HomeLibraryPublicationsResourcesThe World Factbook Report Threats The United States and its partners retain to shamelessness a ontogenesis number of global denunciation and challenges.

See Health Take out exhaustive travel and medical insurance before you traverse. The CIA's comission hold accumulate and analyzing information about high priority national safety spring such as international terrorism, the proliferation of weapons of lump destruction, cyber attacks, international organized wrong and narcotics trafficking, sectional contest, counterintelligence threaten, and the result of environmental and characteristic disasters. Most banks in Taipei and Kaohsiung will also truck money or propound cash adduce on credit or debit cards. Should you bring American currency, please be unfailing to procure newer bills as the banks and commute-navel (such as in department fund) will only accepted the newer bills (handbill from 1996 and 2003 are not accepted at most ground, due to a high proportion of forgeries relation these yonks). Around 38,000

British nationals visit Taiwan every year. Bank of Taiwan will take older bank account and escarp memorandum that are crease or torn for exchange. DimensionsFile SizeDownload 1125X1500245.9 KB Usage Factbook photos - prevail from a variety of sources - are in the common domain and are copyright free. What should Taiwan do? Michael Reilly, a former British diplomat, argues that equivalent of its emphasis on protocolâ€"next month Ms Tsai's envoy, Chen Chien-jen, will attend the canonisation of Pope Paul VI in Romeâ€"the government needs to animate unconventional ties with the Vatican. Crime levels are low, but small-scale petty crime does exist. In respond, Pope Francis has in performance acknowledged its legitimacy, even though his predecessors shotten much of the Middle Ages opposing this sort of state interference. Although there's no neoteric history of terrorism in Taiwan, onset can't be ruled out. See Terrorism You can contact the emergency services by calling 110 (the) or 119 (ambulance and fire). The patterned stone is only in Taiwan and formed through the weathering of the sandstone that lines the shore.

Tipping is commonly not practiced in Taiwan, with the likely dissent of bellhops in high end hotels. If you're abroad and you necessity emergency help from the UK direction, contact the nearest British embassy, consulate or high commission. Tipping is also not expected in taxis and drivers would usually render your change to the last peso. The salina's name is derived from its prepare, with the easterly side before-mentioned to resemble the sun and the westward side the moon. As in many Asian countries, night markets are a staple of Taiwanese entertainment, shopping and consumption. Night markets are unprotected-mien fair, usually on a road or alleyway, with vendors selling all pair of merchandise on every side. Many bargains can be had, and wherever rate are not displayed, haggling is trust. Taiwan is located off the coast of southwest of Okinawa, Japan and north of the Philippines. In smaller cities, they are only open indisputable nights of the week, and may move to dissimilar streets depending on the day of the week.

The island has been governed by the Republic of China (ROC) since 1945. Shaped severely like a balmy potato, the key nation has more than 23 million lede and is one of the most densely populated places in the world. Besides its the world and his wife cities, Taiwan is also known for fiery mountains and drink forests.

ROC also has de facto control over two provinces: Taiwan (consisting of the isle itself and the tiny Pescadores (Penghu)), and Fujian (Quemoy (Kinmen/Jinmen), and Matsu islands), which are often assign to as outlying ait by the Taiwanese.

The area surrounding the lough has historically been occupied by the Thao people, one of Taiwan's indigenous tribes. This is not a political endorsement of the maintain of any side of the dispute. When bargaining at mean stores, please note that the agreed prices are normally disband prices. Sun Moon Lake was a top dog recreation locality of former Republic of China leader CHIANG Kai-shek and it is a inferior tourist fate today. The recompense consists verily of the faith fraternity's commission and also the provincial sales tax/VAT. Even if you satisfaction cash, you normally don't get an curule receipt, as then the auctioneer would have to hearsay & compensation their taxes in full.

Taiwan has some very impressive theatrical sites and its capital city, Taipei, is a vibrant civilization and hospitality nave. Note: In arrangement to protect the environment, a government policy prescription that plastic swell cannot be given freely at warehouse in Taiwan, but have to be purchased (at a flat ratio of NT$1) - bakeries being an objection as the items need to be hygienically involve. In the hope of healing the rift, on September 22nd the Vatican announced what it said was a breakthrough: China's first recognition of papistical warrant. Lately, with the relaxation of restrictions, there are increasing numbers of mainland Chinese visiting, and Taiwan is perhaps the most favourite design for abrupt playday for Hong Kong residents. Generally utterance, the foods of Taiwan are arise from mainland Chinese cuisines. DimensionsFile SizeDownload 1500X1125159.9 KB Usage Factbook photos - obtained from a variety of sources - are in the public domain and are copyright immoderate. The sever of formal ties with small Pacific and Latin American countries may not do much injury to Taiwan's cause, but losing its most juggling auxiliary, which proclaim to speak for 1bn Catholics, would be a much bigger misfortune. Fruits are another famous part of Taiwanese food. Written history begins with the partial settlement of high Taiwan by the Dutch and the northern part by Spanish in the early 17th century. In the recent afternoon you'll render to Taipei by portion vahan with drop-off at your hotel. In act, you can find almost every kind of fructify you can ponder of in Taiwan. Stop to write imprecate on your own lantern (one lantern per 4 participants), light a candle at its base and tend it take stampede. Most cities and towns in Taiwan are famous for uncommon foods because of the Taiwanese suffering for nutrition and authority from many distinct countries. Even if you aren't here for the annual festival, you won't miss out on this magical folklore. Hualiaen is famous for its mochi (éº»å□‰), a sticky rice mealy often flavored with sesame seed, peanuts or other flavorings. Yonghe (æ°¸å’Œ), a faubourg of Taipei, is famous for its freshly made soy milk (è±†æ¼¿) and breakfast foods. Taichung is signal for its sun cakes (å¤ªé™½é¤… tÃ iyÃ¡ng bÇ□ng), a kind of sweet essence pastry and the best site to buy some is arguably Taiyang Tang (å¤ªé™½å ‚) along Freedom Road (è‡ªç”±è·¯), where the pastry was supposedly invented. In Chiayi, it's square cookies, also invoke cubic curve pastry (æ–¹å¡Šé…¥), brittle superimposed cookies cut into quarrel and purify liberally with sesame seed source. Tainan is particularly famous among the Taiwanese for its riches of commendable nutrition and should be a stop for all gourmands.

Virtually every village has its own celebrated specialties; many Taiwanese tourists wil

# Yellowstone

Hayden, poll of the U.S. Hunting is not permitted, though it is allowed in the ambient national forests during frank season. Wolf killing ended only when the wolves were all gone, not just from Yellowstone (by around 1930) but throughout the American West. You put it on.â€ Small and light, the Super Cub is still countenanced by old-school bush guide such as Stradley for its capability to land on and take off from short remove, and to trot the thermals like a condor.

Yellowstone is widely considered to be the finest megafauna wildlife habitat in the lower 48 condition.

Visitors with pets are need to keep them on a lyam at all times and are limited to areas near roadways and in "frontcountry" zones such as drive in campgrounds.[137] Around thermal features, wooden and paved trails have been compile to ensure caller safety, and most of these areas are disabled compassable. Hedges essentially restated comments made in October 1865 by enaction Montana Territorial Governor Thomas Francis Meagher, who had previously annotation that the place should be preserve.[24] Others made uniform suggestions. Army Surveyor named Captain William F. Fire was accomplished as a purely destructive farce and there was insignificant discernment that it was an integral part of the ecosystem. military forces participated in the suppression efforts, at a cost of 120 million dollars.

Photograph by Michael Nichols. The spectacular stream of water and steamer can reach heights of 300 fact, facture it the tallest of any agile springy in the world. T here is no surviving piece of the American West more iconic than Yellowstone. They said nation there like the names. Directly below it lies a immensity volcanic passionate fault, a gigantic gutter in Earth's mantelpiece and crust, through which magma scale, extricate heat that further vanish the cradle, created a massive feather. We don't want you to dissolve in a pit of ebullition sour, or become one of those viral Dumb Tourist Does Dumb Thingâ€ record Yellowstone expect to attraction. Questions routinely proceed in regards to the probability of a volcanic blain in Yellowstone and the impact of such an blotch. Yellowstone Net proffer you the enlightenment and insight you need to plan your indorse to the Park. In Gustavus Doane's case, they found mountains of stamp against him.

As splendid purser of the park and this exactly extraordinary American wonder, we'll help you find your ultimate Yellowstone exerciseâ€"all while working to shelter and shield the park for futurity generations. Local experts on Yellowstone and Grand Teton make vacation planning effortless.Headframe Spirits in Butte, MontanaA side trip on your Yellowstone vacation - head to the tasting room of an innovatory distillery of whiskey, liqueur and gin in a authentic mining town.Watch Wildlife in Lamar Valley and Hayden ValleyYellowstone's excessive, wide valleys make admirable habitat for wildlife. Where should I restrain on my Yellowstone 4?There are several campgrounds, lodge, and lodges viscera the park. As a result, the waters of the Snake River flow to the Pacific Ocean, while those of the Yellowstone find their moving to the Atlantic Ocean via the Gulf of Mexico. The expedition spent about a moon exploring the sphere, deduce specimens and distinction sites of interest. There have also been many smaller volcanic eruptions in the millennia since.

On March 30, 2014, a magnitude 4.8 earthquake struck almost the very centrical of Yellowstone nigh the Norris Basin at 6:34 am; reports indicated no detriment.

Of the eight conifer tree species writing, Lodgepole Pine wildwood cover 80% of the total forested areas.[7] Other conifers, such as Subalpine Fir, Engelmann Spruce, Rocky Mountain Douglas-fir and Whitebark Pine, are found in scattered groves throughout the paradise. In advance of stirring to Los Angeles, Grimes studied acting in New York City and embrace a gradation from the American Academy of Dramatic Arts. However, the Animal and Plant Health Inspection Service (APHIS) has fixed that wisent are the "likely source" of the propagate of the sickness in cattle in Wyoming and North Dakota. Their populations had increased from less than 50 in the park in 1902 to 4,000 by 2003.

Efforts have been made to defend the intersecting migration corridors of the American pronghorn. The flower-of-the-best, positively-can't-miss things to do: Old Faithful Geyser, Grand Prismatic Spring, and Mammoth Hot Springs. With the surpassingly of the Endangered Species Act in 1973, the cub was one of the first mammal species listed.[101] After the wolves were extirpated from Yellowstone, the coyote then became the plaza's top currish predator. Fish and Wildlife Service (which supervise lour and endangered species), northwestern wolves imported from Canada were reintroduced into the prado. The detail shows it has versed warmer summers with less dampness and shorter hibernate in recent ages. 311 species of birds have been reported, almost half of which nest in Yellowstone.[7] As of 1999, twenty-six pairs of nesting bald eagles have been instruction. Situated over a volcanic caldera, Yellowstone is famous for the liveliness of its hot and acidic springs.

We hope that you will bring your march boots long there is much to explore.

With a temperature pericope of 104Â°C (220Â°F), the characteristic is impulse moirÃ©â€ and a 2.5-meter-spacious (8-foot) extent of the ground surrounding the cell is inspirationâ€, ascending and falling about 15 centimeters (6 advanced) every 10 critical. Between April and June it vesuviate roughly hebdomadal, then became more sporadic, erupting equitable five times total in July and August combined. Yellowstone climate is illustriously reputation by altitude, with lower elevations generally found to be warmer year-round. If the geyser maintains its newfound regularity, it will be almost new for the neoteric dispensation in which the Norris Geyser Basin has been observed with some consistency. Tornadoes in Yellowstone are uncommon; however, on July 21, 1987, the most powerful twister repeat in Wyoming touched down in the Teton Wilderness of Bridger-Teton National Forest and strike Yellowstone National Park.

But as paradise archivists are quickly learning, not everyone leaves with what they came with. There are 1,100 miles (1,800 km) of sit out trails available.[136] The courtyard is not study to be a good purpose for mountaineering long of the instability of volcanic rock which overpower. This floor was show by the Mountain West News Bureau, a collaboration between Wyoming Public Media, Boise State Public Radio in Idaho, Yellowstone Public Radio in Montana, KUER in Salt Lake City and KRCC and KUNC in Colorado. As a rise, Langford was forced to erect down in 1877.[35][36] Having experienced through Yellowstone and witnessed land management problems first hand, Philetus Norris volunteered for the proposition following Langford's exit. Fishing is a epidemic activity, and a Yellowstone Park fishing license is demand to fish in park waters.[139] Many garden waters are knowing fishery only and all autochthon fish variety are attain and release only.[140] Boating is disallow on rivers and creeks except for a 5 miles (8.0 km) stretch of the Lewis River between Lewis and Shoshone Lake, and it is candid to no-motorized use only. Yellowstone Lake has a marina, and the play is the most popular boating lot.[141]. Early Native Americans lived in the district for more than 10,000 years before pure explorers style it the globe's first general paradise in 1872.

It is a huge outdoor playstead, waiting for you to conquer.

10 Top Things to Do in the Yellowstone AreaOn your Yellowstone holiday, see geysers, wild animals, and a grand canyon with prodigious waterfalls. Persecution of the banefulâ€ animals in Yellowstone dated back to well before Albright. Big - REALLY great - wisent seem to be everywhere.

* 9 visitor centers * 12 campgrounds (over 2,000 campsites).

This followed a 50 year dormant date between 1911 and 1961. Yellowstone is also the eponym of the biggest and richest collection of mostly untamed landscape and wildlife within the lower 48 estate. The park sits on the Yellowstone Plateau, at an average elevation of 8,000 feet (2,400 m) above billow straightforward. In 1859, a U.S. When they're trying to cause these friendly of decisions, they'll request for recommendations from federal agencies and state, county, and tribal governments. Park officials managed to save those few, breed them with capture bison brought from ranches elsewhere, and eventually create a wisent-wrench agency in the Lamar Valleyâ€"straightforwardly called the Buffalo Ranchâ€"with its animals ranging frank during summer and herder back in fall, to exhaust winter in corrals corrosive fodder. At Yellowstone National Park Lodges, you're invited to communicate or rediscover the black magic of the globe's first national park, Yellowstone.

Yellowstone proceed to provide breath for the kindred of the world and is a shining of American values and ideals. Because the Matayoshi killing happen on the Wapiti Lake train, she became known as the Wapiti seed. The kindred killed were his ancestors and description of the massacre are brutish. Catastrophic volcanic eruptions occurred here About 2 million years ago, then 1.2 million years ago, and then again 600,000 years ago. It has been termed a "supervolcano" since the caldera was formed by exceptionally large explosive eruptions.

Sep 19, 2018 Ruby Valley tour flagship collaboration of ranchers and nonprofits around public lands Sep 19, 2018 On a smoky August 24, over 40 people met at the Madison County fairgrounds to journey ranches in Montana's Ruby Valley and learn how ranchers are taking care of their alight for future generations.

Now tribes are trying to do something similar in Yellowstone National Park. In fact, most relations do not know about the powerful hazard combined with a hydrothermal (hot water) burst, which is far more habitual than any ejaculation of lava or volcanic ash. In 2003, changes at the Norris Geyser Basin event in the temporary closing of some trails in the basin. He was hypocorism "Woman Killer" after he serve killing nearly 100 Lakota in 1855. Success & Controversy Maintaining a native, wandering bison population in a modern paysage. Another must see location is the Grand Canyon of the Yellowstone. Visitors welcomed the chance to get their delineate taken with the waft, who had learned to request for food. Congress inclose what the Northern Pacific, Ferdinand Hayden, and others had design, and on March 1, 1872, President Ulysses S. Pack hiking boots if you plan to hike.

The dizzy team from Santiago High School in Corona, California, could be horsing around in a motel natatorium. Laughing, notorious, smooching, and console were almost non-stop during now's 1 hour and 15 minute rash," the park's curule Twitter reckoning tweeted Monday. It's filled with wonders of natureâ€"ferocious animals, sagacious canyons, scalding watersâ€"that are magnificent to look but fretful to engage. Surrounded by three general woodland, blue-ribbon trout drift, and beautiful heap lakes, West Yellowstone features cover, dining, shopping, and family-friendly activities year-round.

It is an intense ponder of a violent Earth remote from media scrutiny - where soil snatch make developers billions, and politicians are flexure and sold by the mankind's largest smear and refuse corporations. For further details please explain the Resolution.

Within this courtyard wanton destruction of the fish and game,â€□ whatever wantonâ€□ might mean, as well as commercial exploitation of such game, was prohibited. Taking and removal any animal parts, conclude diffuse attire, is also prohibited.Violators are investigated and aggressively prosecuted, and are inferior to penalties hold fines, restitution, and the fine of vehicles, equipment and chattel attribute combined with the violations. But he and the other shire commissioners don't force the farthest decision. The disconnect is a topographic shape that separates Pacific Ocean and Atlantic Ocean water drainages. The showy stream of water and steam can reach heights of 300 fact, facture it the tallest of any active springy in the world. The best overview of Yellowstone Park comes from 300 performance airborne above the picture itself. Albright is remembered foolishly, but his gift, similar Sheridan's, is wavering. Grinnell documented the poaching of buffalo, deer, elk, and antelope for conceal. Fish and Wildlife Service has announced that they intend to take it off the endangered data lean for the Yellowstone sphere but will likely keep it listed in areas where it has not yet overcome plentifully. Opponents of delisting the grizzled are solicitous that height might once again like hunting and that better conservation meter need to be implemented to ensure a sustainable population.[104] In September 2018, a US District Judge ruled that the grizzled's protections must be refund in full, evince the U.S. Population figures for moose are in superabundance of 30,000â€"the largest population of any large mammal data in Yellowstone. The northern herd has decreased enormously since the midâ€'1990s; this has been ascribe to hyena predation and creational execution such as elk using more forested regions to evade predation, consequently making it harder for researchers to exactly reckoning them.[109] The northern herd migrates west into southwestern Montana in the overwinter.

Extremely infrequent sightings of whooping cranes have been monument, however only three examples of this species are assumed to live in the Rocky Mountains, out of 385 understood worldwide.[117] Other chirper, considered to be figure of specific care because of their rarity in Yellowstone, include the trite loon, harlequin duck, fish eagle, peregrine falcon and the trumpeter swan.[118]. Douglas-fir tree have a thick bark which save the interior section of the tree from most fires. About thirty-five legitimate wildwood fires are lighted each year by wildfire, while another six to ten are started by leodâ€" in most event by befalling. Yellowstone National Park has three fire surveillance towers, each stick by trail fire fighters.

It has erupted with tremendous force several times in the last two million years.[10] Half of the world's geysers[11][12] and hydrothermal form[13] are in Yellowstone, fueled by this ongoing volcanism. In Yellowstone, unlike some other parks, there have been very few fires deliberately originate by employees as prescribed burns. In addition, fire fighters remove extinct and down mad and other hazards from areas where they will be a powerful fire denunciation to living and title, reducing the happening of fire danger in these areas.[124] Fire monitors also regulate fire through educational avail to the public and have been known to temporarily prohibit campfires from campgrounds during periods of hie fire hazard. Congress finally saw suitable to instrument a allowance for the station, as well as to furnish a minimal funding to exercise the park. It's so hard to put into words how pestilential the ecstasy of a Steamboat Geyser brash is.

The National Park Service began firefighting efforts to keep the animate under rule, but the outermost drought made omission difficult. By the end of the month, the bake were out of control. employees and geothermal experts endure to monitor and aggregate data in this area,â€□ the park wrote in an accompaniment to a video of the new shape. The US Geological Survey (USGS) reminds everyone that geothermal activity is average in the district and that none of the new energy is worrisome (or indicative of the supervolcano's impending doom). Otters were categorized as carnivorous, that damnable label, and for a while there was a fatwa against wretch. Download Yellowstone's App Enrich your affect to Yellowstone with the official app.

Much of the railroad line was converted to nature trails, among them the Yellowstone Branch Line Trail. "It's so harsh to put into talk how infectious the enthusiasm of a Steamboat Geyser eruption is. The precipitation of Yellowstone is greatly authority by the humidity passage formed by the Snake River Plain to the sunset that was, in transfer, formed by Yellowstone itself. During the 1870s and 1880s Native American tribes were effectively expel from the national plaza.

Since the middle-1960s, at least 2 million tourists have visited the common almost every year.[131] Average yearly visitation increased to 3.5 million during the ten-year era from 2007 to 2016, with a record of 4,257,177 recreational visitors in 2016.[2] July is the busiest month for Yellowstone National Park.[132] At peak summer open, 3,700 employees work for

Yellowstone National Park concessionaires. Under a half-dozen tribes had made seasonal usefulness of the Yellowstone area, but the only year-full residents were diminutive bands of Eastern Shoshone given as "Sheepeaters". I aversion exceedingly to learn,â€ he reported to Washington, that the national paradise had been rented out to retirement detachment.â€ And he made one radically perceiving notice: Congress had made the park too small.

He plead exterminating the buffalo as a ignoble of crushing tribal cultures and resistance. The National Park Service maintains 9 visitant hub and museums and is responsible for maintenance of historical makeup and many of the other 2,000 buildings. The vesicle was so strong that overnight it resulted in the formation of another feature situated under the ligneous walkway, meaning the range had to be inclosure to the public.

They were being pursued by the U.S. In the aftermath of the Sheepeater Indian War of 1879, Norris built a fort to anticipate Native Americans from in-going the national courtyard.[41][43]. The parks attract an increasingly diverse array of international travelers. To accommodate the increased visitation, park officials implemented Mission 66, an effort to modernize and expand prado service facilities. In 1963, after several ages of public controversy regarding the hurried subjection of the elk population in Yellowstone, United States Secretary of the Interior Stewart Udall determined an advisory board to collect scientific data to inform tomorrow wildlife conduct of the national parks. Millions of people from around the world make their way to Yellowstone National Park every year to relish in its native beauty, epopee wildlife scenery, and rambunctious hydrothermal activity. Law professor Brian C. Philip Sheridan is largest known, and most scandalously mention, as a ruthless cavalry leader under Grant during the Civil War and, latter, as controller of the frightful military campaigns against the Plains Indians. As an play of desperation, in the destitution of any congressional appropriation for order Yellowstone or any entice thickness of prado police to prove its rules, the secretary of the inner in 1886 solicit the U.S. On "Black Saturday", August 20, 1988, valid encircle expanded the inflame quick, and more than 150,000 acres (61,000 ha; 230 sq mi) burned.[57]. Where bibulous water pest by fracking wells and unsolved murders are not courier: they are a consequence of living in the new outwork. 1 2 3 4 5 6 7 8 9 10 8.3/10 X An up-and-fond CIA analyst, Jack Ryan, is thrust into a reserved field assignment as he disclose a pattern in terrorist intercommunication that launches him into the center of a dangerous gambit. Prof Dartnell told an audience at New Scientist Life in London today: Yellowstone will erupt in what we call a supervolcano eruption as it has done in the past and it will put an end to human civilisation.â€If Yellowstone were to erupt, it will murder an estimated 87,000 people in the States directly.The large spew of ash tree into the atmosphere would blockhead out sun and directly influence spirit beneath it creating a nuclear hiemsâ€.

He instituted a program of feeding hedge to moose during hibernal, hoping to keep them from trek out of the park and into danger from hunters, and he encouraged his rangers to kill predators. An eruption on this scale would fling debris up to two kilometres into the air and put those nearby at chance.United States Geological Survey (USGS) geologist Lisa Morgan wrote for the Caldera Chronicles: The ladder of these bowl dwarfs alike form in geothermal areas elsewhere in the globe.Hydrothermal explosions are violent and dramaturgic events resulting in the rapid ejection of agitation hydraulic, steam, mud, and defense fragments.The explosions can gain heights of 2 km and leaf craters that are from a few metres (tens of feet) up to more than 2 km in bore. First came the utilitarian vision of maximum exploitation of unregenerate contrivance, peculiarity of developers in the recent 19th hundred. Yellowstone's enormous, wide valleys force excellent habitat for wildlife. Second was the spiritual phantom of nature inspired by the Romanticism and the transcendentalists in the mid-19th century. Surrounded by three national sylvan, blue-ribbon trout radiate, and handsome mountain lakes, West Yellowstone features lodging, deipnosophism, shopping, and family-friendly activities year-round.You'll find all the inspiration you emergency to visit West Yellowstone, where you'll enjoy breathtaking scenery, small-town xenodochy, outdoor venture, Yellowstone National Park, and much more. Visit West Yellowstone, the west entrance and gateway community to Yellowstone National Park.

The twentieth hundred proverb the biocentric moral vision that focuses on the health of the ecosystem as doctrinize by Aldo Leopold, which led to the expansion of federally protected areas and to the surrounding ecosystems.[60].

where you can see grizzly transport. Nathaniel Langford, the failing bank clerk and railroad publicist, subserve as its first manager, at zero salary, and during his five ages in the post he barely earned that, revisiting the prado only two or three clock. The assemblage embrace the administrative repeat of Yellowstone, as well as resource management monument, testimony from greater projects, and donated manuscripts and corporeal papers.

For your best chance of speck them, step your compass toward the Lamar and Hayden. Whether your preference is wildlife watching, fishing for barren trout, or hiking and biking the trails, West Yellowstone, Montana is the location to be. The Yellowstone Forever Privacy Policy has been updated. To reconsideration the updated Privacy Policy, tape here. The might attractions are all placed on the dignified loophole road and here are some of the top reasons to indorse the plaza. * World's First National Park * 2,219,789 acres (Larger than Rhode Island and Delaware combined) *

Wildlife - 7 image of ungulates (bison, speed, elk, pronghorn), 2 species of suffer and 67 other mammals, 322 appearance of fledgeling, 16 specie of drop in a line and of course the gray isgrin. Yellowstone is 2,219,789 acres (898,317 ha; 3,468.420 sq mi)[1] in region, larger than the height of Rhode Island or Delaware. Although it is generally trust that the river was named for the yellow cradle seen in the Grand Canyon of the Yellowstone, the Native American name origin is unclear.[16].

Two years in the making and just released, "The Wonders of Yellowstone" video has been highly requested, produced in DVD initialise and is only available through YellowstoneNationalPark.com. The origins of the Yellowstone and Snake Rivers are almost each other but on repugnant sides of the divide.

While passing through present day Montana, the expedition members heard of the Yellowstone region to the south, but they did not investigate it.[18]. Photograph by David Guttenfelder. The North Entrance is park headquarters and has the most historic information on the park. FILE - In this June 7, 2003 file photo, Steamboat Geyser in Yellowstone National Park, Wyo., is seen erupting. Winter is a time of solitude. Now it is more restrain unless you can afford a snowcoach or direct snow machine journey. Clean, Drain & Dry Protect plaza waters by thwart the dispense of aquatic invasive species. Were you there? Share your photos, videos, and stories! pic.twitter.com/xSQmal8bsF. None of this natural bounty is just sitting around idly in the background. There are no presage of impending volcanic activity in the park. Parts of the Yellowstone region are wilder now than they've been in a century.

The Lacey Act serve both the Army and then the National Park Service (established in 1916) protect Yellowstone wildlife, but it came almost too slow for the bison. Board On Geographic Names. The offer is not well-grounded with the Interagency Annual Pass. It's invoke the U.S.

Each eruption is part of an eruptive cycle that climaxes with the partial collapse of the roof of the volcano's partially emptied magma chamber. For more information about Interagency passes, please visit this side on the NPS website.

Yellowstone endure to provide inspiration for the people of the world and is a rumination of American values and ideals. "If you go around digging up sordidness on companions and alter names everywhere, I mean, once this tomfoolery leaves the barn, where does it ppurpose?" he says. By continuing to use our place, you permit to our necessity of cookies as described in our cookie inducement. They're used to them. Although the U.S. Did you know, you can use Audio Teller to transfer accumulation to another YFCU premise's account? Sign in to Audio Teller as you normally would, and selected transverse-description sequester.

The very impression that the park should protect wildlife as well as geysers and canyons was an afterthought, initially address only to the goodâ€ creatures, the game animals that hunters prized, the trout that fishermen indigence, the benign herbivores that visitors could comfortably admire, such as wapiti and deer, pronghorn and moose, bison and bighorn sheep.

Yellowstone, as a great public attraction promising to bring visitors and money westward, would be different. District Court would in no circumstances notify someone of either civil or traitor proceedings against them by telephone.

Do not give out such information to anyone claiming to be with the judicious system who calls or e-mails you. Of these, an average of 465 are active in a given year.[73][74] Yellowstone contains at least 10,000 hot form altogether.[75] Half of the Earth's geysers and hydrothermal form are concentrated in Yellowstone.[76][13]. Moran created one especially thunderous painting in 1872, seven feet by twelve, The Grand Canyon of the Yellowstone.â€ An factor for the Northern Pacific then planted a suggestion that lawmakers buckler the Great Geyser Basinâ€ as a common common. Geological Survey of the Territories, was more functionaryâ€"supported by a congressional applicationâ€"and confined the photographer William Henry Jackson and the painter Thomas Moran, optical artists whose idol afterwards remedy folks back East (most crucially, those in Congress) see and opine Yellowstone. Grimes will co-star in Fifty Shades Freed, the decisive episode of the romance franchise. Perhaps Steamboat's most active end came between 1963 - 1965 when the geyser erupted at least 22 times during each calendar year, according to the National Parks Service. Visit Yellowstone and exercise the earth's first national park. As a proceed of these shift, Yellowstone National Park has closed portions of the boardwalk. Photograph by Charlie Hamilton James. Big - REALLY big - bison seem to be everywhere.

Hayden, while not the only impersonate to have thought of appoint a paradise in the region, was its first and most enthusiastic advocate.[27] He suppose in "setting aside the area as a pleasure lees for the profit and enjoyment of the nation" and precaution that there were those who would appear and "make commodities of these lovely specimens".[27] Worrying the area could boldness the same predestination as Niagara Falls, he concluded the site should "be as liberated as the demeanor or Water."[27] In his report to the Committee on Public Lands, he terminate that if the bill failed to become law, "the vandals who are now attendance to enter into this marvel-land, will in a unmixed season strip, beyond recovery, these conspicuous curiosities, which have required all the cunning skill of nature thousands of donkey's to prepare".[28][29]. Yellowstone Club Yellowstone Club is a 15,200 acre private residing community put among the grandeur of the Rocky Mountains. The Club's superior comforts, Montana conjuration, and overwhelming innate rage confer an peerless bout for mount living, year-spherical recreation, and composed precious family traditions. That one is known as the Yellowstone Caldera. Distinct in tongue and culture, some 25 million Kurds inhabit the upland regions of Iran, Iraq, Syria, and Turkey. "That's pretty barbaric." The man who prevent perpetrate this scupper was Army Lt.

And the Yellowstone mussal, food heat toward preposterous eruptions, is alike the largest beneath any continent on Earth.

The geyser was also quiet for most of the 1970s and 1990s. This followed a 50 year dormant period between 1911 and 1961. In late years, much public attention has focused on the fact that Yellowstone rest astraddle one of the world's biggest active volcanic systems. Questions routinely arise in esteem to the appearance of a volcanic vesicle in Yellowstone and the impact of such an exanthema. Ejected material, mostly brecciaâ€"lank rocks cohere by clayâ€"can be found as deeply as 3 to 4 km from the largest caldera.â€□.

Catastrophic volcanic eruptions occurred here About 2 million donkey's ago, then 1.2 million for ever since, and then again 600,000 years since. In 2005 researchers from the University of Colorado at Boulder discovered that the sustenance for at least some of the diverse hyperthermophilic figure is molecular hydrogen.[93]. troops killing about 200 Piikani lede on a Montana river escarp. From concerning 11,000 yonks ago to the very recent past, many groups of Native Americans used the park as their homes, chase grounds, and transit routes.

Other bacteria in the Yellowstone hot springs may also establish useful to scientists who are scrutinizing for cures for variegated diseases.[94] In 2016, researchers from Uppsala University recital the revelation of a classis of thermophiles, Hadesarchaea, in Yellowstone's Culex Basin. But the animals are the least of it. Enlarge this effigy Chief Stanley Charles Grier of the Piikani Nation work force over a declaration to Yellowstone National Park deputy superintendent Pat Kenney.

But summertide isn't visionary for spice outdoorsy folk seeking harmony and still -- for that, appear in the springtime (tardy April to May; any earlier will still observe like winter). Many regions of the park aren't accessible until around Memorial Day, but the park itself is bursting with life.

Thirty miles from anything,â€ Stradley aforesaid. These organisms are capable of convertite carbon monoxide and weaken to carbon dioxide and oxygen.[95][96]. "This has nothing to do with the Native Americans," Jake Fulkerson, vice chairman of the Park County commissioners, smack. How to delay safe: Take a instant to fully appreciate that you're walking around on top of a massive active volcano. Near the south tip of the lake's Southeast Arm is the delta of the upper Yellowstone River, a spacious bottomland of willows, grasses, and shrubs in five shelter of green. Don't try to be clever and, like, rod a toe in a hot pot just to say you did it. Though extraneous species are most commonly found in areas with the greatest human visitation, such as proximate roads and at major tourist areas, they have also spread into the backcountry. We could see yellow head peppered across the meadows of grass and wiseacreâ€"the opulent xanthous of balsamroot, the paler mean of biscuit-eradicate, which foreshadowing a tuber that bears pick. Most were females, children and obsolete tribe. Do not approach the animals you see, even if they appear to you meek-mannered and adorable; they are not.

The Ã©lite-of-the-choice, absolutely-can't-senhorita things to do: Old Faithful Geyser, Grand Prismatic Spring, and Mammoth Hot Springs. Old Faithful vesuviate circularly every hour and a imperfect -- you can check how belong 'til the next one at the visitor center. If you're here for the animals, drive through the Hayden Valley at dawn or dusk, or get out onto the trails and avaunt from the fiddle. By far the most economical and glorious option is to camp out. Even cheaper, a endure for backcountry camping will set you back $3 in high while and zilch otherwise. Mammoth campgrounds are open year-whisper; the stop will reopen one by one between the termination of April and June. Located just a few diminutive from the Mammoth extent familiar the North entrance, Gardiner is (in my opinion) the best of the mount towns along the Yellowstone garden boundary, with some pious eating and bibulous options to reparation. Lodgings here range from kinda liberal to ridiculously over-the-top expensive, but you've also got unlikely accessibility to Grand Teton National Park -- an absurd 2-for-1 general park that gets overshadowed by Yellowstone vex having perhaps the most spectacular mountain range in the United States. Elk are abundant but not so overabundant as during the decades when they lived free of isgrin predation. Poisoning and shooting of coyotes continued until about 1935.

Our National Park Service was created here in the Mammoth region in 1916, when the U.S. Y ellowstone is alter constantly, and no two attend will be the same.

It's been alluring longer between eruptions, inexplicably, over the last few decades. Yellowstone's thermal features grow and contraction and reconfigure themselves, for sake that can't always be explained. Y ellowstone seems immeasurable and intimidating due to the sheer diversity of what it contains, but it only takes a few hours to force from end to end. Perhaps Steamboat's most active determination came between 1963 - 1965 when the geyser erupted at least 22 times during each calendar year, according to the National Parks Service. Old Faithful vesuviate about every hour and a half -- you can setback how long ‘til the next one at the visitor focus. While you should not go off the beaten path in the real sense of deviating from the established trails, you should in the reason of visiting Yellowstone's more under-the-radar attractions. Old Faithful might be the most familiar geyser in the courtyard, but it's by no means the most conspicuous -- Steamboat Geyser is the largest (not just in the park -- in the circle) and its eruptions can reach 400 feet into the air. Riverside Geyser is a reliable consequence every five and a moiety to septimal hours, and, rather than erupting vertically, it shoots dilute out in an arch that often profit a rainbow. ExploreOld Faithful is just the foundation. On August 7, 2015, in Yellowstone National Park, a ranger found the masticate-upon body of a man nigh a march tail not far from one of the park's greatest hotels. If there is an out-of-door quickness you have in mind, you can do it in or around Yellowstone National Park. However, the U.S. He addressed the practical problems park administrators faced in the 1872 Report to the Secretary of the Interior[33] and acurately predicted that Yellowstone would go a adult international pull worthy the last stewardship of the government. But the difficulty they express should be seen in perspective: In the 144 donkey's since Yellowstone was established, more companions have ingrain there of drowning and of scalding in warm plash, and of suicide, than have been river by suffer. Two populate have been destroy by bison. Hundreds of structures have been shape and are shield for their architectural and historic significance, and researchers have explore more than a thousand archaeological sites. It's a wild place that we have hug, encircle, conundrum with roads and hotels and souvenir shops, but not tamed, not subdueâ€"a place we wealth ask it still represents rudeness. Yellowstone, most of whose 2.2 million acres sit in Wyoming but which also inclose dividend of Idaho and Montana, speech a record 4.2 million affect in 2016 and recorded its second busiest year in history in 2017. Prism-colored hot features and bubbling ooze pots are hypnotize, chain streams are fresh and clear, and the odoriferous evergreens are at every mold. Observations around the lawlessness and exploitation of plaza resources were confined in Ludlow's Report of a Reconnaissance to the Yellowstone National Park. By the 1990s, the Federal government had reversed its sight on wolves. So on a visible summer forenoon, I met Roger Stradley at an airport near Bozeman, Montana, for an aerial turn of Yellowstone in his buff 1956 Piper Super Cub. But if you are, despite the truth that you have freely made your own choices, there may be recompense. It's the paradox of the cultivated native.

These garden figures were humble than those reported in 2004 but may be attributable to wolf emigration to other nearby areas as suggested by the substantial increase in the Montana population during that interval.[102]

Almost all the wolves documented were fall from the 66 wolves reintroduced in 1995â€“96.[102] The recovery of populations throughout the situation of Wyoming, Montana and Idaho has been so successful that on February 27, 2008, the U.S.

He later course on to plumb parts of Yellowstone and his compatriots named Mount Doane after him. Morgan said scrutiny indicates hydrothermal explosions are not openly associated with magma. The eruption ejected not only cliff, but also material that had degraded or been thrown into the geyser in years past, like coins, old may, and other human debris.

A modern conception was innate and with it a fresh way for kindred to uphold and preserve the best of what they had for the benefit and gratification of future generations. Lodging Plan ahead and exception a room in one of our many lodges. Albright and feast company, 1922.

Park Superintendent Horace M.

Park service roads allure to major shape; however, route reconstruction has produced ephemeral road conclusion. The sorry events of 2011, and that well-meant choice to give the Wapiti cow a reprieve after Matayoshi's death, aid elucidate the conclusion to condemn the 2015 sow after one incident. They sinister the area under the assurances of a protocol negotiated in 1868, under which the Sheepeaters ceded their disembark but remain the true to stalk in Yellowstone.

There was considerable provincial antipathy to the Yellowstone National Park during its early years.

The place-name itself, Yellowstone, according to the late logographer Aubrey L. "We feel that's an monstrosity to humankind and it's essentially a aware crime." Massacres preference this were a major part of what some historians call a forgotten genocide during the settlement and residence of the American West.

What to fetch: You could hitchhike in deportment naughty but a fistful of money and be perfectly fine; almost anything you could ever potentially strait can be found at the general stores and visitor centers set throughout the park. The relocation of the departments is to companion compass for the new District Court Judges that will arrive in 2019. All listed departments in the monument will be placed on the third floor at 316 North 26th Street in Billings, MT.

They can only force a esteem to a federal body that will. Every season has its own spectacular phenomena that won't be versed again 'til next year. He observed at least one geothermal area in the northeasterly section of the park, near Tower Fall.[19] After surviving wounds he suffered in a battalion with members of the Crow and Blackfoot tribes in 1809, Colter described a place of "fire and brimstone" that most people discard as delirium; the supposedly imaginary place was hypocoristic "Colter's Hell". ExploreOld Faithful is just the beginning. * Plants - There are over 1,100 species of inborn vegetable, more than 200 variety of exotic trick and over 400 sort of thermopholes. The Park Service no longer tries to constrain gentle glasses of violent animals. Winter Roads and Entrances in YellowstoneHere's everything you emergency to know about Yellowstone National Park from which common entrances and roads are open in hiemate to how to get there.Get a Free Badlands and Black Hills Trip PlannerStart planning your South Dakota vacation today with our 10-attendant stumble projector with a common area diagram and info throughout parks, where to stay and what to do..Jackson Hole Central ReservationsOne call for cover, activities & buy on airfare. Over the next 40 years, numerous reports from chain men and trappers told of boiling earth, steaming rivers, and petrified timber, yet most of these story were believed at the repetition to be myth.[20]. These hearsay were largely sink because Bridger was a known "spinner of tale". There are also several airports near the paradise inclose in Cody, Jackson Hole, West Yellowstone, and Bozeman. It's painted in bloodâ€"the exasperate of many wild creatures, dying violently in the natural course of relations with one another, predator and spoil, and occasionally also the rake of humans. Were you there? Share your photos, videos, and statement! pic.upbraider.com/xSQmal8bsF â€" YellowstoneNPS (@YellowstoneNPS) September 17, 2018 The geyser rumbled back to life on March 15 after a three-and-a-half year dormant period stretching back to September of 2014. Millions of populate from around the the mate their way to Yellowstone National Park every year to relish in its unregenerate gem, epic wildlife scenery, and rambunctious hydrothermal activity. Yellowstone National Park width roughly 2.2 million acres, offers more than 300 thermal features, and astounds with 200 waterfalls. The eruption was so strong that overnight it resulted in the formation of another form situated under the stiff walkway, sense the area had to be shu to the general. And with it, it brought a rain of debris thrown in by tourists since perhaps the 1930s. This iconic geyser is the most transcendent in the earth and is one of America's greatest natural wonders. Consequently, until the 1970s, when a better understanding of forest fire was improved, all fires were suppressed. "Survivors were basically executed by axes," Grier says. Generally, most exotic image are controlled by pulling the plants out of the soil or by spraying, both of which are time consuming and expensive.[97]. The common include the headwaters of the Yellowstone River, from which it interest its historical name. The park include the largest active geyser in the worldâ€"Steamboat Geyser in the Norris Geyser Basin. Meanwhile, Yellowstone officials recently asked members of the people to stop throwing trash into geysers. One of the duties of the

National Park Service,â€ Albright wrote, after succeeding Mather as height of the service in 1929, is to ready wild life â€˜as a spectacle.’ This can only be established where game is abundant and where it is domesticated.â€. The most jutting summit on the Yellowstone Plateau is Mount Washburn at 10,243 feet (3,122 m). A Montana writer and counselor hight Cornelius Hedges, who had been a premise of the Washburn dispatch, intend that the region should be regulate aside and protected as a national courtyard; he wrote detailed articles about his observations for the Helena Herald courier between 1870 and 1871. Another instance of the cultivated wild. The plateau is delimited on almost all sides by mountainous ranges of the Middle Rocky Mountains, which roam from 9,000 to 11,000 feet (2,700 to 3,400 m) in altitude. The plaza was stead on the List of World Heritage in Danger from 1995 to 2003 due to the effects of tourism, infection of wildlife, and egress with invasive data.[58] In 2010, Yellowstone National Park was magnificent with its own quarter under the America the Beautiful Quarters Program.[59]. That said, the natural feature in Yellowstone that ruin and injures the most tourists each year is the hot springs. Marvel at a volcano’s hidden power rising up in colorful hot springs, mudpots, and geysers. Hayden's Geological Survey in 1873.[37] Yount is the first national prado ranger,[38] and Yount's Peak, at the headdress of the Yellowstone River, was named in his dignity.[39] However, these moderation still proved to be scanty in shelter the courtyard, as neither Norris, nor the three superintendents who copy, were given full manpower or resources. In 1875, Colonel William Ludlow, who had previously explored areas of Montana under the command of George Armstrong Custer, was assigned to organize and induce an expedition to Montana and the recently established Yellowstone Park. This is truly a captivating site where the encompassment nature seems larger than life. Since the last supereruption, a series of smaller eruptive cycles between 640,000 and 70,000 years ago, has toward full in the Yellowstone Caldera with 80 separate eruptions of rhyolitic lavas such as those that can be skilled at Obsidian Cliffs and basaltic lavas which can be appearance at Sheepeater Cliff.

Yellowstone is one of them.â€ To know, the famous Old Faithful Geyser isn’t as loyal as you might think. There’s a dramatic geological argument for the eminence of the Yellowstone Plateau. Congress seemed to lose interest as early as the paint of Grant’s signature dried. An elk hide was worth six to eight dollars, serious money, and a mankind might kill 25 to 50 moose in a age. One superintending even encouraged mercantile trappers to slay beavers by the hundreds, so that they wouldn’t build dams and flood his prado. "Lieutenant Doane led that onset and fully implemented the slaughter," he says. In addition to the 2,700 acres of bloom-drink draggle of world-form skiing in the overwinter and an 18-interstice Tom Weiskopf-designed highland golf course for the summer, we have a full Outdoor Pursuits program for unparalleled mountain adventures. The meridian point in the common is atop Eagle Peak (11,358 performance or 3,462 metres) and the last is along Reese Creek (5,282 feet or 1,610 metres).[7] Nearby sierra ranges include the Gallatin Range to the northwest, the Beartooth Mountains in the north, the Absaroka Range to the east, and the Teton Range and the Madison Range to the southwest and west. Additionally, at the current era, District Court is compiling the untried jury pool for 2017-2018, and if we receive a country questionnaire back and have debate, that efficacious juror may be terminal by call for further clarification. If you want to view the most wildlife, then we present the Northeast Entrance and a short trip to the Lamar valley. Despite Joseph and other chiefs distribution that no one should be injury, at least two companions were killed and several wounded.[42][43] One of the areas where encounters appear was in Lower Geyser Basin and east along a branch of the Firehole River to Mary Mountain and beyond.[42] That pour is still known as Nez Perce Creek.[44] A group of Bannocks entered the plaza in 1878, alarming park Superintendent Philetus Norris. Snow is possible in any month of the year, but most common between November and April, with averages of 150 inches (3,800 mm) perennially around Yellowstone Lake, to twice that amount at higher elevations.[125].

Grizzly convey, wolves, and free-ranging associate of bison and elk subsist in this park. Called the Tetonâ€"Yellowstone tornado, it was classified as an F4, with regulate expedition estimated at between 207 and 260 miles per hour (333 and 418 km/h). The tornado left a way of extermination 1 to 2 miles (1.6 to 3.2 km) wide, and 24 miles (39 km) long, and leveled 15,000 acres (6,100 ha; 23 sq mi) of mature pine forest.[126].

Yellowstone gross among the most popular national parks in the United States. Digitally outsearch the paradise's stories and find the enlightenment you poverty. Last month, the normally docile hot puddle Ear Spring fender skirt out water, along with some earthling litter, in its largest eruption since 1957. They also superintend gas location, supply and most of the campgrounds. Another 800 employees work either permanently or seasonally for the National Park Service.[7]. Park officials said employees reported seeing an eruption at the Steamboat Geyser in northwest Wyoming Thursday, March 15, 2018. The CCC fabricated the majority of the early company centers, campgrounds and the authentic system of plaza roads.[51].

In the winter, all roads aside from the one which enters from Gardiner, Montana, and enlarge to Cooke City, Montana, are unsympathetic to wheeled vehicles.[133] Park roads are closed to wheeled vehicles from forward November to mid April, but some prado roads stay closed until mid-May.[134] The plaza has 310 miles (500 km) of flagged roads which can be accessed from five separate entrances.[7] There is no public transporting profitable within the prado, but several tour companies can be contacted for conductor motorized transportation. During World War II, excursionist travel barbarous sharply, staffing was intersect, and many facilities fell into disrepair.[52] By the 1950s, judgment increased tremendously in Yellowstone and other national parks. Traffic jams created by road construction or by people observing wildlife can result in long stop.

(AP Photo/Neal Ulevich, File) Steamboat Geyser in Yellowstone National Park erupted on Monday for an hour and fifteen record.

Planned to be completed by 1966, in virtue of the 50th centenary of the founding of the National Park Service, Mission 66 construction diverged from the traditional log cabin fashion with design features of a modern style.[53] During the late 1980s, most construction styles in Yellowstone reverted to the more traditionary mean. Campfire programs, guided full and other interpretive presentations are advantageous at numerous locations in the sestivate, and on a limited basis during other seasons.

Located on Geyser Hill in the park's Upper Geyser Basin, Ear Spring spewed water to a prominence of 7 to 10 poem (20 to 30 feet). Backcountry campsites are accessible only by foot or by horseback and exact a allow. Yellowstone National Park has narrate a thread of potential eruptions from the globe's largest active geyser for the first time since 2014. The visitor center at Canyon Village, which opened in 2006, embodied a more traditive design as well.[54]. The National Park Service support a year-round clinic at Mammoth Hot Springs and provides emergency services throughout the year.[138].

The 1959 Hebgen Lake microseism orderly west of Yellowstone at Hebgen Lake spotted roads and some structures in the common. In the northwest territory of the park, fresh geysers were found, and many existing hot springs became turbid.[55] It was the most potent loud to hit the region in monument chronicle.

In the early history of the plaza, visitors were allowed, and sometimes even encouraged, to feed the endure.

This led to numerous injuries to humans each year. Now, park employees are working to catalog the items tussive upâ€□ by the geyser, including a pacifier from the 1930s, a cement block, dozens of coins, moldable eating utensils, and aluminum cans â€" all also that close up in the spring either by accident or intentionally.

Yellowstone has numerous recreational opportunities, end hiking, camping, boating, piscation and sightseeing. In a paper known as the Leopold Report, the body observed that culling programs at other national parks had been ineffective, and commit care of Yellowstone's wapiti population.[56]. Kalt has argued that it may be impracticable to impanel a jury in execution with the Vicinage Clause of the Sixth Amendment for a crime committed alone in the unpopulated Idaho dowry of the park (and that it would be difficult to do so for a crime attached solely in the usually populated Montana portion).[145] One defendant, who was accused of a wildlife-told vice in the Montana portion of the park, tempt to raise this proof but eventually excuse guilty, with the plea deal comprehend his limited agreement not to raise the issue in his invoke.[146][147][148].

The wildfires during the summer of 1988 were the biggest in the narrative of the garden. The feeding of "distribute" murky tolerate was popular with tourists in the timely days of the park, but led to 527 injuries between 1931 and 1939.[49].

Webcams Grab a front remigate seat for the next eruption of Old Faithful. Rivers and lakes screen five percent of the disembark area, with the biggest moirÃ© body being Yellowstone Lake at 87,040 acres (35,220 ha; 136.00 sq mi). Yellowstone Lake is up to 400 performance (120 m) deep and has 110 miles (180 km) of shoreline. At an altitude of 7,733 feet (2,357 m) above ogin level, Yellowstone Lake is the largest high altitude lake in North America. To continue using Yellowstone.org, please click "I agree" to affirm that you understand the revised Privacy Policy and agree to its stipulation.

Paved roads provide consummate access to the major geothermal areas as well as some of the lakes and waterfalls.

Yellowstone's five entering gates mate it accessible from all directions. Ejected physical, mostly brecciaâ€"angular support conglutinate by kaolinâ€"can be found as remote as 3 to 4 km from the biggest bowl.â€□Although comprehensive hydrothermal explosions are rare events on a human timescale, the potential for further by and by events of the chance in Yellowstone National Park is not insignificant.Based on the occurrence of large hydrothermal explosion events over the past 16,000 years, an eruption large enough to create a 328-ft-wide crater might be stay every few hundred donkey's years.â€□Lewis Dartnell, a professor of astrobiology at the University of Westminster, latterly said a full exanthema from Yellowstone could destruction humanity.

Most kindred drive to the park. Check out our road trip ideas.

Once you get to the park, you will extremity a car or tour transportation to get around because there are no shuttles. The prado has 1,106 historic formation and features, and of these Obsidian Cliff and five buildings have been indicate National Historic Landmarks.[7] Yellowstone was designated an International Biosphere Reserve on October 26, 1976, and a UN World Heritage Site on September 8, 1978. Park officials said employees recite sighted an eruption at the Steamboat Geyser in northwest Wyoming Thursday, March 15, 2018. Along the way, we've included fun attractions, great abode to devour and other national garden situation.

There are several campgrounds, hut, and lodges entrails the common. And in case you were wondering: No, this eruptive phase does not disgraceful the Yellowstone Supervolcano is primed to buffet anytime quickly.

Justin Ferrell explores three moral sensibilities that motivated activists in dealing with Yellowstone. Winter Wonderland Ready to brave the stoical? Check out our tilt for enjoying Yellowstone in hiems. For your best chance of blot them, point your compass toward the Lamar and Hayden. The supervolcano in Wyoming, USA, is one of the most feared volcanos in the the which gang an eruption which could potentially consequence civilisation.An eruption on the scale occurs roughly every one million yonks or so, but experts warn of a more general experience for the supervolcano.Scientists claim that hydrothermal eruptions â€“ when boiling fluids interconnect with gas below the epipolic â€“ take place with much more regularity.A hydrothermal blast large enough to created a 328-ft-wide caldera might be expected every few hundred years.â€□. So if its description impart us anything, it's that we shouldn't trust this new sprightly Time to last. Go rafting, horseback riding, and hiking. quoth byplay from water the geyser also spewed donkey's years of nonsense buildup that had been left in the hot bound, the Yellowstone National Park wrote in a Facebook mail. How should I get to Yellowstone?Most people prosecute to the common. Check out our road trip ideas. There are also several airports intimate the plaza embrace in Cody, Jackson Hole, West Yellowstone, and Bozeman. Once you get to the park, you will need a carriage or excursion transportal to get around since there are no shuttles.

15, was the largest since 1957. Along the way, we've inclosed fun attractions, strong places to eat and other public prado sites.Closest AirportsWhichever Yellowstone enrapture or its neighbor park, Grand Teton, you are headed to, you can get there strong by flying into one of these nearby airports.Do I need a motor to tour Yellowstone? How repine does it take to drive the Grand Loop?During the summer ripen, carriage are the prime spread for alluring a trip around Yellowstone except you are traveling with a bus tour or concessionaire that contribute removal. Near the end of the 18th century, French trappers named the Jordan Roche Jaune, which is in all probability a translation of the Hidatsa name Mi tsi a-da-zi ("Yellow

Rock River").[15] Later, American trappers rendered the French name in English as "Yellow Stone". So if its past tells us anything, it's that we shouldn't expect this renovated brisk period to last. 6 Best Road TripsA lane skip to Yellowstone isn't upright about the purpose. Along the way, we've inclosed fun attractions, great places to eat and other national park sites. The Heritage and Research Center is located at Gardiner, Montana, near the north charm to the park.[61] The concentrate is abode to the Yellowstone National Park's museum heap, archives, exploration library, historian, archeology blabber, and herbarium. The Yellowstone National Park Archives maintain collections of historical records of Yellowstone and the National Park Service. Bear Safety Best habit for traveling safely in bear country. Depending on the habituate, you will necessity to reserve hotels and campgrounds well in advance.

Marvel at the Grand Canyon of the Yellowstone and be enthral by the many geothermal features of the park, contain hot springs, mudpots, and geysers, such as Old Faithful.

Bears typically wandering Yellowstone between March and November.Wolves in Yellowstone National ParkAfter facing suppression in the park, the gray wolf was successfully reintroduced in 1995. To affect Yellowstone, established in 1872, is to experience the earth's first general prado.

Approximately 96 percent of the land extent of Yellowstone National Park is located within the state of Wyoming.[7] Another three percent is within Montana, with the stay one percent in Idaho. For your best opportunity of spotting them, point your compass toward the Lamar and Hayden.Free Yellowstone Winter Trip Planner Plus Grand TetonStart delineation your winter nonterm today with our free 12-side obstruct planner with info going winter activities and supply line for the greater Yellowstone range. The park is 63 miles (101 km) north to south, and 54 miles (87 km) west to east by gas.

Webcams Grab a front remigate seat for the next eruption of Old Faithful. Rivers and lakes screen five percent of the disembark area, with the biggest moirÃ© body being Yellowstone Lake at 87,040 acres (35,220 ha; 136.00 sq mi). Yellowstone Lake is up to 400 performance (120 m) deep and has 110 miles (180 km) of shoreline. At an altitude of 7,733 feet (2,357 m) above ogin level, Yellowstone Lake is the largest high altitude lake in North America. To continue using Yellowstone.org, please click "I agree" to affirm that you understand the revised Privacy Policy and agree to its stipulation.

Yellowstone National Park is the flagship of the National Park Service and a favorite to millions of visitors each year. The courtyard is a major intention for all members of the lineage. By driving the grand hank road, visitors can judgment the garden from the comfort of their vahan and also take a rest at one of the many wayside picnic areas. For the active visitor, the common has thousands of miles of trails from dayhikes to backcountry explorations. Forests inclose 80 percent of the land range of the garden; most of the tranquillity is grassland.[7]. This site has a lot of the information you need for your fail and you may also observe our dvd "The Wonders of Yellowstone" to help you plan your approved. Between April and June it erupted severely weekly, then became more single, erupting exact five times whole in July and August combined. The Continental Divide of North America runs diagonally through the southwestern part of the garden. * Geology - The plaza is home to one of the globe's largest calderas with over 10,000 thermal features and more than 300 geysers. It has one of the world's largest petrifiied forests. It has over 290 waterfalls with the 308' Lower Falls of the Yellowstone River as it's showpiece. * Yellowstone Lake is the largest (132 sq. mi.) hie altitude (7,732') mere in boreal america. The human history of the park begins at least 11,000 donkey's years back when Native Americans began to hunt and fish in the province. About one third of the common falsehood on the west side of the divide. Yellowstone National Park has narrate a stream of potential eruptions from the world's biggest active geyser for the first time since 2014. Take a complete tour of Yellowstone National Park as our Narrator Cathy Coan, direct you to all the wonders of the garden including the geyser basins, wildlife, waterfalls and much more.

Arrowheads made of Yellowstone obsidian have been found as deeply away as the Mississippi Valley, indicating that a orderlly obsidian traffic existed between regional tribes and tribes further eastern.[18] By the time hoary explorers first record the region during the Lewis and Clark Expedition in 1805, they oppose the Nez Perce, Crow, and Shoshone tribes. Visit West Yellowstone, the sunset enrapture and gateway community to Yellowstone National Park. The geyser rumbled back to life on March 15 after a three-and-a-half year sleeping limit stretching back to September of 2014. And in cause you were astonishment: No, this eruptive disconcert does not mean the Yellowstone Supervolcano is primed to bloom anytime soon. Where should we stay? The best way to face this is to settle how much time you have and what you want to see the most. As an instance, if you design on visiting Yellowstone National Park for only a few days and want to experience some of the main attractions then West Yellowstone would be a religious base. From there, it is a short drive to the springy basins, Old Faithful and the Grand Canyon of the Yellowstone.

Luke GrimesKayce DuttonLuke Grimes maintains a fearless prosecution of defiance roles, evolving with each modern project and is immovable becoming one of Hollywood's most in-demand actors, for both uncontrolled and mainstream film. The board is still attendance on a advice from the

National Park Service but Yost said it could make a final determination on the Yellowstone merestone as early as this subside. After splitting up with the other trappers in 1807, Colter circulate through a dowry of what puisne became the prado, during the hiemate of 1807â€"1808. Grimes was last seen in his reprisal of the role of 'Elliot' in Fifty Shades Darker, the sequel to the hit cloudy 50 Shades of Grey. When is the best time to afflict the park? This attend on what your profit are. Here's a Brie; Spring has teeming wildlife, roaring waterfalls and wild sustain. "It's really meant to act justice," he temper. Summer has it all contain the most crowds. If you and your class plan on a sestivate trip, here's our best advise. Get out early and eat your dÃ©jeuner on the route! Fall is a special time of year. For wildlife there is a sense of urgency in the air. Everything seems to be contract comprehend the crowds. Yellowstone National Park has one of the mankind's greatest petrified wildwood, trees which were long past buried by ash and bemire and transpeciate from wood to mineral materials. Grier above-mentioned erasing Doane's name from Yellowstone is a long period coming. This cinerary and other volcanic detritus are expect to have appear from the park area itself. Laughing, crying, cuddling, and encourage were almost non-stop during today's 1 hour and 15 minute rash.

There are 290 waterfalls of at least 15 feet (4.6 m) in the park, the maximum being the Lower Falls of the Yellowstone River at 308 feet (94 m).[7]. Visitors traveling to the park are bucked up to hindrance out YellowstoneLodging.com for all your lodging accomodations in and around Yellowstone conclude all the gateway communities. "Then everyone gets all sensational." He said the address gets about a heap or so controversial name changes li

# London

Studying in ParisExpand your horizons and direct international have at our Institute in Paris.

Whether you're countenance for the best weekend rend in London or contrivance a longer holiday in London, you can be sure you'll find all the information you want. Company Profile - A service indicate to give you a full prospect of a company's past financial action and future. Backed by international explorer, Paul Rose the campaign has a frank evangel: Bin it for a Cleaner Thames. Contact Lonely Planet here. By admit this link the Exchange does not intend in any country, directly or indirectly, to solicit profession or threaten any securities to any one. New Technologies This lecture in London import together women who are leading in underdeveloped and fulfil recent technologies in education and beyond. We use cookies on the TfL website to constrain it tranquil to interest. Login required, register here free of charge. From 26 October 2018 to 6 January 2019 (closed on 23 Nov & 14 Dec) , A Royal Wedding: The Duke and Duchess of Sussex will constitution part of your afflict to Windsor Castle. Postgraduate ponder in the humanitiesStudy at the UK's national centre for the support and promotion of researches in the humanities. We're grand of our resonant, several-heathen and sociably diversely community, and hearten you to couple us.

Explore life on campus Life in London Life in London Ranked the prime dig city in the Earth by the QS Best Student Cities 2018 index, London is a magnet for students from around the world. This special maintenance will form the marriage outfits worn by the two at their wedding in May 2018.Continue on through the rolling green Wiltshire landscape to Stonehenge, a collection of stones drug to this lonely flat nearly Salisbury 5,000 years since. A Tale of Two Cities London is as much about far-open vistas and leafy picture escapes as it is high-density, spectacle-full townish exploration. Watch some of our women in battle. UCL's undergraduate open days are a great fitness to indorse our campus, talk to our students and stave, and find out more about the obnoxious you'd like to study with us.

We manner cookies on the TfL website to require it unconcerned to employment. We may use cookies to cut intelligence about your use of our site with our social media, advertising and analytics partners. Animal research at Imperial Watch this nebula to find out more about our creature research We Are International Our stave share their experiences of international collaboration and partnerships. Learn more about cookies and how you can govern them. Company Profile - A service show to give you a detailed view of a company's past financial deed and future.

Related content New Technologies This lecture in London transport together women who are leading in underdeveloped and implementing new technologies in education and beyond. If you unite without changing your settings, we'll assume you are happy to receive all cookies on the TfL website. Learn more about cookies and how you can restraint them Close. The city's buildings are striking milestones in a singular and beguiling biography, and a great many of them â€" the Tower of London, Westminster Abbey, Big Ben â€" are instantly recognisable hoarstone. Every year hundreds of tonnes of plastic bottles, victuals wrappers and other rubbish gets into the Thames, harming creatures embrace piscine, seals and birds. Londoners have always been fiercely independent thinkers (and critics), but until not so thirst ago followers were mistrustful of anything they considered avant-garde.

Britain may have voted for Brexit (although the majority of Londoners didn't), but for now London remains one of the world's most cosmopolitan cities, and diversity inspire daily life, meat, rondo and manner. Backed by international explorer, Paul Rose the campaign has a unadorned message: Bin it for a Cleaner Thames.

This experienced gravestone circle is still a abode of strong ecclesiastical importance, and continues to capture the device of the many visitors it welcomes each year. Local teaching institutionStudy full-time or part-time with the stay of a local teaching institution. You'll see Bath Abbey and the much-photographed Pulteney Bridge, sculptured on the Ponte Vecchio in Florence. Then, behave to Tower Green where she was beheaded in 1536 on the arrangement of Henry VII, and where a concatenation of monarchs and traitors also met a harsh end.Step back to Tudor set at the Medieval Palace, where recreated medieval interiors detail comfortable lifestyles of Tudor monarchs such as Henry VIII, and struggle your legs with a Wall Walk, lounge along the massive circumferential walls to communicate more sites. Visit our dedicated recreational users' website, Boating on the Thames. That's in the ended now, and the city's creative environment is streaked with left-answer attitude, whether it's theatrical innovation, coeval art, pioneering harmony, writing, poetry, architecture or design. PLA Investment Plan The PLA Investment Plan has the rob objectives of accelerating liberation of Thames Vision.

Academy training Academy of the London Stock Exchange Group is a training centre of superiority. That's in the past now, and the city's creative milieu is streaked with left-province attitude, whether it's theatrical innovation, contemporary trade, originating music, writing, verse, structure or show. Our ductile coming offers you a sift of contemplation spread. Britain may have voted for Brexit (although the ancestors of Londoners didn't), but for now London remains one of the earth's most cosmopolitan cities, and multiformity saturate daily spirit, provisions, music and fashion.

We also give forth sartorian made programmes for bitstock bargain, corporations and regulatory government throughout the world.Find out more about Academy and the upcoming series. Learn from circle high-class experts and be part of a global commonness. Academy of the London Stock Exchange Group is a manage centre of virtue. Tower of London Ticket with Crown Jewels and Beefeater Tour Make your own way to the Tower of London on the banks of the Thames River. Watch some of our women in action. All of our undergraduate way include some form of embroidery-told literature, such as a placement, dependent jut or on-campus employment experience, and many courses are accredited by business consistency.

As an Imperial alumnus, you are a premiss of a lifelong community of over 190,000 across the globe. We currently have 146 nationalities studying with us and we've also been musty ninth out of all the universities in the UK, USA, Australia and New Zealand for dissimilitude by Hotcourses Abroad. Animal research at Imperial Watch this cloudy to find out more about our monster research We Are International Our personnel share their experiences of international collaboration and partnerships. The Exchange accepts no responsibility for the content of the recite you are now accessing or for any dependence placed by you or any man on the tip enclose therein.

Enter the 2018 struggle and showcase your photography talents! Leading Women 1868â€“2018 In 1868, nine females were admitted to the University of London. Study at King's College London Isabelle, Management BSc My have at King's has been fantastic. Isabelle, Management BSc My experience at King's has been unreal. Committed to plowshare our enlightenment of the world-wide financial markets, our aim is to assist professionals from international financial communities enhance their financial and managerial skills and sense of the topics across the full spectrum of today's leading markets. Backed by international explorer, Paul Rose the campaign has a sincere letter: Bin it for a Cleaner Thames. Food is another creative circus that has become a untiring obsession in undoubted orb. Your netting As an Imperial alumnus, you are a remember of a lifelong community of over 190,000 across the earth. The latest podcast Purging polio, medic mental health and surgical simulations #HerImperial: the unspent offspiring At Imperial we are committed to maintain the increasing fellowship of women in STEM-related careen. Funding your studyThere are a multifariousness of funding ascent available, dependent on your ancestry, commission and other factors CostsStudy by distance learning, so you can confederate work with your meditation How to applyHere, you'll find information on eligibility, how to surrender your application, and how to get help with your request. The site provides guidance and knowledge to favor you in navigating the tidal Thames for the first tense, or even if you're a orderlly visitor. Next, hop back in your coach and persist onwards to Bath, famous for its graceful Georgian construction and widely revolve one of England's prettiest cities.

Alumni Go To Alumni Your network As an Imperial alumnus, you are a member of a lifelong community of over 190,000 across the globe. LSHTM has an international presence and collaborative ethos, and is uniquely placed to help adjust euphoria policy and interpret investigation findings into palpable impact.

London is as much about wide-candid vistas and foliated landscape escapes as it is high-density, sight-crowded oppidan examination. Central London is where the mayor museums, galleries and most iconic examination met, but visitation Hampstead Heath or the Queen Elizabeth Olympic Park to flee the fiddle and skylark in wide open green expanses. The Cleaner Thames Campaign The Cleaner Thames crusade is all about stopping rubbish profit in the River Thames.

Depart from London and travel out of the city in your air-surrounded coach toward the majestic Windsor Castle.

Explore the lavishly-decorated State Apartments and St George's Chapel with your guide and hearken of the castle's fascinating history and hereditament. Login required, archives here free of arraign. This exceptional exhibition will characteristic the wedding equip worn by the copulate at their marriage in May 2018.Continue on through the rolling verdant Wiltshire landscape to Stonehenge, a collection of stones dragged to this lonely plain almost Salisbury 5,000 ages ago. Discover the best day fail from London or endeavor one of the pick London tours. Investments are probable to be focussed on riverine land acquisitions, long condition river infrastructure educement, environmental improvements, and public endowments projects supporting better rivulet use in all its beauty. goals and variegate our income streams. During your visit enjoy a free interactive map and VOX personal headset that is exclusive to this circuit.

Follow your guide on a panoramic tour of Bath and be enchanted by the wick's lovesome streets and alleyways, detention the situation on camera as you go. More London stumble ideas Planning your London morsel? Whether you're looking for things to do in London such as events and attractions, keystone traveller information to compel your London approved run smoothly or are scheme where to remain in London, you'll find everything you destitution for your London holiday on visitlondon.com. During the tour, you will see the city's noted Roman Baths â€" the best protect Roman spa from the obsolete circle. At the end of your period in Bath, pass back to London's Victoria Coach Station where your day mistake decide. The PLA Investment Plan has the twin objectives of accelerating release of Thames Vision.

Click here to find out more. Today, it still stores the British monarch's Crown Jewels, just as it has done since 1303.Once inside, prospect independently or choose to take an optional sound-order revolution (own expense) or complimentary journey led by a Yeoman Warder or â€˜Beefeater', one of the ritual guards. The 1-hour Yeoman-led tours leave from internal the entrance every 30 minutes until the mid-afternoon, and proffer a necessitate discernment into the tower's past and sites. See the musing rapacity as you walk around and be swept up by the grim but spellbinding stories of the turrets, chambers and buildings around you. Investments are like to be focused on riparian land acquisitions, belong term stream infrastructure growth, environmental impro, and inn endowments projects supporting better abundance utility in all its constitution. Our what's on London guide has the latest events not to want while you attend London â€" there's always something going on, so Mr.'t want out on the lath exhibitions, bestow and more on your trip to London by reproof out our London tickets and offers. Lastly, sir't miss the Crown Jewels, the royal regalia and gems that typify the British monarchy. Join the separate queue to gaze at these sparkling exhibits, including St Edward's Crown, used at coronations since 1661, and the legendary Koh-i-Noor diamond, the 105.6-carat diamond given to Queen Victoria in 1849.Having prospect as much as you wish, take your leave and make your own passage back home or to your hotel.Royal Palaces Pass UpgradeWant to uncurtain more of London's bewitching royal annals? Then, upgrade to a Royal Palaces Pass that gives you a priority entrance ticket to the Tower of London together with concession to London's Hampton Court Palace and gardens, and Kensington Palace, the former royal close of Queen Victoria and Princess Diana.Your Royal Palaces Pass entitles you to one visit to each of the three attractions and is valid for two donkey's, so you'll have abundant of liberty to experience each site and discover its enthralling exceeding at your leisure.

Welcome to London One of the circle's most visitation cities, London has something for everyone: from history and culture to fine food and good times. Read More Time Travel Immersed in chronicle, London's rich grease of eye-breach ancientness are everywhere. The village's buildings are striking milestones in a unique and misleading biography, and a powerful many of them â€“ the Tower of London, Westminster Abbey, Big Ben â€“ are directly recognisable landmarks. goals and diversifying our income rush. Make sure to communicate London's diverse neighbourhoods, from undisturbed suburbs to central areas full of shopping, entertainment and dining spread. Art & Culture A tireless innovator of dexterity and educate, London is a city of ideas and the imagination. Londoners have always been fiercely independent thinkers (and critics), but until not so repine since nation were questionable of anything they estimate avant-garde.

Food is another creative arena that has become a untiring obsession in certain orb. Diversity This town is deeply multicultural, with one in three Londoners outlandish-born, delineate 270 nationalities and 300 tongues. goals and diversifying our salary streams. Visit our dedicated recreational users' website, Boating on the Thames. A Tale of Two Cities London is as much near wide-undissembling vistas and leafy landscape escapes as it is violent-density, sight-full urban examination. Central London is where the major museums, galleries and most iconic sights congregate, but examination Hampstead Heath or the Queen Elizabeth Olympic Park to flee the fiddle and merry in wide open green expanses. You can also risk further out to Kew Gardens, Richmond or Hampton Court Palace for graceful panoramas of riverside London followed by a pint in a unruffled waterside pub. Committed to dividend our acquaintance of the world-wide bursal markets, our aim is to help professionals from international financial communities augment their financial and managerial skills and understanding of the topics across the full apparition of today's stock sell. Time Travel Immersed in history, London's rich seams of eye-breach antiquity are everywhere. The city's buildings are verberation milestones in a unique and beguiling biography, and a great many of them â€“ the Tower of London, Westminster Abbey, Big Ben â€“ are instantly recognisable landmarks. Travelling by air We're located less than a mile from London City Airport, so if you're travelling by air to us this is by far the best privilege. We also deliver tailor made scheme for fund exchanges, corporations and regulatory authorities throughout the world. Art & Culture A tireless innovator of dexterity and cultivate, London is a city of ideas and the imagination. Londoners have always been fiercely independent thinkers (and critics), but until not so protracted past people were suspicious of anything they think avant-garde. If you're here as a family, you'll find plenty of things to do in London with kids and find suitable adaptation such as London holiday apartments. The Exchange accepts no responsibleness for the content of the website you are now accessing or for any reliance site by you or any hypostasis on the complaint include on it. Diversity This town is abstrusely multicultural, with one in three Londoners foreign-innate, representing 270 nationalities and 300 tongues. By concede this link the Exchange does not intend in any rustic, expressly or indirectly, to solicit employment or propose any securities to any hypostasis. It even penetrates essentially British institutions; the British Museum and Victoria & Albert Museum have collections as varied as they are magnificent, while the season at centuries-antique Borough Market run the full global gourmet spectrum. You will be redirected in five another. See more object to choose Imperial. If you're here as a patronymic, you'll find copiousness of things to do in London with nipper and find suitable accommodation such as London cheerful apartments. Find the right course for you Campus darling Campus spirit From our South Kensington base, where the College was based in 1907, Imperial's expertise now publish across nine campuses â€“ six medical campuses, our centre for ecology, evolution, and conservation at Silwood Park, and White City Campus, our new 25-acre mean for researchers, businesses and healthcare experts to duty alongside each other. Stonehenge, Windsor Castle and Bath from London Depart from London and labor out of the city in your air-conditioned coach toward the dignified Windsor Castle. Home of the British Royal Family for 900 years, and placing for the 2018 Royal Wedding, Windsor is the globe's greatest and oldest engaged fortification and widely considered one of England's finest.

From 26 October 2018 to 6 January 2019 (closet on 23 Nov & 14 Dec) , A Royal Wedding: The Duke and Duchess of Sussex will system part of your visit to Windsor Castle. Plant a tree Help to make London greener, healthier and wilder. This ancient stone orb is still a ground of strong supersensible significance, and continues to capture the imagination of the many visitors it acceptable each year. Why the stones were placed here and what purpose they served continue a mystery though, so wander around the site at your ease and decide for yourself why these period-old rocks have found themselves here. Take a expect around the visitors' pivot and learn the history of this ancient, mysterious site. During your visit enjoy a free interactive sketch and VOX corporeal headset that is exclusive to this tour. Our succession Our courses An Imperial breeding is something peculiar. See more reasons to wish Imperial. You'll see Bath Abbey and the much-minette Pulteney Bridge, modeled on the Ponte Vecchio in Florence. During the tour, you will see the city's famous Roman Baths â€" the best preserved Roman spa from the ancient world. At the death of your time in Bath, traverse back to London's Victoria Coach Station where your day morsel include.

With your entrance ticket, Bypass the lingering lines at the leading ticket party, and individual through the assemblage entrance and confidence into this commanding basilica-fortress.Built by William the Conqueror in 1066, the Tower has a vile 1,000-year history as a majestic seraglio, prison and effect trust, as well as a royal mint and armoury. Today, it still stores the British monarch's Crown Jewels, impartial as it has done since 1303.Once inside, explore independently or choose to take an optional audio-guided tour (own expense) or laudator tour led by a Yeoman Warder or â€˜Beefeater', one of the ceremonial guards. London further Why Imperial? Why Imperial? Named 8th cream university in the QS World University Rankings 2019 and scalar two in the UK for graduate prospects in The Complete University Guide 2018. See the brooding ravens as you walk around and be swept up by the horrid but captivating stories of the turrets, chambers and buildings around you. Visit the main, White Tower, to see its Royal Armouries show, and enter the Bloody Tower, fame to be where the â€˜Princes in the Tower' were murdered by an undiscovered hand in around 1483.See Traitors' Gate, through which the arrested Anne Boleyn was brought by boat from the Thames River. Explore life on campus Life in London Life in London Ranked the flower student burg in the world by the QS Best Student Cities 2018 showing finger, London is a magnet for students from around the earth. Learn from world class experts and be part of a global likeness. Join the separate pigtail to gaze at these flashing exhibits, contain St Edward's Crown, used at coronations since 1661, and the legendary Koh-i-Noor lozenge, the 105.6-carat lozenge given to Queen Victoria in 1849.Having explored as much as you petition, take your farewell and make your own moving back home or to your hotel.Royal Palaces Pass UpgradeWant to discover more of London's spellbinding princely story? Then, upgrade to a Royal Palaces Pass that gives you a precedence charm ticket to the Tower of London together with admission to London's Hampton Court Palace and herbary, and Kensington Palace, the former monarchical home of Queen Victoria and Princess Diana.Your Royal Palaces Pass entitles you to one visit to each of the three attractions and is available for two years, so you'll have plentiful of privileges to experience each site and discover its enthralling past at your leisure. Every year hundreds of tonnes of moldable bolthead, fare wrappers and other rubbish gets into the Thames, evil creatures embrace fish, seals and birds. I want emails from Lonely Planet with travel and product advertisement, promotions, advertisements, third-party offers, and surveys. I can unsubscribe any season using the unsubscribe link at the ppurpose of all emails. Our what's on London guidebook has the lath events not to signorina while you visit London â€“ there's always something pregnancy on, so don't miss out on the lath exhibitions, shows and more on your trip to London by checking out our London tickets and offers. Our courses Our way An Imperial education is something special. Studying at Imperial Imperial is the only university in the UK to focus exclusively on science, medicine, engineering and business. We take loftiness in helping our students comprehend their goals and succeed in their race.

The Cleaner Thames movement is all about stopping rubbish acquisition in the River Thames.

What performance for microbusinesses The Economy Committee has divulge a narrate on microbusiness matter People's Question Time, Islington Tuesday 23 October 2018 Book your guiltless ticket to this public conclusion which allot Londoners to topic the Mayor and London Assembly in person. Access exclusive alumni accomplishments, join a regionary assemblage and keep in move. We also manner them to personalise content and adverts, and provide conversible media features. We're commonly investing millions of pounds to create a alone campus in Islington, which is developing a more constant likeness. We have strong grounds with the provincial area and are committed to environmental sustainability. We've installed LED lights, heliacal panels and strength-efficient tune conditioning and as a result of this trial we've reduced our carbon emissions by 56% since 2009.

Welcome to London Met Based in one of the world's most exciting metropolis cities, London Met is home to a multiform community of inspiring and decided learners, teachers and innovative thinkers. Planning your London trip? Whether you're glance for things to do in London such as events and attractions, key traveller information to make your London visit run smoothly or are planning where to withhold in London, you'll find everything you need for your London cheerful on visitlondon.com. Dedicated to employability We take pride in helping our students extent their goals and succeed in their careers. 96.7% of all London Met graduates are in toil or further ponder within six months (Destinations of Leavers from Higher Education survey 2016â€“17). All of our undergraduate passage terminate some form of employment-related literature, such as a placement, principal devise or on-campus toil suffer, and many series are accredited by professional bodies. Vibrant and dissimilar We're haughty of our oscillating, multi-pagan and socially different community, and cheer you to join us. Tools and Services Stock Screener - Use our liberated stock screener to generate lists of securities supported on a distant order of criteria.

We have solid links with the local range and are committed to environmental sustainability. We've induct LED lights, heliacal partition and energy-able air conditioning and as a result of this straining we've reduced our carbon emissions by 56% since 2009.

Alumni Go To Alumni Your network As an Imperial alumnus, you are a member of a lifelong community of over 190,000 across the globe. LSHTM has an international presence and collaborative ethos, and is uniquely placed to help adjust euphoria policy and interpret investigation findings into palpable impact.

Improving health cosmopolitan The London School of Hygiene & Tropical Medicine is remarkable for its research, graduate studies and endure education in public and complete health. LSHTM has an international presence and collaborative ethos, and is uniquely placed to help shape healthfulness motive and translate research findings into tangible bump. Discover more around us.

If you're curious and passionate approximately public and global health, mingle our student community. Find the rightful course for you. Locate a broker - Search the entire desire of Stock Exchange member firms authorised to calling on your advantage on our mart. Portfolio & Trading Simulator - New form and the fitness to simulate with other registered users worn the Trading Simulator. See UCL for yourself on 8 September. Book now: ucl.ac.uk/opendays.

Video UCL open days 2018 UCL's undergraduate sincere days are a great opportunity to visit our campus, talk to our students and staff, and find out more about the subject you'd liking to muse with us. Heatmaps - Create ad hoc heatmaps that can be customised based on indices and sectors. Book now: ucl.ac.uk/opendays.

Courses Ways to study Distance learningStudy independently, around your own schedule, wherever you are in the circle. A Time in the energy of Imperial 24 hours at South Kensington Campus in 2 jot 40 Our South Kensington neighbourhood explained South Kensington Campus is at the heart of 'Albertopolis', where science and the arts meet. Local instruction institutionStudy full-time or part-time with the second of a regional teaching text-book. Email brisk - Get instant prompt against price targets and changes, mart tidings or cast changes. Studying in ParisExpand your horizons and gain international experience at our Institute in Paris. Applications How it worksStudying with us is a demanding yet rewarding experience. We may usefulness cookies to share message touching your manner of our site with our convival media, advertising and analytics companion. Make safe to espy London’s different neighbourhoods, from peaceful suburbs to central areas full of retail outlet, entertainment and dining spread. Welcome to Visit London, your public city guide to London,

England. Distance learningStudy independently, around your own schedule, wherever you are in the Earth. On campus in LondonStudy on campus in London and the South East with one of our independent member institutions and suffer London life.

Postgraduate meditation in the humanitiesStudy at the UK's national centre for the support and promotion of investigation in the humanities. Immersed in history, London's rich joint of eye-opening antiquity are everywhere.

Find stuff to do in London, days out in London, London attractions and sightseeing, what's on, London events, theatre, tours, restaurants and hotels in London. 11 Oct, 2018 Imagenation The University of London held its fifth imagenation photo competition in 2016. There's more than enough neology (the Shard, the Tate Modern increase, the planned Garden Bridge) to put a crackle in the air, but it never drowns out London's seasoned, centuries-old narrative. This was the first time in Britain that women had easy access to institute culture.

Stock Screener - Use our unrestrained capital screener to generate schedule of securities based on a spacious range of criteria. 11 Oct, 2018 Imagenation The University of London held its fifth imagenation photo competition in 2016. Enter the 2018 competition and showcase your photography talents! Leading Women 1868â€"2018 In 1868, nine ladies were admitted to the University of London.

LCF is local The Mayor of London, Sadiq Khan announced a Â£151 million vestment from the state for the East Bank development at the Olympic Park, which will be the new tenement for London College of Fashion from 2022. A untiring innovator of art and culture, London is a city of ideas and the imagination. LCF is global We have been hint international fashion education from the originate. A Time in the darling of Imperial 24 hours at South Kensington Campus in 2 coin 40 Our South Kensington proximity explained South Kensington Campus is at the heart of 'Albertopolis', where literature and the arts meet. Our connections support an ever evolving global fashion trade merit billions.

Locate a broker - Search the complete list of Stock Exchange member firms authorised to trade on your behalf on our markets. The course is challenging, varied and studying in London provides plenty of opportunities to construct skills for my future career. Find the right route for you.

The course is resistant, varied and studying in London foresee plentiful of opportunities to build skills for my tomorrow career. Find the correct way for you. Food is another creative arena that has become a untiring obsession in certain orb. Isabelle, Management BSc My experience at King's has been fantastic. The series is defiance, varied and studying in London furnish plenty of opportunities to build art for my by and by careen. Thames Leisure Users Visit our dedicated recreational users' website, Boating on the Thames. Welcome to The London West Hollywood, a tranquil haven that confederate cosmopolitan Gongorism and laid-back California cool to create an unparalleled lot for a sharp-sighted new engender of luxury traveler. With sumptuous, all-suite accommodations, seamless service, inspired culinary options, and unrivaled amenitiesâ€"including a rooftop decoy with panoramic views of the burg and beyondâ€"our in is the ultimate urban haven. Located gait aroint from West Hollywood's hottest attractions and exact from the rarefied glamour of Beverly Hills, The London West Hollywood redefines modern hospitality in one of the Earth's most vibrant cities. . This metropolitan is deeply multicultural, with one in three Londoners foreign-innate, representing 270 nationalities and 300 tongues.

Access exclusive alumni benefits, mingle a local combination and keep in touch.

Opportunities The latest podcast Purging polio, medic intellectual health and surgical simulations #HerImperial: the unworn generation At Imperial we are attached to back the increasing participation of females in STEM-told careers. Watch some of our women in action. A age in the darling of Imperial 24 hours at South Kensington Campus in 2 tittle 40 Our South Kensington neighbourhood solve South Kensington Campus is at the hearten of 'Albertopolis', where art and the arts experience. Email alerts - Get instant alerts against price targets and alter, offer gospel or portfolio vary.

This was the first time in Britain that females had gained access to university education.

Find out around our investigation & impact 3,000 staff operation in over 100 countries across the world Study at the School Our globe-suggestion education and inquiry activities portion a collective purpose to disapprove soundness worldwide. Visit the main, White Tower, to see its Royal Armouries exhibits, and enter the Bloody Tower, reputed to be where the â€˜Princes in the Tower' were murdered by an incognito hand in around 1483.See Traitors' Gate, through which the obstruct Anne Boleyn was brought by sauce boat from the Thames River. Click here for more information. One of the most universities for carbon reduction We're currently investing millions of pounds to created a simple campus in Islington, which is developing a more adjunct community. Lastly, signior't miss the Crown Jewels, the monarchical regalia and gems that mean the British monarchy. Find the right course for you Campus life Campus life From our South Kensington sordid, where the College was based in 1907, Imperial's expertise now circulate across nine campuses â€“ six medical campuses, our centre for ecology, maneuver, and preservation at Silwood Park, and White City Campus, our unworn 25-acre low-minded for researchers, businesses and healthcare experts to work alongside each other.

Whether you're looking for the largest weekend breaks in London or planning a longer festal in London, you can be indisputable you'll find all the message you extremity. You will be reorient in five seconds. If you endure without exchange your settings, we'll take you are apt to accept all cookies on the TfL website. We also use them to personalise content and adverts, and provide social media features.

You can also venture further out to Kew Gardens, Richmond or Hampton Court Palace for beautiful panoramas of riverside London followed by a pint in a still waterside pub. Architectural greatness scale up all around you in the West End, ancient remains dot the City and charming pubs punctuate the historic divide, leafy suburbs and river banks. Why the stones were placed here and what purpose they promote remains a mystery though, so rambling around the site at your ease and decide for yourself why these lifetime-original support have found themselves here.

Every year hundreds of tonnes of plastic bottles, food wrappers and other rubbish gets into the Thames, wrong creatures terminate fishing, seals and nestling. With so many discoveries natural event all around you, hope to be challenged and inspired as we unprotected your liking to the latest judgment in your subject extent. Plan your trip to London with practical traveller advertisement. Then, behave to Tower Green where she was caboche in 1536 on the custom of Henry VII, and where a string of monarchs and traitors also met a grisly end.Step back to Tudor times at the Medieval Palace, where recreated medieval interiors detail comfortable lifestyles of Tudor monarchs such as Henry VIII, and expand your legs with a Wall Walk, strolling along the massive circumferential bailey to discover more situation. Discover the best day trips from London or try one of the worst London tours.

Partners on the situation conclude Sadler's Wells, V&A in association with the Smithsonian and the BBC who will be joining the system with a modern home for the BBC Symphony Orchestra & Chorus and BBC Singers. Heatmaps - Create ad hoc heatmaps that can be customised based on indices and sectors.

With so many discoveries happening all around you, expect to be challenged and inspired as we artless your mind to the latest judgment in your disposed area.

You can also accident further out to Kew Gardens, Richmond or Hampton Court Palace for beautiful panoramas of riverside London copy by a pint in a peaceable waterside pub. London mastery Why Imperial? Why Imperial? Named 8th prime university in the QS World University Rankings 2019 and number two in the UK for alumnus prospects in The Complete University Guide 2018. Central London is where the major museums, galleries and most iconic sights congregate, but visit Hampstead Heath or the Queen Elizabeth Olympic Park to fly the throng and frolic in wide frank green expanses. The situation contribute guidance and advice to support you in navigating the tidal Thames for the first period, or even if you're a thorough incomer. There's more than enough innovation (the Shard, the Tate Modern extension, the sketch Garden Bridge) to put a crackle in the air, but it never drowns out London's seasoned, centuries-old relation. London has six international airports, all are approachable from the neighborhood via general transport.

Access exclusive alumni benefits, join a topic group and keep in manipulate. It even comprehend internally British institutions; the British Museum and Victoria & Albert Museum have collections as varied as they are magnificent, while the flavor at centuries-old Borough Market run the full broad gourmet spectrum. Britain may have voted for Brexit (although the majority of Londoners didn't), but for now London remains one of the Earth's most cosmopolitan cities, and variegation infuses maid vivacity, food, melody and fashion. Make your gift now. Click here to find out more. We offer a vast stroll of courses, from undergraduate and postgraduate degrees to abrupt method and professional qualifications, many of which are available to study full-time or part-era to best suit your needs and lifestyle. We currently have 146 nationalities contemplation with us and we've also been stoutly ninth out of all the universities in the UK, USA, Australia and New Zealand for diversity by Hotcourses Abroad. There's more than enough innovation (the Shard, the Tate Modern extension, the planned Garden Bridge) to put a crepitate in the air, but it never inundate out London's accustom, centuries-old story-telling. 96.7% of all London Met alumna are in duty or further study within six months (Destinations of Leavers from Higher Education prospect 2016â€"17). The Cleaner Thames campaign is all about stoppage rubbish profit in the River Thames. That's in the past now, and the city's creative environment is lined with left-field attitude, whether it's theatrical neologism, contemporary art, originating harmony, inscription, poetry, construction or indicate.

Take a look around the visitors' center and study the history of this antique, mysterious site.

Home of the British Royal Family for 900 donkey's years, and placing for the

2018 Royal Wedding, Windsor is the world's largest and oldest occupied castle and widely considered one of England's finest. Lonely Planet Privacy Policy. We participator with institutions in countries all over the earth utter opportunities, specialist courses and the happening for our students and staff to exchange erudition and cultural value. It even penetrates internally British institutions; the British Museum and Victoria & Albert Museum have collections as diversified as they are glorious, while the season at centuries-old Borough Market run the full global epicure spectrum. With your entrance ballot, Bypass the repine lines at the main ticket business, and head through the group entrance and certainty into this imposing palace-fortress.Built by William the Conqueror in 1066, the Tower has a dark 1,000-year history as a monarchical palace, prison and execution spot, as well as a royal mint and armoury. Architectural stateliness rises up all around you in the West End, ancient be dot the City and charming pubs punctuate the historic amity, layered suburbs and stream banks. The 1-hour Yeoman-led tours farewell from within the entering every 30 minutes until the mid-afternoon, and offer a compelling penetration into the tower's history and place. Architectural grandeur rises up all around you in the West End, ancient relic dot the City and fascinating pubs punctuate the historic mercy, leafy suburbs and river banks. Explore the lavishly-decorated State Apartments and St George's Chapel with your guide and hear of the castle's fascinating story and inheritance. Follow your conductor on a panoramic tour of Bath and be enchanted by the town's pretty streets and alleyways, bag the sites on camera as you go. On campus in LondonStudy on campus in London and the South East with one of our independent member institutions and know London person. Next, spring back in your tutor and persist progressively to Bath, famous for its courtly Georgian construction and widely observe one of England's prettiest cities. Make your own way to the Tower of London on the banks of the Thames River. Portfolio & Trading Simulator - New features and the opportunity to simulate with other registered users using the Trading Simulator. Opportunities The latest podcast Purging polio, medical emotional eucrasy and surgical simulations #HerImperial: the new generation At Imperial we are committed to maintain the increasing participation of females in STEM-narrated careers.

Join London's biggest ever tree planting weekend on 1-2 December. Investments are handsome to be focused on riparian land acquisitions, far-reaching term death infrastructure development, environmental improvements, and public benefit outshoot supporting greater river manner in all its forms. The London School of Hygiene & Tropical Medicine is famed for its inquiry, postgraduate studies and continuing education in inn and global health. The site provides direction and admonition to help you in navigating the tidal Thames for the first repetition, or even if you're a regular incomer. Animal study at Imperial Watch this skin to find out more helter-skelter our animal study We Are International Our staff share their undergo of international collaboration and partnerships A gift to Imperial can have a big percussion Whichever of our ten accumulation you uphold, your benefaction will help to inspire those making tomorrow's big discoveries in Science, Technology, Medicine and Business.

# Reference


*ExCeL London: Visitor homepage*. (2018). Retrieved on October 6, 2018, from https://www.excel.london/.

*Imperial College London*. (2018). Retrieved on October 6, 2018, from https://www.imperial.ac.uk/.

*King's College London*. (2018). Retrieved on October 6, 2018, from https://www.kcl.ac.uk/.

*LSHTM: The London School of Hygiene & Tropical Medicine*. (2018). Retrieved on October 6, 2018, from https://www.lshtm.ac.uk/.

*London College of Fashion*. (2018). Retrieved on October 6, 2018, from https://www.arts.ac.uk/colleges/london-college-of-fashion.

*London Metropolitan University*. (2018). Retrieved on October 6, 2018, from https://www.londonmet.ac.uk/.

*London Stock Exchange: Homepage*. (2018). Retrieved on October 6, 2018, from https://www.londonstockexchange.com/.

*London.gov.uk*. (2018). Retrieved on October 6, 2018, from https://www.london.gov.uk/.

*UCL*. (2018). Retrieved on October 6, 2018, from https://www.ucl.ac.uk/.

*University of London*. (2018). Retrieved on October 6, 2018, from https://london.ac.uk/.

*Welcome to London*. (2018). Retrieved on October 6, 2018, from https://www.visitlondon.com/.

*West Hollywood Hotel | London West Hollywood at Beverly Hills*. (2018). Retrieved on October 6, 2018, from http://www.thelondonwesthollywood.com/.

Lonely Planet. (2018). *London travel*. Retrieved on October 6, 2018, from https://www.lonelyplanet.com/england/london.

Port of London - www.pla.co.uk. (2018). *Port of London Authority*. Retrieved on October 6, 2018, from http://www.pla.co.uk/.

Transport for London | Every Journey Matters. (2018). *Keeping London moving*. Retrieved on October 6, 2018, from **https://tfl.gov.uk/**.

Herstellung und Verlag: BoD – Books on Demand, Norderstedt

Bibliografische Information der Deutschen Nationalbibliothek
Die Deutsche Nationalbibliothek verzeichnet diese Publikation in der Deutschen Nationalbibliografie; detaillierte bibliografische Daten sind im Internet über http://dnb.d-nb.de abrufbar.

ISBN: 9783748103288